Always Kiss Me Goodbye

A Memoir

ALWAYS KISS ME GOODBYE

www.jenniferoslerbolton.com

Editing and design by Jennifer Osler-Bolton
Distribution by Red Jacket Publishing

THE HOLY BIBLE: EASY-TO-READ VERSION (ERV). 2013, 2004, 1987. Bible League International. Used by permission.
Batterson, Mark. Draw the Circle : The 40-Day Prayer Challenge. Grand Rapids, Mich., Zondervan, 2012.

Cover and wedding photographs: Marta of Perfect Wedding NYC and Wedding Packages NYC
Author and family photographs: Whitney Michaels of Whitney Lee Company

Some names and identifying characteristics have been changed to protect the privacy of the individuals involved. While the author has made every effort to provide accurate information at the time of publication, neither the publisher nor the author assumes any responsibility for errors or changes that occur after publication.

ISBN: 979-8-9924734-4-5 (paperback)

Always *kiss me* Goodbye

A MEMOIR

Jennifer Osler-Bolton

where hope is written
RED JACKET
PUBLISHING

To God.
Without You, there would be no story.
I love you. I trust you. I need you.

Photo taken by Amanda Osler
September 19, 2016

Grief is the price
WE PAY FOR LOVE
Queen Elizabeth II

Dear Reader,

I've been staring at a blank page for years. I've known I was given something to say, but have never really known how to say it. I've lost count the number of times I'd start to write and then quickly erase. But the pressing on my heart kept getting stronger: "*write it down.*"

I couldn't get it out of my head. The thoughts never felt scary, nor did they feel confusing. It was my own subconscious trying to convince me I wasn't ready to write. For months, I kept receiving signs of encouragement to put pen to paper (or fingers to keyboard). Whether it was from strangers on the internet or family and friends pushing me towards a goal, the pressing continued to get stronger.

I asked God what He wanted me to do. He consistently answered, "*write.*"

I didn't know if I could do it. I wasn't sure if my mind could coordinate with my heart, but I decided to try. I prepared myself to relive the most traumatic experience of my life up to this point.

Laced throughout these pages is my journey with God and my hope in His promises, but this book is not about being a perfectly poised Christian. The truth is I'm not a fan of 'pretty faith.' I don't buy the Christianity that is sold today as a promise that everything will be better when we say 'yes' to God. That has the potential to create pretty-looking faith which crumbles when the trials arrive.

I can say this because that's how my faith used to be. In these pages, you'll hear my story about coming to God as a twenty-year-old newlywed, but I didn't really know Him. I was going to church, reading my bible, praying, doing all the Christian things - but loss and hardship filled years of my life after saying 'yes' to God. Ryan and I endured miscarriage with our first pregnancy; my father-in-law died unexpectedly; our marriage suffered years of drunkenness, dishonesty, and financial ruin which led to separation as we stared divorce in the face. I wondered about the promises God made about watching over my life, protecting me from harm, and His plans not to hurt me (Jeremiah 29:11). I assumed church equated God to which I was a dedicated participant; however, it was human hands I was reaching for, not God's sovereignty. I expected church would carry my faith, making my burdens light and my days easier.

But in 2016, I discovered that church and God are not one in the same. I decided to go deeper with God, discover His supremacy and let go of the human hands I was clinging to for dear life. In the middle of a soul-searching, faith-seeking journey towards connection with God, my husband was killed. My world was ripped from underneath me and my heart was shattered. I was confused: *"but... You promised?"* As I sat with God, I finally got it: faith isn't Sunday mornings, Hobby Lobby signs, familiar phrases, quoted scripture or cute tattoos – all of which I've done, I've purchased, I've said and I have.

There is nothing on earth that can guarantee a "better life" and that is the biggest misconception about church and God. I assumed I was protected from hardship because I said 'yes' to God. I assumed I was safe from physical harm because I said 'yes' to God. I claimed that I didn't see Him as a wish-granting Genie (after all, I wasn't a millionaire), but just as I believed church equated God, I believed faith equated safety. Faith is knowing there is no promise for a better *life* - only a better *eternity*. It's knowing the protection is over our souls, not our desires. It's trusting that God is next to us in the hardship, not preventing it. It's believing that our time on earth is for His purpose, not our gain. It's knowing that Jesus' sacrifice is for our salvation, not our success.

Within my experiences and journey with God, I learned how to trust God with the occurrences and outcomes of my life. I discovered how to listen for, and then discern, His voice. I learned the noise of the world will easily drown His out, which taught me to seek Him, and only Him, in every single moment.

This is a story about dismantling polished religion and discovering beauty within the mess of raw faith. Although this book might appear to be about a Hallmark-style love story with a happy ending, it's about a greater love: God's - and what He can do with a willing heart. It's about trusting His devotion, provision and protection; believing His promise that nothing will be wasted and everything will be used for good. It's about leaning into the comfort of His arms and being willing to follow His lead regardless of where He goes. It's about learning how to listen for His voice while sifting through the noise of others. It's about personal discovery of the true meaning of trusting God and realizing that polished religion isn't the same as deep faith.

Faith is understanding what it means to truly trust God in all things, and then willingly, vulnerably, and courageously walking towards the front lines of spiritual war saying, *'Here I am, send me.'*

§

You may read my story and feel that you can't relate because you're not a widow or a widower. Maybe you don't have a relationship God; maybe you're skeptical of an invisible creator. Maybe you don't believe He exists and you're reading this out of sheer curiosity or support for me.

All of that is ok – because I don't share my story to convince you there is a God, although I do hope you will see Him throughout these pages. The truth is, we've all been hurt by loss and leery of hope - that is why I share my story.

We all have been forced to say goodbye to someone, or something, when we weren't ready to. Maybe it wasn't a spouse or a partner – maybe it was a friend or a friendship. Maybe it was a parent or the hope of having the parent/child relationship you always wanted. Maybe it was a sibling. Maybe it was a job; maybe it was a house. Maybe it was a pet. Maybe it was your first car. Maybe it was an item taken from you. Maybe it was that necklace you lost. No matter the type of loss, it was time that was stolen from you.

Unfortunately, none of us are immune to loss. But I believe, with all my heart, that there is power in **hope**, and that is why I tell my story. We all have the ability to rebuild, to rise, and to heal at our own pace, in our own way. And no matter where you are on your journey, I want to remind you that you are not alone. You are capable. You are worthy of healing. And you are most certainly worthy of happiness.

I've heard the phrase: "my loss will not be my story." It's usually said in an effort to minimize a deep level of heartache.

But what if we allow it to be? What if it's our story that will bring light, perspective and hope to others? We can allow our heartache to evolve us into better humans, and I promise, it won't take away from what you've lost and where you've been. We can hope for our future without fearing it will erase our past. Hope doesn't mean you have to forget your pain; it means you choose to keep going in spite of it.

I'm not writing as someone who has all the answers or as someone who has "moved on" from loss. I'm here as someone who has learned to move forward with it. I've learned it's possible to carry pain and joy at the same time. I've learned our grief does not define us - rather, it's our ability to rise from it, to keep dreaming, to keep loving, that defines us.

Each day that we live through heartache, we become emotionally and spiritually stronger. We become more resilient and we find new ways to LIVE, even if it looks different than it once did. I don't live the same as I did before Ryan died. His death changed me for the better and because of that, his life lives on through me and with me.

If you are currently walking through a journey of loss, I pray you know this: your grief is valid, your feelings are real, your journey is yours and this is <u>not</u> the end of the story you will tell.

If you find yourself not walking through loss right now, I ask you to remember that hope is something we can offer to others. A kind word, a gentle gesture, an open heart - these small acts can make all the difference to someone who feels lost in their own pain.

Thank you for being on this journey with me. As you read through my heart on paper, I want to encourage you to embrace YOUR story and hold on to hope. No matter what you're going through, no matter how heavy the weight may feel, know that there is always a way forward. You are capable of finding hope again and you deserve to live freely in the world you now see differently.

I am living proof that healing is possible, hope is real and faith is powerful. My prayer is that as you read ahead, you are reminded of your own strength and endurance while being gently held by a God who absolutely adores you - and He's not done writing the story you will tell one day.

Prologue

I couldn't stop swinging my leg. I was sitting in the waiting area of the DMV with my right leg crossed over my left as I waited for my number to be called. I looked down at my hands, which were holding a piece of paper whose words proved to everyone that my life had changed.

The air felt stiff and musty. There was a quiet groan of low voices and printers working behind the desks. I looked around at the group of us waiting patiently to be called upon. I wondered what business brought people into a place like the DMV. It felt like such an official place: the place where name changes happen after marriage or divorce, the place where nervous teenagers come to take their driving test, and the place that collects our money for the vehicles we drive and the ones we sell. I wondered if anyone was there for the same reason I was.

I glanced at my watch. For some reason, time crawls when waiting inside the DMV. Each number called feels like a winning lottery ticket as we all double-check our ticket and sigh in disappointment when we realize it's not our number. I examine my wedding ring, wiggling it on my finger in an effort to elicit sparkle underneath the dim fluorescent lighting. Even the diamonds look bored.

Over the crackling of a speaker, I finally heard my number, "G12." I swiftly jumped up and approached the woman behind the desk.

I smiled politely. "Hi, I need to order new pink slips for my vehicles."

She didn't smile in return, she simply reached out her hand to take my paperwork. I unfolded the larger document and placed it onto the counter along with my driver's license. Without any emotion, the woman loosely held my driver's license in one hand while looking over the document in the other. Despite my driver's license confirming my existence, it was that piece of paper that had become my identity. She glanced at me with sympathetic eyes.

It was my husband's death certificate.

Chapter 1

1995

"Hello?"

Any time the phone rang in our house, I ran to answer, assuming the caller would be looking for me. I was standing in the family room of my parents' home with the receiver pressed against my right ear as the white cord coiled itself around my wrist.

"Hey, can I come over?" It was my friend, Jason. He was a year older than me and would often come by my house after school in his blue truck. He was the friend I could call when I had a craving for a chili cheese burrito from Taco Bell, and I knew he would go get it for me.

"Sure!" My parents were great about allowing my friends to come to the house whenever I wanted (as long as it was before my 9:00 p.m. curfew).

"Cool. I'm gonna bring a friend with me."

"Ok, who?"

"Ryan Osler," I didn't recognize his name, which surprised

me because I spent a lot of time with Jason's friend group.

"Ok, sure!"

Jason didn't live far from my house and was at my door ten minutes after we hung up the phone. I was only fifteen years old and too naïve to understand why he was coming to my house on Valentine's Day. The doorbell echoed as I skipped in its direction. Jason was standing in front of his friend with a big smile on his face and a boxed chocolate heart in his hands. He was quick to give me a hug and I could feel the sharp edge of the box digging into my back as he brought me in close. When I pulled away from his arms, I could see his friend behind him. He was wearing a baseball hat and was staring at the ground as he swayed back and forth.

"Hi!" This kid was obviously shy, so I forced him to acknowledge me.

He looked up and mumbled some kind of greeting and I immediately took notice of his features. This kid was cute. His long blonde hair was flipping upwards beneath the back of his hat, his hands were awkwardly tucked into the pockets of his jeans, his white shirt looked as though he'd worn and washed it a million times, and his faux Timberland work boots were peeking out beneath his light blue, loose legged jeans. He didn't smile at me. In fact, he barely looked at me and said nothing more than whatever he mumbled when I overwhelmed him with my greeting.

Having been to my home several times before, Jason comfortably walked in and greeted my parents. After a quick hello, my parents went back to the family room to watch television, leaving me, Jason and my new friend Ryan, to talk about whatever teens of the 90s talked about, which in this case was nothing.

My parents, being absolute geniuses, purchased a ping-pong table for my brother and I that Christmas, and they set it up in the middle of the living room. They cleared out the couches that were never used and allowed my brother and I to take over the entrance of our home with our friends. As I mentioned before, I spent a lot of time with Jason's friend group and when they would come to my house, the ping-pong table was our entertainment. We were loud and obnoxious, screaming at each other while hitting that little plastic ball across a bright green table. My parents never asked us to be quiet, never asked us to be careful about accidentally hitting the walls, and never asked my friends to leave (well, unless it was after 9:00 p.m).

I tried talking to Jason's friend, but he didn't offer much conversation. He kept his head down, so rather than get to know him, I studied his white baseball cap and noticed how well (and questioned how long) he wore it. The bill of the hat was red and the stitching on the front of the cap was the same color, although I couldn't read what it said. I asked him about it and he shrugged.

This kid was clearly not interested in talking. So, I challenged him to a game of ping-pong. Without looking at me, he grabbed one of the paddles that were always left sitting on top of the table. I immediately served the ball to him. The rhythmic tapping of the plastic ball seemed to bring a smile to his face, and suddenly, he was laughing. I became so focused on our game that I didn't realize Jason was no longer in the room with us.

There was a secondary family room that my parents added onto the house, which was connected to the living room. Just beyond the ping-pong table, through the large doorway, was another television, a pair of couches and my dad's computer desk. Ryan hit the ball over my head and it went sailing into that other room. Jason was seated at my dad's computer desk facing the direction of the ping-pong table looking anything but amused.

"Hey, your friend is really cute," I whispered to him. He didn't acknowledge me. Instead, he stayed seated in my dad's computer chair, and I ran back into the living room determined to break the shell of this cute, shy kid.

It wasn't long after my comment that Jason said he needed to leave, which meant Ryan needed to leave, as well. I walked with them outside, and as soon as Ryan got into Jason's truck, Jason pulled me aside and let me know exactly why he came to my house that night. I was too young to put it together; I assumed we were really good friends, and I felt terrible that the feeling was not mutual. Not only was it not mutual, but that night I went to bed determined to find out more about his friend.

At school the next day, my best friend, Jaemie, and I found each other during our fifteen-minute break between classes. We were both familiar with Jason's group of friends, so we headed in the direction of where they were gathered beneath a tree. I don't know how I never noticed him before, but on this particular morning, I immediately noticed that white hat with the red stitching and that long blonde hair flipping out from beneath it.

I confidently walked over with a bounce in my step and placed myself right in front of him. I could feel my backpack hit the top of my butt as my feet landed inches away from where he was standing.

"Hey Brian," I said with full confidence.

He smiled just big enough for me to see the dimples I hadn't noticed the night before. But he didn't say anything. I could hear Jaemie talking to somebody else, so I decided to join in on that conversation since obviously this kid wasn't going to talk to me. The bell rang across campus signaling that our break was over.

He grabbed his binder and started to walk away. As he passed by, he smiled at me (well, he was either smiling at me or the ground) and Jaemie said loudly, "Bye, Ryan!"

My eyes widened as I turned to look at her. "Ryan?? Why didn't you tell me??" I was mortified. No wonder he smiled as big as he did, I called him by the wrong name. As I replayed that moment in my mind, I could hear Jaemie's muffled laughter. I went to class, and for the rest of the day, I did everything to ensure I would not see Ryan again.

§

It was Friday night and these were my favorite nights: sleepovers at Jaemie's house, talking to boys on the phone in her room (I wasn't allowed to have a phone in mine), and staying up late in the depths of girl talk.

There was a boy that had been pursuing Jaemie for a while and she told him about the crush I was brewing on his friend, Ryan. Before I had a chance to protest, Chris and Ryan showed up at her house. Chris drove a small black truck, and from what I was gathering, it seemed that Ryan didn't have transportation of his own.

It was another night of me trying to crack Ryan's shell. I didn't get too far. When Ryan and Chris were leaving, Jaemie and I walked outside with them. This felt like a repeat of three nights earlier; however, this time, Ryan's driver wasn't annoyed with me.

I watched Ryan walk across the street to Chris's truck and get into the passenger seat. Chris got into the driver's seat but he didn't start the engine. It looked like they were talking and before I could decipher their body language, Ryan got out of the truck and started walking back towards the house. I assumed he must've forgotten something, although I didn't know what since he didn't arrive with anything other than that white hat, white t-shirt, blue jeans, and faux Timberland work boots. The same exact thing he was wearing when I first met him.

He was walking straight towards me. I could hear Chris saying something from across the street but I couldn't focus on anything other than the sound of Ryan's boots against the concrete of the driveway.

"Chris said I have to kiss you or he won't give me a ride home."

I was fifteen years old. Standards and expectations didn't exist for me yet. I wanted this boy to kiss me and I didn't care that his ride home was being held for ransom.

"Well, ok. Then kiss me." Teenage Jenn was bold and confident. I didn't move. I stood there and watched this nervous kid lean into me. His hands on my shoulders felt like he was trying to maintain balance rather than trying to pull me in, and suddenly his lips were on mine. Just as fast as they were upon me, his lips were off me. He mumbled something to me and then crossed the street to his chauffeur in the black truck.

I turned around to find that Jaemie had gone inside. When I entered through the front door, she was sitting at the foot of the stairs eagerly awaiting my report on the kiss.

"Well?? I knew Chris was going to do that, I told him to do that," she was very proud of herself and her secretive planning.

As I walked into her kitchen for a glass of water, I answered, "that was terrible."

§

Although our first kiss was awkward and uncomfortable for us both, it seemed to break the ice. When I saw him at school three days later, I had a note for him. Back then, cell phones were for rich people and texting didn't exist. If we wanted to connect with someone, there was no such thing as 'swiping' or 'DM'ing.' We had to go full contact. It was terrifying. I don't recall what I wrote; probably some generic talk about the weekend or how much I hated my math class. But whatever I wrote, it worked. He wrote back to me.

This continued on for the rest of the school week. We exchanged phone numbers and would talk on the phone after school when we could. Rumors were floating around that Jennifer Yniguez and Ryan Osler liked each other, and eleven days after we first met, we became official.

It was a Saturday night and I tagged along on a babysitting job with a girlfriend of mine. I wasn't in charge, and I wasn't being paid, so I was on the phone with Ryan instead.

"Do you want me to ask you?" His voice was quiet and low,

nearly a whisper.

"Ask me what?"

"You know. Do you want me to ask you?"

He was right. I knew exactly what he was trying to ask me. But I wasn't going to make this easy for him.

"Ask me what?"

"You know what I'm going to ask you."

"Do you want to ask me?"

"Do you want me to ask you?"

"Only if you want to." I knew he liked me, but I didn't want another forced 'kissing situation' to take place.

After a long, nervous pause he finally said, "will you go out with me?"

I smiled so big it made my cheeks quiver. As though I had been expecting this question for months, I coolly answered, "yeah."

"Ok. I have to go. I love you." He rushed off the phone so quickly, I don't think he heard me say, "I love you, too." I hung up the receiver and glanced at the analog clock sitting on the kitchen counter beside the phone.

Saturday, February 25th, 1995. 11:12 p.m.

I didn't need to write it down. I was never going to forget the moment I became his. And even if we didn't actually know what it meant to love someone at fifteen years old, we would spend the next twenty-one years learning together.

Chapter 2

2016

It was the beginning of August, and Ryan's 38th birthday was fast approaching. My parents were looking for gift ideas and I came up with the perfect one.

"Garth Brooks is going to be in concert in September. How about tickets to the concert?" It wasn't an odd suggestion. We loved going to concerts and had received tickets, as well as given each other tickets, multiple times throughout our years together. My parents were happy to oblige.

Going to concerts was our favorite thing to do together. I've lost count of the number of shows we attended; if concert-going was a hobby, we were collectors.

It was Sunday, September 18th, and we were both looking forward to a date night with some good ol' country music. Ryan, a firefighter for Ventura County Fire Department, worked a twenty-four-hour shift the day before, and by the time he got home from work in the morning, I was already at church preparing to lead Sunday school for a room full of kindergarten-aged children.

I glanced down to see my cell phone ringing; it was Ryan. I sent his call to voicemail and quickly followed it up with a text: "what's up babe, can't answer right now"

"Nothing babe I just missed you and wanted to say hi."

"I miss u too babe, I can't wait for tonight!! And some good food! And maybe even a beer! ;)"

"Whaaaaaaaaaaaaaat."

"We need to find a good restaurant around there"

"Yes and a hotel"

"Haha I wish"

"Why not it's going to be so late."

"I have to work babe"

"Take it off."

The concert was at a venue located an hour and a half from home, and although he was off work the next day, I was not. We had every excuse not to make the drive that night: he was tired from the shift before, I had to work the next day, the venue was over an hour away, and it was going to be a very late night. Instead, we headed down early, battled the crowds, and endured the long wait for a table at JT Schmid's in Anaheim.

I was in the middle of a fitness challenge and had been strict with my diet and exercise, but that night there were no rules: I enjoyed a beer while we waited for a table, we ordered loaded nachos to go with our greasy burgers and beer. Over dinner we daydreamed about our future, planned our retirement and laughed at the memories we made over our twenty-one years together. We didn't talk about money or our children. We were enjoying the night as if we knew it was the last time we'd sit across from each other over dinner.

When we arrived at the venue, we found our seats and settled in. We had seen Garth Brooks in concert before (including being part of his television special when he went through his "Chris Gaines" phase), but we waited for him to take the stage as if this was our first time seeing him perform.

Before the show started, Ryan offered to get drinks so I wouldn't have to miss a moment of the concert. He darted away, and after several minutes passed, the lights in the venue went dark. I immediately pulled out my phone to capture Garth Brooks' entry. I was screaming in anticipation when I felt Ryan's presence beside me. Holding our drinks, he started yelling in excitement with me. For the next two hours, we sang every word to every song. Knowing it was his mom's favorite song, Ryan called her as Garth Brooks sang "The Dance," I took multiple videos of Garth performing, and I never noticed that we stood for the entire concert.

As the show began to wind down, Ryan yelled into my ear that he was going to get some coffee because he'd need it for the ride home. I asked him to get me a coffee, as well. I wanted to stay awake with him as he drove. After the concert ended, we walked back to our car, hand in hand, talking in excitement about the show and how well Garth Brooks entertains each time.

As Ryan drove us home, I posted a video on social media. It was a short clip of one of the songs I recorded and the only video I posted. It was Garth Brooks on stage acoustically singing his song, "If Tomorrow Never Comes."

The video captured these lyrics:

"...would she ever doubt the way I feel about her in my heart?

If tomorrow never comes, will she know how much I loved her?

Did I try in every way to show her every day that she's my only one..."

Of all the songs he sang, of all the song clips I recorded, of all the ones I chose to post - it was that one. I had no idea that was our last date, and I'm glad I didn't. Had I known, I would've put so much pressure on us to enjoy our time together. I would've calculated our conversations and made sure we said everything we needed to say. I would've cried through each song; I would've been consumed with making sure I memorized every detail of the night. I would've been lost in what I was losing.

Despite getting home at 1:30 a.m. and regretting not taking the day off, I was up early the next morning to get the kids ready for school and myself out the door to work. I worked as a pediatric medical scribe and I loved my job despite its hour long commute each way.

I arrived home from work that night to find Ryan in the kitchen preparing dinner. Music was playing, our twelve-year old daughter Amanda was helping in the kitchen, and our eleven-year old son Brandon was on the trampoline in the backyard. I went upstairs to change out of my uniform, and I could hear Ryan singing as he was making refried beans in the kitchen beneath our bedroom.

When I returned to the kitchen, I found myself smiling effortlessly as I watched him prepare dinner. I pulled out my phone and started taking photos. As I captured him, he begged me not take his picture because his hair was a mess. I promised I wouldn't post them on my social media accounts. I turned around and captured Amanda chopping tomatoes, and then I went outside in an attempt to capture Brandon's bouncing in our dimly lit backyard.

As I made my way back into the house, I was overwhelmed with gratitude in that moment. *Overwhelmed.* My heart felt as though it were about to burst as I watched my little family in our flow of togetherness. As the rice cooked, Ryan brought me outside to the front of the house to show me all that he had done while I was at work. He spent the day working around the house: he put together the trampoline that he had taken down during a wind storm, he replaced all the lights in the front yard and he cut the grass and trimmed the bushes.

We stood across the street looking back at our house. The trees were beautifully lit, the steps leading up to our house had a warm glow, and the laughter of our two children on the trampoline filled the quiet neighborhood.

"It looks great, babe, thank you for doing all that," I said as I touched his shoulder.

When we entered the house, a notification on Ryan's phone interrupted the music playing through speakers in the family room.

It was 7:40 p.m. "They're looking for someone to fill the water tender," he said as he put his phone back down. There was a fire burning near Vandenberg Air Force Base in Lompoc and Ventura County Fire already had a strike team in place, but they needed to send a water tender to assist the firefighting efforts.

"Should I take it? It'll be easy money," he said.

We were in the process of saving money to put a pool in our backyard. It was the first time in our married life that we were finally on top of our finances; we didn't have any debt and we could focus on Ryan's dream to have a pool.

After years of being married to a firefighter, I answered him as I always did when it came to overtime and strike teams, "whatever you want to do, babe." We didn't go through a summer without Ryan being on a strike team. The year before, he was gone for almost three weeks as he was sent to a fire in Riverside County (south from our home), and from there, he was sent directly to the Rough Fire circling Hume Lake (north from our home). Our family was used to this routine.

He agreed to go, and as soon as his acceptance was acknowledged, everything shifted in the house. He ran upstairs to shower, pack his out-of-county bag with extra clothes and toiletries, and change into his uniform. I went outside to let the kids know their Daddy was called to a fire. I then went to the kitchen, turned off the stove, and made him a cup of coffee.

I could hear his heavy footsteps moving quickly upstairs. The water tender was hoping to leave at 9:00pm; it would take Ryan approximately an hour to get from our house to the station, and he had to first stop at his own station to get his gear. I heard a giant thud as his bag hit the floor in front of the stairs. I walked his direction with a hot cup of coffee in my hands and our kids in tow.

At 8:19pm we began our "Daddy is leaving on a fire" routine. We knew the drill: walk Daddy to the door, hugs and kisses goodbye, watch him drive away and wave until he was out of sight. I quickly snapped a photo of Ryan as he walked out the door in a hurry. The photo was blurry and the kids were an equal blur of motion as they chased after him. He loaded his car and then came back to me. I handed my phone to Amanda so I could wrap my arms around him.

She took a photo. 8:20pm.

She captured our last moment together. Our very last hug.

Ryan's face is buried into my neck, his eyes are closed, and he's holding me tightly with his right arm, while holding that cup of coffee in his left hand. We held that hug longer than we usually would. "Strike team hugs" were always different because we didn't know when he'd be home again. It could've been a couple days or a couple weeks, and hearing from him while being away wasn't a guarantee.

When we broke our embrace, the kids each hugged him and then the three of us stood on our porch as we watched Ryan get into his car and back out of the driveway.

He stopped when his car entered the street and rolled down his window, "tell Terry I'll help him move that bed when I get back!"

I said I would and stuck out my arm to wave goodbye. The kids were waving frantically as he drove away from home, the energy from their time on the trampoline coursing through their veins. "Bye Daddy!!"

And he was gone.

I walked the kids back into the house, told them to go upstairs to shower and get ready for bed, and I started cleaning up the kitchen. My phone rang. It was Ryan. With wonder about why he was calling, I answered the phone, "hi babe, what's going on?"

"Nothing, I just miss you already."

I smiled and softly giggled as I said, "I miss you, too, babe."

Chapter 3

September 21, 2016

It was an ordinary Wednesday morning in September in Southern California. Despite being the day before the official end of the summer season, the air was already warm at 6:15 a.m. as I was leaving the gym. As I walked to my car, I noticed a text from my husband: *"Good morning babe I love you."* He sent it at 6:07 a.m. I responded as I walked, "Good morning babe, just leaving the gym. I love you!" I jumped into my car and made my way home.

As I was nearing the house, I received a phone call from my cousin. I answered and could hear she was crying.

"What's wrong?"

Through sobs, Katie said, "I'm pregnant." She and her husband were not expecting this surprise. With three young children and a small townhouse, she was overwhelmed by this news. I listened to her, secretly smiling because I was thrilled to know we'd be welcoming another baby into our family. I reminded her that God doesn't make mistakes. I encouraged her with reminders of God's plans for our lives, even the plans we don't expect.

The morning continued as every morning did: waking the children, making sure they got themselves ready for school as I got ready for work, school drop offs and then enduring the hour-long commute into the office.

My mom and I were nearing the office building in which we worked. Although we worked for the same pediatric practice, we only drove together once a week. I traveled between our two office locations three days a week, but on Wednesdays, I stayed at our primary office, which is where my mom always worked. Waiting in the left turn lane, the only sound in the car was the ticking of the blinker. My mom was driving; I had been looking at my phone, but placed it in my lap to look up and count the number of cars ahead of us. Once I saw we'd be at the light for a while, I picked up my phone again.

Within that brief moment, a text had been delivered to me. It was Brandi, the wife of Ryan's captain.

8:13 a.m.

"Hey Jen what is the name of the doctor office you work at?"

I worked for a pediatrician and several of my friends brought their children to my office, so this wasn't an odd text for me to receive.

"Hi! The Pediatric Group of Southern California (Dr. Barnhard)"

"What's the address. Is it off of Burbank Blvd"

"Yes!"

"Ok thanks honey"

I thought nothing further of our text exchange and returned the phone to my lap.

Out of habit, I picked up my phone after a couple of minutes had passed. This time, I saw that I missed a phone call from an unfamiliar number. While still in my hands, a notification appeared on my phone that the unknown caller left a voice message.

"Hi Jennifer, this is Mark Lorenzen with Ventura County Fire Department. I'm going to try calling you again."

Mark Lorenzen was the Fire Chief of the department for which my husband worked. *"Why the heck is the Chief calling me,"* I whispered as I dialed his phone number.

He answered in the middle of the first ring. "Hello?"

In my bubbliest voice I answered, "hi Chief, this is Jenn Osler, I'm returning your call."

The rest of the conversation is in fragments of my memory:

"Ryan was assigned to the Canyon Fire... There was an accident with the water tender... He was killed."

We hadn't made that left turn yet. We were still waiting to move.

"What? You're joking."

"I'm so sorry..."

I felt the car turn left as we crossed over the familiar railroad tracks. My mom placed her hand on my shoulder. I don't know if I screamed. I don't remember what I said. The only thing I can clearly recall is yelling to the Chief, "what am I going to tell my kids??" I was bent over in the passenger seat of the car. My body was folded in half. I could hear my mom's voice but I had no clue what she was saying.

"We're coming to your office," the Chief said.

"No. I'm going home. Go to my house."

I hung up on the Chief, and then realized that Brandi wasn't asking for my office address because she was looking for a new pediatrician. She was asking for the address because the Chief was looking for me.

I don't remember arriving, but somehow my mom and I were in the parking lot of my office; the one I told Brandi about. I heard my mom talking to someone, but didn't know who. I felt the car turn as my limp body was pushed against the door by gravity. We were heading back to the freeway that would take me home.

It was quiet again.

I later learned that Ryan was in the passenger seat of a California OES (Office of Emergency Services) water tender. The water tender is a truck that seats only two people and its purpose is to transport water supply to fire engines or brush rigs where there is no immediate water available. In other words, it was the least dangerous task a firefighter could be given on a wildfire. The accident occurred early morning (approximately 6:20am according to reports) as another Ventura County Firefighter drove the water tender eastbound on Highway 246 towards the Canyon Fire at Vandenberg Air Force Base in Santa Barbara County. The weather conditions were listed as being dark with dense fog reducing visibility levels. I'm told that the water tender struck a roundabout on Highway 246 at Purisima Road and an overcorrection of the vehicle caused the water tender to roll, killing my husband in the process. The words "dead on arrival" became descriptive of my husband's condition, and I did everything to block that phrase from my mind.

"He has to come home. This isn't real. It's not. He's coming home." Over and over again I repeated this to myself. My voice became a whisper. "It's not real. He's coming home." My stare was blank. My phone was being loosely held in my hands. My words were on repeat: "it's not real."

Forty-five minutes later, we rounded the corner onto my street. I saw a department vehicle parked in front of my home. *"Oh my God..."* In the driveway stood a man of stature, dressed in uniform, beside him was my father and I realized that must've been who my mom called. I doubled over. I couldn't lift my arms. My head felt heavy as it rested against my knees. I suddenly felt hot air hitting my body. My dad opened the passenger door and immediately covered me. I could hear his voice, he was sobbing. I felt the moisture of his tears against my cheek. I couldn't unbuckle my seatbelt. My dad must've done that for me. My weak legs climbed out of the car.

"Let me get you a chair. I'll grab a chair. Come sit down. Let me get a chair," my dad sounded frantic.

"I don't want a chair. I don't want to sit."

I approached the very tall, soft-faced man. He was a Chaplain with the fire department; he looked familiar, although I couldn't place where I had seen him before. Without any emotion I asked, "were you the one who was there the night my father-in-law died?" I'm not sure if he answered my question. I'm not even sure if he was the Chaplain I was thinking about.

He offered his condolences; his eyes appeared heavy. I think I interrupted him: "does his mom know yet?" He softly whispered, "no."

"Someone needs to go tell her. Right now."

She lived a mile away from our house, and I knew she would be there because she worked from home. I also knew she kept the local news on the television in her office, and I knew it wouldn't be long before Ryan's death was being talked about on her television screen. I heard my dad offer to go with the Chaplain to her house. I stood in my driveway, trying to imagine her opening the front door to find the Chaplain waiting for her. I felt physically ill. I closed my eyes as they drove away, wishing she didn't have to open the door.

A noise forced me to open my eyes again. I saw my neighbor, Terry, in his driveway across the street. He reminded me of a young Santa Claus. He was always working, always building, and seemed to always be wearing denim overalls. I walked slowly toward him, and the memory of Ryan promising to help Terry when he returned home flashed through my mind. Terry had on those overly worn overalls. He didn't say a word. He put his hands up in the air; I could see his bottom lip curl as he tightly wrapped me in a hug as though he were trying to take away the truth. We stood in the middle of the street, crying. His wife, Trish, rushed to me, quick to cradle me in her arms. I can still hear her voice, sweet but cracked, as she tried to comfort me.

We stood in the middle of the street. I watched as my next-door neighbor, Chase, and his wife, Collette, emerged from their front door unaware of what was happening. Trish ran to them. Terry and I were talking, but I don't recall the words. Chase came running our direction, Collette closely followed behind him. More hugs. More words. The five of us stood in the middle of the street staring at my house. Two nights earlier I stood in the same spot with Ryan as we stared back at the house. Everything appeared the same but suddenly looked different.

As we stood in the street, a white truck rounded the corner at a speed that was too fast for our neighborhood and abruptly parked in front of my house. Out of the truck jumped a man whose face was a mix of disbelief and tears. "No, it's not true, is it? Not Ryan. Not him." It was my husband's best friend, Roger.

One by one, more cars appeared in my driveway and parked on the street. In numbers were fire Captains and Chiefs entering my home, their condolences beginning to sound like a standard greeting. My home was a single girl's dream with uniformed firefighters taking up a majority of space. But for me, it was a nightmare.

Someone mentioned that the Fire Chief was on his way to my home. I nodded in acknowledgment, but silently turned my gaze toward the dining room table. I went straight to the cupboard beneath my kitchen sink, grabbed a bottle of cleaner and a dust rag. I made my way through the blue uniforms and random people in my home and began dusting my dining room table. My mom came over to me in disbelief and asked what I was doing.

"The Chief is coming; I can't have a dusty table. I have to get the house ready." Ryan held every rank in high respect (even refusing to call his captain by name while on vacation with him and his wife). I remember hearing my husband speak highly of Chief Lorenzen and I knew he would be mortified to have a dusty table welcome his Chief.

My mom took the rag out of my hand, "you don't need to worry about the table," she said. I let her take the rag and said nothing as she continued to wipe down the table for me.

The Fire Chief seemed to appear on my doorstep within minutes. His eyes were soft but sorrowful. This was my first time meeting the Chief and as he stood before me, I envisioned the minutes leading up to our phone call. My empty heart was filled with sympathy as I realized he also received a phone call that morning. The domino effect of this accident was enormous and it all started with someone having to make a phone call. He repeatedly apologized for having to tell me over the phone, "…I needed to get to you before you heard about it somewhere else."

I was advised by Chiefs to leave my children at school. It was determined best to let them finish their day while more people arrived to inform me about what would take place over the next 48 hours. No sooner had I been directed to leave my children at school was I approached outside by another firefighter.

"Do your kids have a phone?"

"My daughter does," I answered hesitantly.

"Then you need to go to the school right now and get her. It's already in the news. His name and everything."

Panic swept over my body. I pulled my phone out of my pocket. The screen was flooded with text messages, missed phone calls and voicemails. I had notifications in every social media outlet. I opened Facebook and sure enough, there he was. His handsome face. His smile. His name.

Article after article was about the firefighter who died in a roll-over accident on his way to fight a fire. Post after post was about the department mourning the loss of their comrade. Word after word was about the man who was supposed to come home to his wife and his children. Photo upon photo was the man I called my husband.

My parents offered to get the children and bring them home.

"No. I will go get them."

Just as I was about to leave, a woman appeared on my doorstep, Sharon. Less than a year earlier she was teaching me about grief, the grieving process, and steps towards healing through the Grief Recovery Method. I had been there to grieve the loss of a relationship in my life, but I could've never anticipated how her wisdom would be used a short time after learning from her. I could see so much pain in her eyes. I stood still as she wrapped me in a hug. My body felt too weak to return her embrace. I told her I was going to get my kids. She gently held my shoulders as she reminded me to be direct when telling my children. "Say the words, say the words," she reminded me.

Death is a scary and uncomfortable topic as it is, and when it comes to discussing death with children, it's natural to want to protect them from the harsh truth. Phrases such as "daddy is gone," "daddy went to heaven," or "we lost daddy today" sound gentle to the ears but run the risk of confusion within their precious minds. Their innocent thoughts begin to wonder, "where did daddy go? When will he get back? Daddy is lost? Can we look for him?" I could hear the echo of Sharon's teachings in my ear as she looked me in the eyes: "Be direct, and then walk them through the truth."

I nodded and slowly walked to the passenger side of a car

waiting for me; it belonged to Mahal, my closest friend and Roger's wife. A Chief, a Chaplain and Roger followed behind in a separate vehicle. As we left the safety of my home, I tried to grasp the gravity of what was about to happen.

My stare was as blank as my mind. My limbs felt numb, and my body felt as though it would float away had it not been for the seatbelt holding me down. We first went to the school of my twelve-year-old daughter. I walked into the front office, followed by a group of solemn faces behind me. The woman behind the desk immediately stood as we entered; I noticed the puzzled look on her face.

"I need to get my daughter. Her father died this morning." My voice was lifeless.

I don't know what happened after that. I remember standing in the office, swaying back and forth as I waited for her. The room felt musty and drenched with sadness.

What was likely only minutes felt like an hour of waiting. And then, I saw my daughter approaching the office. I hadn't taken my eyes off the window, but she seemed to appear out of thin air. The principal of the school and a school counselor were waiting for her outside. I watched her through the window and realized I was witnessing the last moments of her normal life. My heart pounded in fear as I prepared to take her world from normal to broken. Her blonde hair bounced as she walked, and her smile towards the principal and the counselor indicated that she had no idea what was waiting for her once she stepped into the office.

As soon as she entered, she stopped. She didn't come to me.

Instead, she stood still, staring at me, and then slowly glanced at the faces behind me. Her voice shook when she said, "Mommy, what's wrong?"

I walked toward her, grabbed her hand and led her outside. She was nearing adolescence, but with her hand in mine she felt so little. We stopped a few feet away from the door. I hugged her tightly as I tried to gather the courage to tell her. She pulled away from my hug, "Mommy?"

I placed her face in my hands and brought her eyes to mine.

"Baby, there was an accident this morning..." I had to pause as I watched her eyes search mine. "...Daddy died this morning."

Her eyebrows furrowed, creating deep valleys between her eyes. I watched her lips quiver as they distorted into a frown too deep for her youthful face. Her bright blue eyes were drowning in the tears that hadn't fallen yet. I immediately pulled her into me, holding her head against my chest. I don't know how long we stood there. I don't know at which point I released my grip on her. But eventually, we broke our embrace. We walked in silence.

Once in the car, she whispered, "does Brandon know?"

I turned to look at her face. Her once fair skin was now red with remnants of black mascara painted on her cheeks. I remembered Ryan's disdain the first time he saw Amanda wearing mascara; he wasn't ready for her to grow up but she was ready to blossom. It broke his heart to admit she was maturing. That same mascara now stained the face of his little girl.

"Not yet. We're going to the school now."

The distance between the two schools is just over a mile, but the drive felt as though there were a hundred miles separating them. The car was silent. When we arrived at my son's school, I asked my daughter to wait in the car with Mahal. As I entered the office with a cloud of gloom behind me, I asked the woman behind the desk to call for my son. I turned away, my stomach in knots as I waited for him. I could hear Roger talking to the women behind the desk. My back was facing them, but I could hear their expressions.

I walked out of the office. I needed fresh air. I looked towards my right, expecting to see my son walk down the corridor. But instead, he appeared to my left.

"Mama, what's going on? Why is there a fire [department] car here?"

Just as I did with my daughter, I grabbed my son and held him close to me. I barely had him in an embrace when he started pushing me away, wanting an answer. I cupped his small face in my hands. His eleventh birthday was less than two weeks ago but as I held his face, all I could see was the two year-old playing catch with his dad for the first time.

I inhaled deeply, afraid to exhale.

"Baby, there was an accident this morning..." I paused, catching my breath before altering my son's life, "...Daddy died this morning."

He didn't cry. He looked behind me at the bright yellow Suburban parked in the driveway of the school. "What?" He was confused. "Dad died? How?"

"There was an accident with the truck he was in, and he died in the accident."

I could see that he needed to cry, but his body refused that release. I wrapped him in my arms, resting my cheek on the top of his head. "I'm so sorry, baby," the words barely emerged from my mouth. I placed my hands on his back, and started leading him towards the car. The silence in the air was painful. I watched my son stare at the Chief and the Chaplain as we walked past them. They nodded in his direction, acknowledging his presence.

As soon as we were in the car, I turned to face both of my children. They were staring at each other. There were no words.

I broke the silence. "There are going to be a lot of people at our house right now. Do you want to go home? Or do you want to go to a park or somewhere else?"

With tiny voices they both agreed to go home. We drove in silence. I kept turning around to look at my children. My daughter's face was filled with worry; she wouldn't take her eyes off me. My son was staring out the window; I could see the thoughts running through his mind.

We seemed to arrive at our house within a matter of seconds. There were more vehicles surrounding my home. My front door was open. There were people scattered all over my property, several I recognized and many I did not. In a daze, my children and I walked towards the front door of our home. As soon as we crossed the threshold, the three of us were separated. It was as if we were caught in a wave that crashed upon us, forcing us to separate. The kids were immediately smothered with hugs and words. Men who never met them but knew their father approached with forced smiles and gentle handshakes.

I was pulled away by a couple of men in uniform. In hushed voices I was escorted to my front porch.

"They're starting the procession to bring Ryan's body home. I know this is a hard question to have to answer, but where do you want him to be taken?"

Ryan and I hadn't spoken about this. Each time I would ask hypothetical questions about our eventual deaths, he would refuse to discuss the topic. I didn't know what he wanted; I didn't know where his body should be received. I didn't know.

But, as surely as I did not know, I felt the answer come to me naturally: "Conejo Mountain." It came out of my mouth as though Ryan and I had discussed this several times in the past. Conejo Mountain is the resting place of Ryan's father, who died fourteen years earlier. In the time since his father's death, Ryan visited the cemetery only twice: once when his grandmother died and most recently a year before his own death. I had no reason to recall the name of that particular funeral home and cemetery. It was located an hour away from our house, and Ryan's father and grandparents were the only souls I knew resting there. But when I was asked in that moment where I wanted my husband's body to be taken, the answer came to me as though I had been prepared for this day.

More questions were coming:

"do you know how you would like for his body to be prepared?"

"would you like to go to the cemetery to watch the procession?"

"there's news coverage of the procession, would you like to see it?"

I chose not to go to the cemetery to welcome the procession. When asked, I was told I needed to give an answer sooner rather than later due to the length of time it would take us to get to the funeral home. Without thought, and in a panic, I quickly answered: "No. No, I don't want to see it."

It's one of my deepest regrets to this day.

I imagined watching a slow-moving black hearse carrying not only my dead husband, but a dark feeling with it. I didn't want to see or feel that darkness. I wanted to stay with my children in the safety of our home.

Months later, I would do a Google search of my husband's name and come across a video from a local news channel that documented the arrival of his body. I saw a beautiful white hearse pull into the front of the funeral home. A red carpet lined the walkway where the hearse parked, and several uniformed men decorated the border of the carpet. Their arms were tautly raised with their hands against their foreheads in salute of their fallen brother. I watched as two men opened the rear doors of the hearse and gently remove the gurney on which my husband's lifeless body laid. The American flag was draped over him and I could see the familiar outline of his body.

Immediately, my heart was filled with regret. I should've been there. I should've been there to welcome his body home. I should've been there to feel his body through the fabric of the flag. I should've been there to lay my head on his chest. I should've been there to hold his hand before an embalmer took possession of it.

Instead, he was received by his brothers in the fire service, and I am grateful to each of them for being there to welcome him home.

§

Later in the afternoon, I approached Chief Lorenzen and asked him to follow me outside. He followed closely behind me as I walked him towards the side of my house, where nobody else stood. News vans had been driving past my home, and local sheriffs were parked on the street below to keep them from coming our direction. Outside, hiding on the side of my house beside three large trash bins, I asked the Chief about the accident. More specifically, I asked how Ryan died. I had an image in my mind of Ryan slowly dying and his last thoughts being riddled with fear of leaving me, our children, and his mom behind. I hated that thought. I hated imagining him worried about us as he took his last breaths. In my imagination, I saw fear in his eyes. I heard him apologizing for not coming home. I hated imagining my husband worrying about us as he lay dying on a street. I hated it because I knew he would. I knew that would've been his heart. He would've died feeling guilty for leaving his family.

"I don't want to know details, but can you tell me how Ryan died? Was it fast or..." my words trailed off. I didn't know how to finish that question.

The Chief softened his expression and looked towards the ground. He knew what I was wondering.

"It happened so fast, I don't think he knew what happened," he finally said. His voice was gentle and his eyes were empathetic. I nodded in understanding, thankful to know (or at the very least, believe) that Ryan's final moments were not filled with the fear or worry I imagined. I still don't know the details of the accident. The police reports have been offered to me, but I don't want them. I don't want to know. I don't need to know. I have in mind that Ryan closed his eyes and opened them to God, and that is all I want to envision.

The rest of that first day was a blur, except for a moment that occurred in the late afternoon. I stepped outside and sat down on the steps leading up to my front door. The sky was crystal clear. The sun was warm on my skin and its glare was forcing me to squint. A very gentle breeze was causing wisps of hair to stick to my face. It was the kind of day that made you grateful to be alive. I felt a small presence next to me. It was my son. He sat down, getting as close as he possibly could.

"Hey buddy."

"Hi mama."

We sat still, allowing the sun to melt our arms together.

"Mama, is Daddy really dead?"

My heart dropped. "Yeah, buddy. He is."

He said nothing. We sat in silence for another minute.

"His heart will never beat again?"

I was staring at the ground in front of me. "No, buddy."

The only sound was the murmuring of people inside our house and the leaves being rustled by the breeze that once made me grateful to be alive. Together, we sat. Although inaudible, I had a feeling we were both focusing on the sound of our beating hearts.

Chapter 4

I've always been active on my social media accounts. I had been operating a public Facebook page that grew by thousands; it was titled Spiritually Single, which was inspired by my blog of the same title. What began as a group for women married to men who didn't regularly go to church became a sanctuary for married and single women alike. I had grown it enough to host giveaways and take the role as a guest blogger for the popular website, Girlfriends Pray. But my favorite thing to do was share some kind of encouragement each day with the women in this group.

The morning of Ryan's accident, but before I learned of it, I posted a photo I saved from Pinterest. In black script, bordered by gold-colored arrows, read the words: "Where God guides, He provides. Isaiah 58:11." I didn't share any thoughts beyond a red heart emoji beneath this photo. I didn't feel that it needed any explanation. It spoke loudly to me, and after my cousin's phone call about her pregnancy, I sent this photo to her as a reminder that God would provide whatever she was going to need. I had no idea how those words would speak to me a couple of hours later.

In addition to Spiritually Single, I was active on my personal Facebook page and Instagram account, typically posting something each day. By nine o'clock that night, the only thing the public heard from me was silence.

As night fell onto my part of the world, the house became quiet as there were only a handful of people remaining. I sat down at my dining room table and picked up my phone. In the midst of the afternoon chaos, I had only one thought in regards to my phone, and it wasn't about social media: *"I wonder if Ryan saw my text."* Unlike me, he kept the read receipts on his text messages.

"Good morning babe, just leaving the gym. I love you!"

Read 6:17 a.m.

He read it two minutes after I sent it, and possibly only a couple of minutes before the accident.

When I looked at my phone that night, the screen was littered with notifications. I knew what was behind each red dot - the condolences I didn't want to read. I hesitantly tapped on Facebook. As soon as it opened, my husband's face was staring back at me. My 'friends' were reposting articles and videos that had been shared by news networks across the country. More red dots within the app glared at me through my screen. People tagging me in posts, writing on my Facebook page, sending private messages - it was so kind, but it felt like too much. I didn't acknowledge any of it.

Instead, I answered the prompt at the top of my screen: *"what's on your mind?"*

I opened the photo album on my phone. I knew exactly which

picture I was looking to find. I shared it four months earlier with words honoring my husband on International Firefighter Day. It was one of my favorite photos. I captured Ryan's silhouette walking out the front door of our home as he was leaving for the 2013 Rim Fire in Yosemite. I quickly snapped the photo as he headed out to load the car with his gear. I don't know why I took the photo; I'd like to believe that I was intentionally capturing moments for him to look back upon during his retirement years, but in truth, I don't know what prompted me to capture that moment. I selected that photo and populated the empty box asking for my thoughts. I finally broke my silence: *"My world stopped today. My love, my all, my hero... #teamOsler #FOURever"*

I publicly posted it, stared at my words in absolute disbelief and put down my phone. I didn't want to see anybody's words or posts because if I read them, it meant that all of this was true.

My body was exhausted and I knew I needed sleep, but I couldn't sleep in my bed. Ryan hadn't slept in our bed for two nights prior to his death, and I was used to him being absent from bed several nights per week due to the job, but this was different. I was afraid to sleep in my bed. I didn't want to wake up with the reality that he will never wake beside me again.

I opted for the couch in my living room. It was big and comfortable and it swallowed my body just enough to make me feel safe that I wouldn't roll off. My children slept on the other sections of the couch and the three of us tried to pretend that sleep was what we wanted instead of what we needed. I don't remember falling asleep and I don't remember waking up, but suddenly a new day was glaring at me through the window.

The house was eerily quiet, as though the walls were trying to pretend that everything was normal. I glanced at my sleeping children and decided I would join the walls in their silence and pretend nothing had changed. But the air felt different, the sunlight peeking through the blinds looked different, and I knew that nothing would ever again be the same.

I reached for my phone. Any time Ryan was at the station or away at a fire, I always woke up to a text message from him wishing me a 'good morning' to start my day. Always. He never went a morning without texting or a night without reminding me of his love. Even if we were angry, he didn't withdraw his love. In nearly twenty-two years together, I can't recall a time when I experienced a day without his declaration of love for me.

There was nothing. No morning text from Ryan. His name had fallen beneath countless text messages from names and numbers of people who took the place of his expressed love. I scrolled past unopened messages in search of his. I tapped on his name and read his message again: "Good morning babe I love you." I stared at it until my eyelids forced me to blink. I couldn't comprehend that any of this was real. How could this possibly be the last message I would ever receive from my husband? I scrolled back through our texts and instantly hated myself for getting a new phone two weeks earlier; I couldn't find our messages prior to that time period. I was angry with myself, angry with Apple, angry with everything and everyone. I read through our text conversation the night before he died. It was about the kids and it had the potential to go sour, but it didn't. My husband went to sleep the night before he died feeling appreciated, and I went to sleep feeling heard. The next morning, those texts would become the last thing I'd have as proof of his love for me.

I still have our texts on my phone. Every once in a while, I scroll all the way to the bottom of my messages. Instead of his name, now it's his old phone number. I open our text thread and stare at our last communication with each other. The specified time of the read receipt stamp on my last message is no longer specific to the hour; it simply says "Read 9/21/16."

I was in the habit of posting inspirational words on my Spiritually Single Facebook page each morning. I typically had a draft scheduled and ready to go, but that morning I stared at the community I built and decided to let them know what took place the day before.

I shared a photo of Ryan and I from our vow renewal in Jamaica. It's a heavenly setting: we're both wearing white, the background was lightened to appear heaven-like, and there is a soft glow surrounding our kiss. As I began to write, I realized that none of the thousands of people on this page actually knew me. I never shared my name or a personal photo. I had to tell them what happened. I hadn't had to do that yet. Up until this moment, everyone I interacted with knew what happened to Ryan. For the first time, I had to say the words out loud to those who didn't personally know us:

"Yesterday my world came to a screeching stop. I'm asking my faithful, wonderful Spiritually Single friends to carry me and my children in prayer as we try to figure out how to go on. My husband, Ryan Osler, was tragically killed yesterday morning while on his way

to fight a fire away from home. Please pray for me and my children and the days to come. #teamOsler"

§

Fire personnel returned to my home later that morning. A chaplain, chiefs, captains, and several others, I'm sure. My dining room table had become a host of quiet conversations. I was sitting with two men from the department, although I can't recall whom. I hadn't yet learned the name of the firefighter who was driving the water tender that took my husband's life. The most I knew about the accident was one firefighter walked away from the wreckage with minor injuries and one was dead on arrival. Despite not knowing his name, I worried about him, whoever he was.

I looked towards one of the uniformed men sitting beside me and didn't take my eyes off him when I softly asked, "how is the driver?" The firefighter turned his gaze away from mine, undoubtedly because the question made him uncomfortable.

"He's doing ok, he's home."

I wasn't sure if he understood what I was asking, so I asked again, "how *is* he?" I changed the tone of my words to signal that I was concerned about his emotional well-being.

The firefighter beside me didn't know how to answer. He could only shrug his shoulders in response.

"Please, make sure he knows I'm not angry with him. I'm not upset with him. I don't blame him."

Without meeting my eyes, the man beside me nodded and said, "I'll make sure he knows."

I lowered my head, placing my face under his, forcing him to look at me. "I mean it, make sure he knows."

I didn't know anything about the driver, but I knew that if it were my husband in the driver's seat of the accident that took another man's life, he would've been emotionally tortured. To this day, I believe that had it been the other way around, the kids and I would've lost Ryan to his torment. I couldn't stop thinking about the man responsible for my husband's death. I genuinely felt no anger towards him. I knew he was tortured with the sights and sounds of that morning. I knew he was forced to replay every minute in his mind. I knew he was going back to the moments leading up to the accident and wishing he had done something different. I knew that my husband's death would be endless suffering on his conscience. And I knew that my anger would serve no purpose, however, my offering of compassion and forgiveness might be able to serve him peace.

"I trust that if Ryan were meant to come home, he would've. I believe that." I truly meant that. It wasn't a thought-out response nor was it rehearsed. It was a conviction I didn't even know I had until I said it out loud.

The firefighter finally looked at me. He shook his head in what I see now as disbelief. Maybe he thought I was crazy, maybe he thought it was the shock talking, but whatever he thought, he offered a gentle smile and said, "I'll make sure he knows."

§

Nobody wanted to, but we needed to talk about the next step: the funeral. Before that discussion, we needed to talk about Ryan's wishes, if he had any, and how I would like to proceed. They sat me down in preparation to begin planning, but I requested that our meeting wait until Ryan's mom and his sisters were present. I refused to make any decisions without their input or awareness. We were all operating in shock and I wanted to ensure that nothing would be a surprise to anybody. As soon as they arrived, we gathered in a circle in my family room. First order of business: what to do with his body.

Ryan and I never spoke about this. I laughed to myself at the irony of the conversation because each time I would ask Ryan about his wishes, he would brush me off and call me morbid for wanting to talk about death.

I knew his mom would not want him to be cremated, so I immediately took that option off the table before she arrived at my home. We didn't even discuss it. The next step would be to go to the funeral home and decide upon burial options. Burial options. As if we were deciding options on a car or upgrades in a home. The men in uniform said they would arrange for transportation and we would go to the funeral home the next morning.

While we were discussing the funeral, a bunting ceremony was taking place at Ryan's fire station in Moorpark. Ventura County Fire Department, Station 42, was Ryan's last assignment. He loved that station. It was new, big, beautiful, and one of the few to have an actual pole to slide down. But his favorite thing about the station didn't involve any of those things; it was his room where he kept pictures of the kids, a drawing from Amanda with a reminder to be safe, and the bed from which he would call me each night before falling asleep. He was proud to call that fire house his home away from home.

The public had been invited to participate in this ceremony as black and purple bunting was draped from the roof of the station, photos of Ryan were placed near the flag pole, the flag had been lowered to half-staff, and flowers dropped off by residents decorated the front of the station. Pictures sent to me later that day showed a somber, reverent, and beautiful scene: numerous uniformed firefighters were present, along with several members of the public, including my pregnant cousin, her husband, and their three sweet children.

§

That night, I again refused to sleep in my bed. The kids and I made ourselves comfortable on the couch for another night of broken sleep. I woke in the middle of the night with a fierce ache in my stomach. I didn't realize that I hadn't eaten all day or the day before. I know there was food in the house because people kept bringing it. My body consumed nothing but somehow emptied everything. I tiptoed into the kitchen because Mahal was sleeping on the couch. '*A banana, I'll grab a banana,*' I thought to myself as I quietly approached the kitchen counter. I stood at my back door slowly eating the banana I selected while staring into the dark sky and watching the twinkling city lights that danced in the distance.

Suddenly, Mahal sat up on the couch. She noticed me at the door and walked over to me. "Are you ok? Do you need something?"

For the first time in two days, I felt peaceful. Genuinely peaceful. I shook my head, "no, I'm ok. I'm going to be ok. It's weird, I feel peaceful." It was an odd thing to say at 3am, and another to feel two days after my husband died. "I really believe it's all the prayers that are being said for us."

"Well, that's good. I'm happy to see you eating a banana, by the way," she whispered. We giggled in silence as I admitted I could only finish half of it and we stared into the sky without saying another word.

I went back to my spot on the couch with my body somewhat pleased I put something in it and my heart ready to attempt sleep again. The next thing I remember, it was morning. I sat up, stretched and turned my body towards the front window of my home and watched our American flag waving in the gentle morning breeze. I slept, which my body needed, but the peace that my heart felt hours earlier was now gone. It was Friday. And this was the day I was going to be forced to acknowledge the reality of my loss.

I was going to the funeral home.

§

A limousine arrived at my house to pick me up, along with Ryan's mom and sisters. We were heading to Conjeo Mountain Funeral Home and my mind was racing with ideas of what might be awaiting our arrival.

It's the most beautiful setting (if cemeteries can be called beautiful) tucked into the hills of Camarillo. As we exited the car, I could hear soft music playing through speakers hidden from view. The employees knew we were coming; they were waiting on us as soon as we walked in. Directly in front of us was a guest book with a framed sign above it: "Honoring Ryan Osler." An American flag stood perched next to the podium and

I noticed there had been a single pink rose placed delicately at the top of the guest book.

As I admired the scene, I was approached by an employee, "someone left that for you when they heard you were coming by."

I picked it up with gratitude for the kindness of a stranger and slowly turned toward the hallway on my left. I saw two uniformed men standing at attention outside of a door. We were escorted in their direction and I felt a flood of fear wash over my body. *'Was Ryan in there? Why are they standing guard? What's in there? Is there a casket in there?'* I silently panicked as I entered the room behind their guarded attention.

I slowly, hesitantly, looked to my right and saw two more uniformed men standing at attention. There was no casket. There was nothing scary waiting for me. Instead, there was a podium between them on which a folded flag was resting. It was the flag that had been laid across Ryan's body when he was being transported from Lompoc to Camarillo. My heart settled and I sat in a chair to observe the simple scene before me. The uniformed men would not look at me; I don't know if they were instructed not to or if they couldn't bring themselves to meet my eyes. They were firefighters. I studied their faces and my heart broke for each of the men in uniform assigned to stand in an empty room to protect the flag that covered their deceased comrade.

We were then taken into a room with a table that felt larger than necessary. As we gathered around it, I imagined how difficult this job must be for funeral directors and employees. I don't recall much, but I do remember being shown options of caskets, firefighter adornments and burial tombs; items I never imagined having to choose at this age. The conversation shifted when it came to discuss how deep Ryan would be buried. Ryan's father died fourteen years earlier in 2002, at which time Ryan's mom purchased a plot for herself next to him. Now, she was giving her reserved space to Ryan. Her son. My soul sank each time I tried to imagine what this must've felt like for her.

As we talked through burial logistics, the conversation turned its focus onto me. My husband died two days earlier. He was 38. I was 36. We had our whole lives to live together and now I was being asked if I had given thought to what I wanted in regard to my eventual demise.

Thinking that burying two caskets on top of Ryan's burial tomb would require a depth that might reach the center of the earth (his mom's casket to be near his dad, and my casket to be near Ryan), I opted for something different: "I would like to be cremated and partially buried with Ryan."

I'm not sure how my mind moved as rapidly as it did to consider that my kids might want to do something with my ashes. In a matter of milliseconds, I flashed through scenes of my own death and imagined my grown children wishing to spread my ashes but being unable to as result of my forced decision.

The funeral director appeared relieved to know that he would not have to configure three caskets in one plot, and he said, "ok, we can do that. We will bury Ryan deep enough to leave space for his mom's casket and some of your remains to be placed in a small box and buried with him."

My remains? I wanted to respond, *"then bury me now because there's not much of my heart remaining."*

As I sat in the limousine on the way home, I twirled the pink rose between my fingers, watching the petals move slightly with each twist of the stem. I smirked at the memory of Ryan avoiding the topic of death due to its morbidity, and yet I had an intensely morbid conversation with a stranger about who will be buried where and how.

§

When the limo pulled up to my house, we were greeted by my parents, my children, and friends who had been waiting for our return, ready to offer hugs to anyone who needed one. "Mommy!" I heard my son's youthful voice calling for me as I stepped out of the car. "Mama!" My daughter was following right behind him with her arms stretched out to receive me. Trying to hold both of them while gripping the folder given to me by the funeral home, the world around us slipped away.

Shortly after my return home, Brandon asked if he could talk to me in my room. We sat on my bed facing each other in silence. Finally, he spoke: "mama, promise that nothing will ever happen to you?" Since the moment I told him that his dad died, I hadn't been apart from the kids for more than a few minutes. I realized that my travel to the funeral home and my time away from them sparked a worry in my son that I, also, might not return home.

"Oh buddy," I said as I grabbed his hand. I stared at him for a moment before giving him an answer I knew he didn't want to hear. "I can't promise you that."

It was the truth. I couldn't make that promise to him. As much as I wanted to promise that nothing would ever happen to me, I knew I couldn't. My son was desperate for a sense of security but I had the responsibility of being transparent and truthful with him. I wanted nothing more than to ease his mind with the promise of a safe and untouched future, but Ryan's death proved that such a promise can't exist.

"Buddy, I can't promise you that nothing will happen to me," I saw his face fall. "But, I can promise you that I will always do my absolute best to be safe." He lifted his eyes to meet mine and I saw a faint smile appear on his face. I stretched my arms out to him and he curled into my lap. As I held him, I closed my eyes, remembered what Sharon said, and reminded myself: *"be direct, walk with them through the truth, even when it hurts."*

That night, I decided to finally look at those red notification dots on my phone. I was exhausted from the day, but I remembered the peace I felt the night before and the awareness I had that it must've been the result of thousands of prayers being said on our behalf. I was ready to read their words. I wasn't consistent on Instagram, but I decided to go through those notifications first. I didn't realize that my account was public, and when I opened it, I was overwhelmed by the number of strangers who found my account and flooded my page with condolences.

I chose to share another photo of me and Ryan in Jamaica. It was a selfie we took after our first day in Montego Bay. In the original photo, our skin is brightly sun kissed and my blue dress accented the sky's perfect sunset glow. It's still one of my favorite photos of us. But instead of posting it in its original color, I made it black and white. The removal of color felt appropriate for the amount of life remaining in my heart.

Beneath the memorialized photo I shared, I finally acknowledged the kindness that I wasn't aware had been poured over me for the last two days. Clearly this audience knew what happened, and I was thankful not to have to explain my loss. For the first time, I read the words that had been shared with me, I allowed the love of others to pour onto me, and the birth of a hashtag that would define us was born:

"Thank you, everyone, for your words, your prayers, your thoughts, and the way in which my husband is being honored. You truly don't know how much you've impacted and held together my shattered heart. #teamOsler #ryanosler #OslerStrong"

Osler Strong. Forever.

Chapter 5

I had been quietly crying out to God through tears during those first few days after Ryan's accident, but I had not gone to the secluded area of my closet to sit with Him in prayer. I couldn't do it. I had no idea what to say. I couldn't gather words. I opened the door to my closet. I stared at the shelving my husband meticulously placed. I looked to my right. In the corner of my small walk-in closet, Ryan brought my idea to life.

§

A year earlier, Ryan walked into our bedroom to find me feverishly purging my closet. Shoes, jackets, clothes, and boxes were scattered all over our bathroom floor.

"What are you doing?" I heard him ask as I was buried deep within my closet.

"I want to create a prayer space."

"In your closet?"

"Yep. Right here in my closet."

"What are you going to do with all this stuff?"

"I don't know yet."

Instantly, he started offering ideas. I heard him leave our

room, but I continued on with my task. Still deep in my closet, surrounded by countless items, I could hear the muffled sounds of his heavy steps climbing the stairs towards our room. I then heard another familiar sound: the release of a measuring tape slapping itself back into place. In a clumsy attempt, he tried to climb over me as I was bent down to organize my shoe boxes. I crawled out of the closet beneath his legs, trying to push past the piles of clothes.

I stood back and watched him measure every nook and cranny of my little closet. I couldn't see his face, but I knew his eyes were full of calculations. That slap of the measuring tape signaled to me that he had finished calculating. In an excitement that nearly matched my own, he told me that he was going to buy shelving so I could better organize my closet.

Within an hour, I was at one store buying decorative storage boxes and he was at another buying shelving. By that evening, he was in the attic sweating off the burger we had for lunch because he wanted to install an electrical outlet.

"Babe, I don't need an outlet in here, you don't have to do all that."

"Yeah, but there's no air circulation in here. What if you get hot and want to use a fan?" That was my guy - always making sure I had everything I could ever need.

Over the next couple of days, I watched my husband turn my once cluttered closet into a space that would become my sanctuary. As it was coming closer to being done, he said to me one night, "go to the store and get whatever you need to make it what you want."

Like any smart woman, I headed out the door before he could change his mind. I purchased several small picture frames, a decorative chair and a small end table, just big enough to hold my bible, a journal, and a couple flameless candles.

I came home to find him still in my closet. His hard work was done and he was placing my new storage boxes on perfectly measured shelves. Excitedly, he showed off the new light he installed so I could have "better lighting," again making sure I had everything I needed. I couldn't wait to start decorating my prayer space. I took notes and cards that had been written to me with words of encouragement, placed those in the picture frames I purchased and hung them on the wall of my closet. Once completed, I stood back and admired my new prayer space. I couldn't wait to wake up in the morning, sit in my space, closed off from all distractions, and spend time with God.

§

God

I didn't grow up going to church. I went on occasion with my grandparents when I spent time with them during the summer, and Easter Sunday was always a guaranteed visit to church. I recall an older gentleman, very tall from what I remember, bald, and always wore thick rimmed glasses. He knew my name but I could never remember his. He would squeeze my pinky finger and make it squeak; I thought he was a magician of some sort because I could never make my finger squeak. I remember sitting in the cushiony pews next to my grandmother trying to be quiet and not laugh at my brother or my cousin, Katie, who were trying equally hard to stay quiet. We would fill out the "Welcome" cards and shove them underneath our legs so nobody would find them. I vividly remember the singing; there was always one woman behind us who sang so loudly she was all I could focus on. I remember my grandmother handing each of us a dollar bill to place on a shiny gold plate as it came down the pew. I always put the dollar bill on the plate, although I never understood why and I wondered who got all the money at the end of church. I remember 'snack plates' being passed down the aisle. I knew we weren't supposed to take a piece of the cracker or a sip of the juice but I remember secretly hoping that one day my grandmother would say, "Go ahead, Jennifer." I wanted a snack like the grown-ups. I knew church was about God and Jesus, but I didn't know who they were.

§

On March 10, 1996, my family suffered a devastating loss. My younger cousin, Heather Rose, suffered a brain aneurysm, killing her instantly. She was only 13 years old. Heather wasn't an average a teenager, though. She was diagnosed with cerebral palsy shortly after birth and with that diagnosis came many handicaps. She could not walk on her own, she could not speak, she could not feed herself. She required assistance to use the bathroom, a feeding tube was placed in her abdomen, she was wheelchair bound her entire life. She would never be what society considered "normal." And although some would say she suffered this diagnosis, she didn't seem to suffer at all. She embraced life. She exuded happiness. She showered everyone with love.

My grandparents helped care for Heather and her younger

brother, Darrel, and they became a second set of parents to them. Every Sunday, my two young cousins attended church with my grandparents and they each grew to know about God and Jesus. Heather Rose, despite what the world viewed as handicaps, appeared to live without limits. She had dreams for her future, she was obsessed with Danny from New Kids on the Block, and she laughed harder than anyone I had ever known. Life excited her and there wasn't a soul on earth who could've convinced her that she should feel otherwise.

Time seemed to freeze the night she died. Her death didn't make sense to me and nobody could give me answers. I was sixteen years-old and I didn't know what to think. I remembered she believed in God and I heard that heaven is where people went after they died, so I assumed she must be with Him (whoever He was) in heaven (wherever that was). I assumed God might be able to deliver a message to Heather on my behalf: "God, if you're with my cousin, can you tell her I said hi?" I wondered if she was dancing, running and talking with her mom who died years before her. I imagined she was happy, sitting with that guy Jesus, telling him about me and the games we used to play.

I found it easy to talk to God, and after that night, I kept talking to Him. I didn't know whether or not I was praying, all I knew was I believed there was a God in the sky and without any physical confirmation, I somehow felt assured He was listening. My requests were always in the same pattern: "protect my family, keep us safe, tell Heather I miss her and I love her. Amen." I knew to say 'amen' at the end of my conversations with God because I remembered hearing my grandfather end dinner-time prayers with that word. I assumed it was something similar to saying 'goodbye' at the end of a phone call.

As I grew more comfortable speaking into the quiet darkness of night, my chats with God began to extend into asking for help with things like school exams, bigger paychecks, and better hair days. After some time passed, I began falling asleep before finishing my conversations with God. Eventually, I was no longer having those talks with Him. Instead, I was jumping into bed, closing my eyes and falling asleep. Everything was going smoothly, my family was safe, and I was certain Heather was enjoying her heavenly home, so I ditched our nightly 'phone calls' and didn't give God another thought.

§

Church

2000

I was twenty-one years old when I met a woman in a local grocery store. It was my first trip to the market since marrying my high-school sweetheart. I was standing in the aisle of frozen food staring at the seemingly endless boxes of pre-made dinners I could serve to my husband (lucky man). A young woman not too far in distance giggled and said, "If only our husbands could see us now!" Somewhat offended, and definitely embarrassed, I laughed along with her and then made my way to the next aisle, where we crossed paths again. We spoke for several minutes; I shared that I was a newlywed having been married a mere two weeks and this beautiful young woman shared that she and her husband led the teen ministry at their church. She invited me to go to her church, to which I politely accepted the invitation and we exchanged phone numbers, although I had no intention of going to church or speaking with her again. A couple of days later, I received a message from the girl I met in the market. I called her back and unbeknownst to me was the beginning of a life changing friendship.

Ryan and I would frequently get together with this woman, Amy, and her husband, Daniel. They were expecting their first child and it was exciting for me to watch as their family developed. For several months, even after the birth of their daughter, we spent countless hours with them and they were gracious hosts and friends. They continued to invite us to church but we always found a reason we couldn't join them.

Then, one day, we ran out of reasons.

§

Walking into the church building was like walking into a family reunion filled with aunts and uncles you've never met but they seemed to know you. We were met with hugs and smiles from several strangers. Prior to this the only people I hugged were my grandparents, my real aunts and uncles, and my husband. I was intoxicated by the excitement our presence brought into the room. For the next ninety minutes, smiles were tossed out from the singers and the minister on stage. From the congregation, shouts of "amen!" reinforced the sermon, which confused me because I thought "amen" was the exit word for prayer. And then there were the shiny plates: one with the crackers and one with the tiny cups of juice. I didn't know what to do when the first plate was handed to me; it was the one with the crackers. Had I been denied the cracker and juice by my grandmother because of my young age? Was I allowed to have it now? Did I have to wait for someone to give me permission? In a panic, I passed the first plate along to my husband, who passed it to the person seated beside him. We repeated the same thing when the second plate, and then a basket, landed in our hands. Neither of us took part of the mid-morning snack or gave money to people we didn't know.

Immediately following the final song, the room was filled with chatter from the congregants. More hugs, more smiles, more introductions to new people, and an invitation to study the bible.

§

Ryan and I were inconsistently attending church for a few months; our decision whether or not to attend depended upon family plans and breakfast cravings. I was enjoying the warm welcome from my new friends each time we'd show up, but I didn't realize their eagerness was attached to a hope we would become members of their church. I didn't know anything more than the name of this local church and that it belonged to a much larger international religious organization. I was repeatedly asked to study the bible, which I interpreted to mean attending a class of some sort. Despite how much I was enjoying the new friends I was making, attending a bible study was not something that interested me; therefore, I declined every invitation.

We were invited to lunch with Amy and Daniel after church on a beautiful afternoon in May. They were house-sitting for one of the elder couples of the church and after consuming a quick lunch, they lead us into the living room for conversation on sofas that were clearly purchased for decoration rather than comfort. Daniel wasn't his usual self. There was a seriousness about him I hadn't seen before. I could see in his eyes that whatever he had to say was not going to be light. Amy wasn't smiling either. She sat quietly beside her husband; I noticed she didn't make eye contact with me. Instead, she kept her eyes focused on Daniel as he began to speak.

"So, you've been coming to church for the past couple of months, where do you see this going? What do you want to see happen?" Daniel's voice wasn't harsh, but there was a sternness to it that indicated we hadn't been taking church as seriously as he would've preferred.

I was confused. I thought church was just a place we could attend; we had been enjoying the people so much, I wasn't aware more was expected of us.

Ryan was silent. I knew he was waiting for me to say something, so I did: "what do you mean?"

With Amy by his side, Daniel launched into an explanation that church was, in fact, not just a place we could attend. We had to become 'members of the body,' which meant we had to make a decision: did we want to study the bible or not?

I was still unclear about what was being presented to us. Having no experience with church or religion, I told Daniel and Amy that I was curious about God and I was enjoying church on Sundays. Again, Daniel asked if we wanted to study the bible. Not really wanting to go to a bible study class, but feeling as though we were running out of free visits to the church, I answered for the both of us: "yes, we do."

Daniel's smile immediately returned to his face and Amy's facial expression relaxed. We scheduled an evening for our first bible study, and where I should've felt excitement, I felt confusion instead. I didn't know exactly what I said 'yes' to, but I knew whatever it was, it was for Daniel and Amy rather than for me and Ryan.

Over the next couple of months, Ryan and I met regularly at Daniel and Amy's apartment for a bible study. Several other people joined and we were always separated: men in one room, women in another. I didn't realize this was a bible study specifically for me and Ryan. I assumed it was a generic study of the bible for all involved; until the night Amy and three other female members of the church discussed the topic of sin with me. In particular, my sin. I was asked to write out a list of everything I'd ever done wrong, from past to present. I was then told to bring the list with me to our next bible study.

I felt naked as I read my list to a room full of women I barely knew. They rebranded my nakedness, calling it "vulnerability," and I could feel their delight in my obedience. Amy told me that after confessing my sin and promising to repent of all sinful behavior, I could continue with bible studies and eventually receive the blessing of church leaders to get baptized.

After doing as I was told and earning approval from leadership, I was baptized. I learned that the gold plates of crackers and grape juice I once thought were snacks were actually symbolic offerings of worship and a time of reflection and remembrance of the sacrifice made by Jesus at the cross. I learned the third plate (or in this case, the basket) was a monetary collection known as a tithe in which members give money each week for the functionality of the church. For the next fifteen years, I rarely missed a Sunday service. I rushed home from work on Tuesdays to grab my kids and race to the midweek church service. I gave my weekly tithe, which created arguments between me and Ryan, who stopped attending because, according to him, something about the church "felt off." I continued going. My life had become the church. I didn't have many friends outside of the organization, and if I did, my job was to convert them. I went to every church occasion, bible-talk, and family-group event. I was told my servanthood to the church was representation of my loyalty to God. I was made to believe that revolving my life around the church and its doctrine is what classified me as a Godly woman. Fifteen years after proclaiming Jesus as Lord of my life, I realized I had become a disciple of the church and knew nothing about the entity I called Lord. So, I set out to discover Him on my own.

Chapter 6

February 2016

I didn't know how to have a relationship with God. I did everything I was taught to do: attend church consistently, contribute financially, meet regularly with my mentor (known as a 'discipler' and assigned by the church), volunteer when asked, take notes during the sermon, have 'quiet times' with God then report about them to my discipler, and invite people to church. I did what I was supposed to do. I was a good Christian. My family members and co-workers knew about my active church-life and rarely did I spend time with anyone outside of the church.

But I never felt the spiritual or emotional connection to God that I heard about from other people. I was no doubt obedient, but my connection was with the church, not to the Creator.

When the idea of creating a quiet prayer space came into my mind, it was in the middle of battling my daughter's recently diagnosed anxiety. Her anxiety did all but physically paralyze her; it was robbing her of normal living. Ryan and I had become mentally, emotionally, and physically exhausted as we did everything we knew to do for her. I was desperate. We had been seeking medical and professional help for Amanda, as well as talking with friends who worked with children of this nature, but there wasn't a solution that worked well for her. I decided it was time to beg. The first week in my new prayer space felt cozy, but I wasn't feeling any closer to God. I assumed having this closed off corner of the world was going to somehow create spiritual depth, but the only thing it gave was a gentle ambiance.

Years earlier I heard someone mention the book, "The Circle Maker" by Mark Batterson. I read it and liked it, but it wasn't something that radically changed my prayer life. In my new pursuit of trying to draw close to God, I went looking for that book but couldn't find it in my personal library ('library' is a loose term; more like, the empty wardrobe I use to collect my books). Assuming I must've given it to someone, I went to my phone to order a new copy. Up popped a different title by the same author, "Draw the Circle." I liked the concept: a forty-day prayer plan. I'm a planner; I like agendas, itineraries, and following instruction. It's the reason I always did well with a personal fitness trainer - "just tell me what to do and I'll do it." So, a prayer plan? I immediately purchased the book.

The package arrived on my doorstep and I tore into it as if it were a surprise gift. The book was smaller in size than I expected and I quickly flipped through the 232 pages of promise.

My alarm went off at five o'clock the next morning. I crawled out of bed and seated myself in the coziness of my closet. Before I opened my prayer journal, I opened my new book. *"Day 1: Get Ready."* The author began speaking of someone named Cornelius.

I sighed at the thought of having to research this Roman man who *"prayed to God regularly"* (p 15) so I could understand the author's point. I continued reading the first chapter feeling as detached from God as I did when I first sat down.

I pulled out my bible, read a little bit and felt nothing. I grabbed for my prayer journal next and wrote nothing. Instead of making an attempt to connect with words, I picked up my phone and googled, "who is Cornelius in the bible." As multiple articles populated my screen, I felt embarrassed. After fifteen years of going to church, I should've known who the author was talking about. I reached for my bible again. The well-worn cover, flexible binding, and marked pages proved that I opened it frequently, but the unmarked pages surrounding the story of Cornelius in the book of Acts proved I didn't spend much time in this area of the bible.

As I read through chapter 10 and the account of Cornelius, I felt ashamed for not knowing this story. It was powerful and thought-provoking. Two men, whose paths should've never crossed due to geography (Peter in Joppa, Cornelius in Caesarea), as well as, ethnicity (Peter, a Jesus-believing Jew, Cornelius, a God-fearing Roman centurion). Both men were praying to God, both received a vision, both were obedient to the call, which led them to each other and ultimately united them in Christ. Two men, two different lifestyles, no reason to ever meet, and yet, God connected them.

Wow. How had I missed this story? I closed my bible and decided I needed to pray. But instead of praying, I simply talked to God like I did when Heather died. "God, I'm sorry I don't know You as well as I thought I did. Show me more. I want to know more about You."

I was a little more eager to get to my prayer space the next morning. I grabbed the book first.

"*Day 2: Established by God.*" I soaked it up. "*Day 3: Amazing Things.*" I kept going, but I hadn't yet done the very thing the book instructed me to do in the introduction: circle my prayer. It felt strange at first. I wrote my daughter's name in my journal and circled her name once. As I lifted my pen off the page, I expected some kind of spark to happen. Nothing. My spirit felt the same, my closet felt the same and the circle didn't do anything.

"*Day 18: Keep Circling.*" I felt weird circling my daughter's name. I didn't feel anything different about this time I was spending with God, but then again, I didn't know what I was supposed to be feeling. After circling my daughter's name for two weeks, I feared I stepped too far into a whimsical idea that a circle drawn by my pen would deliver an answered prayer or, at minimum, a deeper connection with God.

But then I reached "*Day 24: Find Your Voice.*" The author posed a question and it felt as though he was reading my mind, "*so how do we hear the voice of God?*" (p 137). Yes! Exactly! How am I supposed to hear God's voice? Please tell me! Finally, I felt as though I was reaching an answer in my quest to connect with God. "*The first thing you do is open your Bible.*" Done. I nodded my head in fervent agreement. Next? "*...make sure you have no unconfessed sin in your life.*" Okay, I'm listening.

Mr. Batterson didn't go on to give step-by-step instructions, but he did write something I hadn't considered before: "*When too much white noise invades my life and I'm having a hard time hearing the voice of God, I'll often go into a season of fasting. Fasting is like noise cancellation. It helps me tune out the voices I shouldn't be listening to and tune into His frequency. It's still difficult to distinguish between our own thoughts and the inaudible voice of the Holy Spirit, but just like a relationship with a loved one, we begin to discern His voice more accurately. Eventually, it'll be like the voice of a spouse or child. We'll be able to interpret even the subtlest intonations.*" (p 137)

Fasting? No food for a day? I had never been able to accomplish that feat in the past, almost always caving to the pangs of hunger by three o'clock in the afternoon. I didn't immediately toss away the idea, but I also didn't quite understand the concept of fasting. I was only familiar with two types of fasting: no food for twenty-four hours in a desperate plea for answered prayer and Jesus' fast in the desert for forty days, which was not going to be an option for me. At all.

As the day went on, I couldn't stop thinking about the idea of fasting. Feeling recently embarrassed by my lack of biblical knowledge, I asked Google about biblical fasting. I found that fasting wasn't limited to food or time. It could be anything I wanted for any length of time I wanted! The general idea was to fast from something that I enjoy daily, something that I would crave if I didn't have it. A thought came to mind faster than I could stop it from arriving: "*diet coke.*" I laughed at the thought, but also agreed it would be an appropriate thing for me to fast from because Diet Coke was my daily habit, multiple times a day. I would go out of my way to find a McDonald's just to satisfy my craving for a Diet Coke; especially in the mornings on my way to work. Diet Coke was my morning (and afternoon) 'coffee.'

The following morning, I continued in my book, prepared to read an emphasis on fasting, but the author didn't mention it again. I felt the nudge to read Day 24 again. So, I did.

There was an unusual urge I could feel in my soul that this was something I needed to do. *Ok, fine. Let's do it.* I tapped the top of my pen against my lips as I thought about what I would fast from and how long I would go without it. "*Diet coke,*" kept coming to mind and I laughed each time. "*Diet coke, for a month.*" As though I were having an audible conversation with my brain, I said, "*why not make it a year*?" I didn't laugh after I said it. I stopped tapping my pen. I felt my nostrils release a puff of hot air as I smirked in confirmation.

I reached beneath my chair and pulled out a new, unmarked journal. I opened to the first page and with the pen I used to contemplate this wild idea, I wrote, "*Fasting Prayers.*" In a verbal contract with God, I whispered, "*one year. Diet coke. I'll do it.*"

At the time, Ryan wasn't going to church with me, but we spoke often about God. I knew he loved God, but I also knew he struggled with trusting that God was good after seeing so much pain and destruction during his time as a firefighter. I chose not to tell him I was fasting. Part of my reasoning was that I didn't want him to think I was trying to be holy, but the primary reason was I wanted to keep this between me and God.

The first few days were difficult; I didn't realize how much of that carbonated drink I consumed each day. I chose to approach those pangs of craving with a casual conversation with God instead of a well-versed, Latin-laced prayer. *"Ughh, I really want a diet coke, God! But I'm doing this for Youuuu."* I have no doubt God was not entertained by my initial attitude, but as the days went on, my tone softened and my request changed. *"It's for You, God. I want to hear You."*

It took Ryan about a month to realize if I had a drink option, I was choosing iced tea instead of my usual Diet Coke.

"Why aren't you getting a Diet Coke?"

"Oh, it's just a thing I'm trying." He didn't pry any further.

Each morning, my alarm went off at five o'clock. If Ryan was home, I would go downstairs to make us both a cup of coffee and bring it to him while he was in bed. Then, I slipped into my closet for my time with God. I initially began the fast in a quest for answered prayer and connection to God. After two months of committing myself to this time with Him each morning, I noticed something happening.

My prayers weren't being answered, but my roots were growing deeper and I was being trained to go to God first. I was also getting to know God on a personal level. His words jumped off the pages of my bible and landed on my heart with understanding and clarity. I finally *knew* God. I had known *of* God for so many years, but it wasn't until now that I began to know Him on a deep, personal level. I had never experienced Him like this before. I felt attached to Him, as though I would die should I ever be told I couldn't speak to Him. I had a desperation for Him and a love for Him that I couldn't explain.

I began this fast in an effort to change my circumstance, but the whole time He was trying to change my habits. He was training me to depend on Him while teaching me how to pray. Rather than circumstantial prayer, it became a pleading for His wisdom, His guidance, His strength, and His comfort as I walked through circumstance. I was no longer praying for a specific outcome. I was quickly learning that God may not answer my circumstance-specific prayers in the way I'd prefer, but He will always answer prayers for wisdom, guidance and presence. It's as if He were saying, "come and ask me for *those* things and then together we'll get through the other things." As more time went on, I began talking to God about what He needed me to do, rather than what I wanted Him to do.

My experience with God became spiritual, not religious. I could feel Him. I could discern which thoughts were mine and which were His. I noticed the ways in which He would communicate with me through earthly messengers, whether it was a stranger with words specific to what God knew I needed to hear or prayers being answered like the morning I begged Him to move a thunderstorm and He did. It was the way His spirit organically cooled my ego and softened my tongue. It was in my increased patience and seemingly care-free outlook. But the change in me wasn't due to forced obedience or monitored repentance; it was due to genuine willingness, compelling faithfulness, and the utmost reverence for the greatest love of my life: God.

I continued going to church because I enjoyed the worship band and visiting with my friends, but I quickly realized that my roots with God had nothing to do with the preacher, the music, the sermons or even my friends. On a plate of tasty spiritual food, they were the side dishes, but God was the main meal, and He was all I wanted to consume.

I met God in my closet every day without fail. And then, six months into my fast, six months into my authentically deepened and strengthened relationship with God, Ryan was killed.

§

During the afternoon of the day Ryan died, I was asked if I wanted anything to eat or drink.

"I want a Diet Coke," I said. As I stood there waiting for a cold can of the soda I had been denying myself for months, I mumbled in annoyance with God, *"it doesn't matter anyway, does it."* I felt betrayed by God. Apparently, He didn't take my fasting seriously, so neither would I. After all, Amanda's anxiety hadn't resolved, and now, my husband was dead.

The morning after breaking my fast, I didn't wake up early because I didn't sleep the night before. I didn't go to the kitchen to make a cup of coffee because there was nobody for me to serve. And I didn't go to my prayer space because there was nothing I wanted to say. I didn't want to talk to God. I had absolutely nothing to say to Him. I wasn't angry as much as I was in shock. I didn't understand. I had been the most faithful I had ever been in all the years of my Christian walk. I had grown to know God on a deep and personal level, and yet here I was in a world I no longer recognized allowed by a God I felt I no longer knew.

Ryan died on Wednesday morning and I hadn't spoken to God at all. When Sunday morning arrived, I decided I wanted to go to church. I still didn't have anything to say to God, but I knew I needed to be surrounded by worship music, if nothing else. My spirit knew what it needed, even if my heart did not.

I was covered by the protection of my friends as I sat in the back row. I had codes and catch phrases in place with people close to me to act as a signal when I needed out. I could see the pitiful expressions of those who watched me walk through the doors and take my seat in the back, a spot in which I didn't normally sit.

I don't remember anything more than the somber welcome and a monotone sermon from the minister. I don't remember the message he preached. I only remember feeling the heaviness that filled the room.

I don't remember the people, the songs, or the communion. I wasn't there for church. I knew well enough to know that a sermon wasn't going to revive me. I had already known and felt for months that the church building was never where I felt closest to God. On this particular day, four days after my husband was killed, I was at church because I was afraid of getting too far from Him. I was there because I needed the Holy Spirit to push me back towards God. I was not there for church.

The next morning, I went into my closet. I grabbed a new journal, turned on the gentle glow of my flameless candle, and for the first time since my husband died, I sat with God. I couldn't pray for Ryan's return. I couldn't pray for his broken body to be restored on earth. But for months prior, I had been trained to pray for what I needed: God's wisdom, guidance and presence to get me *through* my unanswered prayer. God spent so long training me to seek Him and wait on the prayer He will always answer.

September 26, 2016

"Dear God, it's been 5 days since my world stopped. This morning, I feel at peace. I know it's the thousands of prayers that have been said on our behalf, and I pray that those prayers don't stop. God, I'm begging for your strength and your wisdom. As peaceful as I feel right now in this moment, I know there will be times when I lose sight. I pray that you will protect me, guard my heart, and keep Satan's lies from me. I know Satan wants me to blame you and hate you, I pray that I continue to hear those whispers as lies. Please continue to show yourself to me in ways that I can clearly see you. God, I pray that you stay especially close to my children. I pray that you will guide me and give me wisdom. God, my children are about to begin a journey that is going to be filled with emptiness at times. I pray that you fill their hearts with your love and they feel their heartache lighten. God, I know you are a God of love and I know you would never want to hurt me. I know you are hurting with me, but I also know you see a bigger picture in front of me. God, I pray that your peace stays with me today. Father, I know and trust that you have something incredible planned. You waste nothing. Please stay close to me and the kids. Please keep showing yourself to me in ways that I can see and feel you. I love you. I trust you. I need you."

I closed my journal and sat back in my chair with my eyes closed. I could feel the burn of tears approaching my eyes. *"I trust you,"* I whispered into the air. In a softer whisper, I repeated my words, *"I trust you."*

It was nearing the lunch hour when I went downstairs to

find my children, my family and my friends all waiting for me to appear. I received God's love in abundance through their hugs, smiles, and warmth. And I received His grace when I found a case of Diet Coke waiting for me in the refrigerator.

Chapter 7

Less than one week after Ryan died, summer temperatures were still forcing themselves onto us. As I entered the vanity area of my bathroom, I felt warm air being pushed through the vents above me. I stopped and felt the air hit my face as I looked up expecting I would be able to see the problem.

"*What the hell,*" I mumbled to myself. Assuming the fan was running, but somebody might've turned off the air conditioning, I checked the thermostat with an irritation that somebody must've been in my bedroom. Everything was as it should be. I walked back to the vent in confusion. I checked the vent in my bedroom - warm air. I quickly went into each bedroom upstairs hoping to find something different but was slapped in the face with a push of warm air each time.

I went back to my bedroom. I know what I would've done in this situation had it happened a week earlier. I would've called Ryan and told him that the air wasn't working properly. He would've had me check a couple things while on the phone and then would've resorted to telling me that he would take a look at it when he got home the next day. He could fix anything. That is no exaggeration. Anything. I never had to call a mechanic, a plumber, an electrician, a handyman, anybody – he could quite literally fix everything.

But now, I couldn't call him. I stood there beneath the warm air in my own personal hell. I had no idea what to do or who to call. I lowered myself to the floor of my bedroom and sobbed. "Why are You doing this? Why are You allowing this to happen? Do You even care? Do You really think I need one more thing on my plate? WHERE ARE YOU?" I said each word out loud in between the breaths I had to take while crying.

Exasperated, I went downstairs in search of my phone. I dialed a number I was growing used to repeating.

"Hey Rob, I'm sorry to bother you, but my air conditioning isn't working right and I don't know who to call."

I can't remember what Rob said, but I am certain it was something along the lines of, "don't worry, I'll make some calls."

The day of Ryan's accident, I was asked by the department who I would like to be our family liaison. Who would be our middle-man, our go-to guy, our stand-by-for-whatever-we-needed? A name was offered to me, but I answered by shaking my head in resistance. "No. I want Rob." Rob was Ryan's captain at the time of his death and months earlier, Ryan and I went to Las Vegas with Rob and his wife, Brandi. I had come to know Rob on a personal level and I was aware of how much Ryan respected him. I knew I could trust him. I knew he would do everything possible to make sure I had everything I needed. I knew he would not allow me to endure unnecessary decision making nor would he subject me to making decisions on my own. I trusted Rob because Ryan trusted Rob. More importantly, I could now see why God nurtured that relationship between us months earlier - I was going to need him.

Just before three o'clock I received a text from Rob: "Jake from Stewart Rose AC should be by in an hour or so."

My heart stopped. Stewart Rose AC? That's who was coming to my house? I held my phone in disbelief as my mouth contorted into an awkward smile. "*Stewart Rose?*" I said the name out loud as though I needed to taste it on my lips. I was afraid Rob might've misheard the company name, so when asked by the guests in my home, I only said that Rob arranged for someone to come out to the house.

A very kind gentleman arrived at my doorstep an hour later, just as Rob said. I looked at his van: Stuart Rose Heating and Air Conditioning Co. Just as Rob said. I invited him inside and he went straight to work on the units in my backyard.

A girlfriend of mine arrived shortly after he did and as she came inside, she said, "did you see the van outside??"

"I did," I answered with a smile. I felt a warm sensation consume my body as though God himself was standing beside me.

Brandon *Stewart* and Amanda *Rose*. The names of my two children, and the name of the business that came to my rescue. I didn't think God cared that I was hurting so deeply. I didn't feel that He was near, let alone paying attention to my needs. I felt abandoned by the God who promised He would never leave me. But then He showed up. Through a broken air conditioner He told me I had nothing to fear. He reassured my heart that He was listening, He was near, and I was not going to walk through this alone. It took a moment of broken hope to remind me of His perfect love.

September 28, 2016

"It's been a week. Part of me can't believe it's been a week, the other part of me feels like it's still the day of. God, thank you for your love note yesterday with my air conditioning. I know that was You. I knew it was a love note from you. Thank you for showing yourself to me, especially when I had such a hard day. Father, I know you have a plan in all of this. I trust your will for my life, I pray that you continue to show me all the ways in which you are with me. I love you. I trust you. I need you."

Chapter 8

It was late. I was sitting at my kitchen table going through thousands of photos at the request of the funeral home. I sent a text to my sister-in-law, Jeanine: "I have a ton of photos from the age of sixteen and up, but I don't really have any of him younger than that." Ryan's sisters and I were given the task of sifting through memories frozen in time for the slideshow being prepared for the funeral.

I remember a male voice asking me about a eulogy for Ryan. I didn't take my eyes off my computer screen as I continued to click through each photo trying to manifest Ryan's return home.

"Sure, I'll write it."

Writing is therapeutic to my soul. I journal, I write, I scribble, I take notes, but I knew that writing a eulogy for my husband would feel like stabbing myself in the heart. I opened Microsoft Word and began writing anyway.

"Ryan Stewart Osler passed away in the early morning hours of Wednesday, September 21, 2016 in Lompoc, CA responding to the Canyon Fire."

It was so matter-of-fact, so blunt.

"Ryan was born on August 29, 1978 in Camarillo, CA to Ralph and Cherie Osler. Ryan grew up in the Santa Clarita Valley where he attended elementary school, Jr High School and eventually graduating from Saugus High School in 1997."

More facts. I had never written a eulogy before. I assumed all started with facts about the person whose life was being condensed into essay format. And then came the words I didn't want to acknowledge:

"Ryan is survived by his wife, Jennifer, his high school sweetheart."

I stared at that sentence and hated it. Tears instantly sprang to my eyes. The funeral was scheduled for Monday, October 3rd. We would've celebrated our 16th wedding anniversary four days later on October 7th, but instead of making dinner reservations for the two of us, I was writing a eulogy for my dead husband.

"...and they would've celebrated their 16th wedding anniversary this Friday, October 7th."

I wanted them to know. Whoever was going to hear these words needed to know that we were a success story. A high-school-romance success story. Ryan once told me that he loved telling people how long we had been together: 21 years as a couple, 16 years married. We experienced some of our worst years together (deceit, drinking, drama and separation), but we made it through. We did it, and he loved to share about our breakthrough to the other side. For that reason, I wanted everyone to know that Ryan and I should've been celebrating that week. Instead, our celebration was now a "would've been."

I continued on with the eulogy:

"Ryan is also survived by his two beautiful children, Amanda Rose

and Brandon Stewart, his mother Cherie, as well as his two sisters, Julie and Jeanine."

I hated every minute of it, but I continued on with the factual information about Ryan: his father who died before him, his path that led to the fire service, his work ethic, his hobbies, his love for music. These were the details that described him to those who didn't know him, but were the things the rest of us loved about him. I saved it, emailed it to someone (I can't remember who), and stared at my computer.

"I can't believe I just wrote an f'ing eulogy for my husband," I thought to myself. Whoever the male voice was next to me received the document I emailed and read through it as my mind was still processing what I had just done.

"Great, this is great. Thanks, Jenn."

I weakly smiled for the sake of acknowledgment.

"Yeah, great," I thought as I closed my computer while praying I would close my eyes and wake to find that what I had written was part of a fictional story rather than my reality.

A couple of days later, I was asked to give a shorter version of the eulogy to be printed on the inside of the program that would be handed out at the funeral. I inwardly rolled my eyes. I prayed this would all go away and instead I was being asked to do it a second time. Instead of writing a second, shorter eulogy, I cut apart what I had already written and condensed it into a quick read. I titled it, "Eulogy, pt 2."

Jeanine was at my house that afternoon. I handed over "Eulogy, pt 2" for Roger to read and approve. After he finished, he passed it along to Jeanine, "what do you think?"

"I think it's good, but it's missing something," she said. Ashamed of my own editing, I looked down at the ground as I heard her tapping away on my keyboard. "There," she said as she passed the computer back to Roger. I looked up in nervous anticipation but relaxed the moment she looked at me, smiled, and gave me her signature wink to let me know she was pleased with what she added.

"There were many things that brought happiness to Ryan, but he found the most joy in showing his love for his wife and children by providing for his family and creating meaningful memories together as a family."

I didn't realize that in writing Ryan's eulogy I hadn't made any mention about me and our children, other than the anniversary we should've been celebrating. I spoke of everything that he was to everyone else because he was truly selfless in giving his time and talent to so many. But in that moment, Jeanine reminded me of what truly made Ryan happy, and it was us. Jeanine's addition to my condensed eulogy made me feel loved and seen. I had now gone days without Ryan's daily reminder of his love for me, but his baby sister delivered a message on that day in the form of a fact she knew I needed to hear.

§

As the funeral drew nearer, I was forced to think about what the kids and I would be wearing. Black, obviously, but I didn't have any funeral appropriate dresses readily on-hand. I was standing in my closet when I remembered something incredibly ironic: I did have a black dress and it was funeral appropriate. It was also brand new with tags attached because I purchased it only a couple of weeks earlier. I pulled it out and held it in front of me. A gentle laugh swept over my body as I held it at arm's length. Ryan bought this dress for me. He loved to take me shopping, and even though it wasn't his favorite activity, he found pleasure in being able to say, "just get it, babe!" One afternoon in particular, we were browsing Charming Charlie when I came across a black dress. I didn't need another dress, but Ryan explained that it would be nice for me to have and suggested it for a date night together, and who am I to argue with my husband wanting to buy me a dress and take me on a date? I tried it on, liked the fit, and we brought the dress home with us.

I never got to wear it on the date Ryan suggested we'd have, and he only saw me in it when I quickly popped out of the dressing room to get his approval.

I fell to the floor of my closet, clutching the dress in my hands. *"Oh my God, Ryan picked out the dress I'd be wearing to his funeral."*

Chapter 9

It was the day before the funeral. It had been suggested the kids and I go to the funeral home so we could privately say goodbye to Ryan. The public had already been given the opportunity to pay their respects to the hero they never met. Someone from the department contacted Conejo Mountain to inform them of the time we would arrive to ensure nobody from the public would be there.

I don't remember the drive from our house to the funeral home. I don't remember whose car we were in; I don't remember who was with us, I don't remember arriving. But I do remember walking into the parlor that housed my husband's lifeless body. With my children on either side of me, we stepped into the room. It felt deceiving as we walked in because there was nothing more than bright walls and empty chairs that welcomed us. We stepped inside a little further, and out of the corner of my left eye, I saw it. There was a casket in my peripheral vision, which I could now see was the front of the room. I could see the brightly colored American flag draped over it. The red stripes were beckoning to me as I took steps in its direction. I felt the grips of each of my children tighten around my fingers. My body mindlessly walked down the aisle towards the casket. Sixteen years earlier, I walked down the aisle of a church towards Ryan in excitement as we began our life together. Now, as I walked the aisle of another sacred place towards him, it was because our life together came to an end. Instead of Ryan, there were two uniformed men standing at the end of the aisle waiting to receive me. Members of the honor guard had been respectfully standing guard over the casket 24 hours a day, never leaving him alone.

I could feel the heaviness of my purse hitting against my leg as my children and I paraded down the aisle. We finally reached it. I immediately placed my hands on the casket, laid my head on my arms, and cried. The material of the flag felt rough and stiff beneath my fingers. How could it possibly be my husband, my young, healthy and handsome husband, that was laying lifeless beneath this flag? I tried to imagine his body, his face, and his hands. I wondered what he looked like. I don't recall how long I stood there, and the only reason I know my children were draped beside me is due to the pictures I've seen. I have no physical memory of their weight against me in that moment.

I eventually stepped away from the casket and I could see there were faces familiar to me seated in the chairs I thought were empty. I sat down in the front row of chairs facing the casket. I stared at it, imagining my husband's cradled head, and I started to cry. There was nobody seated next to me. Suddenly, I felt my brother's presence to my left. He immediately placed his arm around me and began to gently rub my right shoulder.

I appreciated his effort to soothe me, but in that moment, I wanted to sit alone in my sadness and feel the heaviness of my grief. I wanted to release what I was carrying on my shoulders and, in that moment, his loving hand added more weight than I could bear. His hand became the only thing I could feel and the only thing that held my focus. It wasn't his fault. He couldn't read my mind and I couldn't form the words. His heart was not only aching for the loss of the brother he'd known since he was twelve years old, but also for his big sister being forced to shoulder a heaviness she didn't ask to carry.

Mahal, having remembered the cue cards placed throughout my home by Sharon, the Grief Recovery specialist, appeared in front of me and asked my brother to move down so she could sit beside me. Years later, I learned that her gesture hurt a lot of feelings, but in that moment at the funeral home, nobody was aware that she knew exactly what I needed. She knew I didn't want to be touched. She knew I wanted to sit alone. She knew I needed space. She sat in the chair beside me and didn't touch me. She didn't speak to me and she didn't soothe me. She let me return to my grief. In that moment, she was the wall I needed around me, and I appreciate her quick action and bold interference.

At some point, it was time to leave. I don't know the length of time that's considered appropriate to stare at a casket, but I knew it was time to go. The kids and I approached the casket one more time. As we started to walk away, my daughter had a panicked look on her face.

"I want to see him," she said. She wanted to open the casket and see him. We were nearly to the door.

"Baby, you can't," I said as tears filled my eyes.

She insisted, "I want to see him, Mom. I want to see Daddy."

Above the heads of people in front of me, my eyes were frantically searching for an answer. I knew she couldn't see him. I didn't know the extent of his injuries, but I knew his body was not prepared for viewing. I made eye contact with Rob. He immediately came over to me and asked if I needed something. I explained Amanda's request to him, and although he already knew the answer, he set off to talk with the funeral director, or at least, that's what I pretended he was doing. I remember looking at something intently as we awaited Rob's return - was it a poster with photos of Ryan on it? I honestly can't remember.

I caught sight of Rob over the crowd of people. He looked at me and silently, sadly shook his head 'no.' I closed my eyes and thanked God for that answer. I knew it was an impossible request and I knew Ryan wouldn't have wanted his daughter to see him like that, regardless of whether or not his body was prepared for viewing, but I also knew his little girl was in need of closure. I grabbed her sweet face, looked into her eyes and said, "baby, you can't see Daddy, and he wouldn't want you to see him like this. I know he wouldn't. I am so sorry, baby. I'm so sorry."

Despite Ryan refusing to talk with me about his wishes upon death, there was one thing I knew for certain: he wouldn't want his children to see him in a casket. The day of his father's funeral, Ryan and I approached the open casket that held the lifeless patriarch of his family. For the next fourteen years, Ryan was haunted by what his eyes saw and he regretted those moments staring at his father's empty body. He hated that that was his last vision of his dad. I didn't need to speak with Ryan about his wishes to know he wouldn't want his own children to live with similar torture.

She looked up at me and whispered, "can everybody leave?"

"Baby, everybody's gone."

"No, I mean, like, even the guys standing next to him."

Rob, watching this conversation take place, walked over to inquire about our needs.

"Can the kids and I have some time alone with Ryan?"

He nodded and walked towards the honor guard to dismiss them from Ryan's side.

The room was silent, but not scary. The walls were bright and the windows allowed beautiful natural light into the room. Together, the three of us approached the casket again. I heard the doors close behind us. I set down my purse and placed my arms on the center of the casket and laid my head down. On my left, my daughter did the same and her eyes met mine. I watched as her fingers traced the stitching of the flag. My son was standing on the other side. We were quiet. There wasn't a sound in the room. I'm not sure how long we stood there, but I didn't want to leave. It was the last time the four of us would be alone in the same room. Silent tears soaked the flag that so beautifully decorated his casket. I smiled at my daughter through the tears.

"We're gonna be ok. I promise," I whispered in hope that it was true. It was the only thing I had promised them since the day he died.

She smiled back at me.

I heard a light tapping come from the other side of the casket. I lifted my head to find my son drumming his fingers.

"Where are we going for lunch?" he inquired.

My daughter and I began to laugh. His sweet innocence brought a sense of relief to my heart as our laughter filled the silent room.

I laid my head back down against the casket. I closed my eyes and imagined Ryan's face. Resting comfortably in his blue jeans, 80's hair band Tesla t-shirt, the brand-new shoes I bought for his birthday just weeks before, and the black silicone wedding ring he asked me to buy a couple of weeks earlier. I smiled imagining my husband resting within. His heart was still but his soul was alive. I could feel it. I kissed the top of the casket. I can still feel the texture of the flag against my lips.

"Let's say 'bye to Daddy," I whispered.

I watched my children each kiss the casket that held their father.

In voices softer than a whisper, they simultaneously said, "bye, Daddy." Together, we walked away, glancing back as we neared the door. That was the hardest thing to do: walking away, leaving him there, knowing that as soon as we stepped out, the four of us would never again be in the same room together. The next time we would be near him would be in front of thousands who also came to say goodbye.

§

The night before the funeral, Amanda's nerves reached their peak. Her stomach could no longer hold itself, and I was of little help to her. Although I did my motherly duty of cleaning her up and making sure she was okay, I had minimal to offer her by way of emotion. I was numb and going through the motion of making sure everyone's clothes were ready, my purse was changed, and my alarm was set.

By six o'clock the next morning, my friend and hairdresser, Danica, was setting up in my bathroom to do my hair and take that pressure off me. The house was dark, but my bathroom was well-lit and showed evidence that I had been awake long before she arrived.

The morning is a complete blur. I don't know how or when we each got dressed, I'm not sure if my kids had anything to eat and I barely remember who was at our house. But I do remember being told that the limousine had arrived and then walking outside to find family members waiting to be escorted to the church. As we all climbed into the limo, I remember someone explaining the air conditioning wasn't working properly. We didn't have time to arrange for different transportation, but there was a promise that before we left to the cemetery from the church there would be a new vehicle with working air conditioning.

The drive from my house to the church was approximately one hour. The car was filled with moments of awkward silence, half smiles, and minimal talk. Each of us were on our way to say goodbye to the same person, but not in the same way. I studied Ryan's mom with deep sympathy as I tried to comprehend the magnitude she faced of losing her son. I watched his sisters who were not only being forced to say goodbye to their older brother, but also preparing to speak in front of thousands as they were going to share stories about him. I followed the faces of my children; so many thoughts ran through my mind. They were too young to be going through this; I felt anger flood my body. My kids didn't deserve this. None of us did, and that's the truth, but they hadn't been given the chance to experience Ryan for decades the way we did. They were at an age old enough to have (what have now become vague) memories with him, yet young enough to experience an entire lifetime without him.

As we drew closer to the church, the anger slipped away. It was as if God was pulling it out of me so I could be present. When the car entered the driveway of the church, I felt my body go numb. There was a huge line of fire trucks; the bright yellow of Ventura County Fire, as well as the classic red from visiting departments. *"Oh my God,"* I whispered to myself. It was the same feeling I had the day of his accident when I saw the Chaplain waiting for me in my driveway. My hands began to shake in nervous anticipation. The car slowly pulled up to the front of the church. As we stepped out, we were greeted by hundreds of uniformed firefighters lining the walkway. I grabbed the hands of my children as we were escorted into the church. The air was silent and heavy. I couldn't focus on anything other than the steps I was taking. I felt my son's hand change from being held to holding mine. My daughter clasped her fingers tighter around mine with each step she took. I didn't know what to do in that moment other than look straight ahead.

The details and logistics of that morning are unknown to me. I recall entering into the church building and being escorted into a private room. There were tables set up with water and small food items, and several family members were there awaiting our arrival. Shortly afterwards, we were accompanied into another room. This room was empty, aside from a large curtain on my left. We were told that Ryan's casket was behind the curtain. The room filled with more people and there was a low murmur of voices in the background. We were quietly told that we could step into the curtained area to have a moment with Ryan. I grabbed the kids' hands and we waited outside the curtain as family members disappeared behind it. After everyone had the chance to privately say goodbye, the kids and I stepped towards the curtain and slowly entered the makeshift sanctuary.

I was thankful this was not the first time my children were seeing their Daddy's casket because despite having seen it the day before, it was still a shock to the heart. We each touched the flag draped over the coffin that was holding the man whose strength was supposed to protect us. The man whose love was supposed to build memories with us. The man whose life was supposed to be spent with us. We were silent. After a few minutes, I faintly said, "let's say bye to Daddy." Amanda and Brandon whispered their goodbyes to an unresponsive box. I closed my eyes and lowered my head, pressing my lips against the flag as I kissed him goodbye one last time. The kids grabbed my hands and we stepped out from behind the curtain to find a gathering of faces waiting for us.

§

Captain Andy Doyle of Los Angeles County Fire was a stranger to me until that day. He approached to let me know the service was ready to begin. We lined up to walk into the church's sanctuary when he stopped me and said, "you and the kids will wait here." I did as I was told and slowly, the room emptied. "You and the kids will follow behind the casket." I instantly felt my hands become clammy, which my son also felt because he let go of my hand to wipe his on his shirt.

Immediately flanked on the side of the casket were those who knew and loved Ryan deeply: his cousins Michael and Keith; his sisters' husbands, Mark and Richard; his best friend, Roger, and my brother, John.

I don't remember the path taken into the sanctuary, but I remember stepping inside and seeing Ryan's face on the large screen at the front of the church. They used a picture of him from our anniversary trip to Jamaica. I couldn't take my eyes off him. I could feel the presence of thousands. The sound of the drums and bag pipes filled my ears. Each step felt heavy. As we approached the front, I finally broke my stare and glanced to my left. I saw a familiar face; one that had been there from the beginning: Jaemie. I watched her spirit break when we made eye contact. I felt my lips curve into a weak smile knowing she was there.

The kids and I were escorted to our seats, and from there, the entire funeral is a blur. I rely on photos, video clips from news broadcasts, and the accounts from others who were there to rebuild the memory of his funeral service.

At the conclusion of the service, the kids and I were again instructed to walk behind Ryan's casket. We exited the building in the same way that we entered: slow, silent, somber, and surrounded by hundreds lining the walkway. I hadn't noticed when we first arrived that there were two fire trucks with their ladders extended and a larger-than-life American flag was hanging between them. I looked up and marveled at the way it was waving in the breeze. I smiled thinking to myself, *"Ryan would love that."* He loved the American flag; he was proud to be a servant to our country.

We were led to gather in an area facing the back of Ryan's fire truck. Engine 42 was decorated with American flags and black and purple bunting. The hose that is normally in the back of the engine was removed and we watched as seven firefighters received Ryan's casket and lifted it into the back of the truck. Helicopters flew over in "missing man formation," a salute to a fallen hero. The helicopters signaled the end of the service and the crowd around us grew smaller as people closed in on our space.

As promised, we had a vehicle with working air conditioning waiting to take us to the cemetery for the burial service. It wasn't another limousine; it was a party bus. I found myself laughing as we stepped inside. It felt ridiculous to be in a bus heading towards the cemetery, but for the first time that day, I felt at ease and my kids had something light in the middle of something heavy.

Escorted by police officers, our convoy began making its way up the busy freeway. Every single Ventura County fire truck was following behind our family bus as we followed the engine carrying Ryan's casket. I stared out the window to my right, completely numb to my surroundings. Several cars had pulled to the right and taken themselves off the freeway as we drove past. People were lining the freeway overpass to watch as a parade of fire trucks drove north. As we pressed on, I noticed a red pickup truck with an American flag hanging from its tailgate parked at a freeway exit. Beside the truck was a man wearing black shorts and a white t-shirt; his face was serious, his posture was erect, and his hand was tautly raised in salute as Ryan's casket passed him. My eyes followed him as we drove by. In all my life, I had never experienced the magnitude of love and respect that was being shown to Ryan and our family. Seeing complete strangers stop to honor Ryan filled me with a gratitude I still can't express.

I asked for the burial service to be closed to the public. I wanted only family members, close friends, and Ventura County Fire personnel to be there. The funeral service had been open to the public and was streamed live on the internet, but a burial is intimate and I wanted to keep it that way for Ryan's family, friends, and colleagues.

Everyone appeared to have arrived long before we did. As we walked towards the gravesite, my breath was taken away by the powerful scene that was ahead. Across from the seats designated for us was a sea of blue uniforms. Hundreds of Ryan's brothers and sisters in the department standing at attention with the sun beating down on them as they faced us. It was overwhelming to see the solidarity of the department.

Again, the memory of what was said during this ceremony is lost on my broken heart, but the memory of watching the flag being removed from Ryan's casket, folded in honorable perfection, and presented to me by the Chief is something that will never leave me. Nor will the sound of radio dispatch honoring Ryan's last call or the sound of the bell signaling his last alarm.

When the service ended, we were immediately surrounded by those offering kind words and gentle hugs. As my children were receiving attention from family members, I caught the sun bouncing off the large, mirrored tomb in which my husband's casket was resting upon. I walked towards it as though it were trying to pull me in. There were hundreds of people around me, but as I stared at the lid that would eventually enclose my husband, the noise of the crowd disappeared. Behind my sunglasses, my eyes were caught in a blank stare. I noticed Ryan's name was etched on the mirrored lid of the tomb I didn't remember choosing. My hands involuntarily gripped the flag I had been given, burying my nails into the folds. My mind was as empty as my stare. My husband was going to be locked in a box, placed into another box, and buried below the ground. I couldn't process that it was *my* husband.

I felt a small presence beside me, but I didn't move. I kept staring. I knew who it was without having to look. Without taking my eyes off the shiny lid of the tomb, I turned my body into her embrace, and wrapped my arms around her. Ryan's baby sister, Jeanine. We said nothing. When she pulled away to look at my face, she winked at me. Her signature wink; the same one she gave when she edited the condensed eulogy. The wink that says, "I got you."

A gentle hand on my arm communicated it was time for us to head towards the private reception at the Commemorative Air Force SoCal Aviation Museum in Camarillo. I nodded and turned to look for my kids. They were both standing behind me, and once again, we were left to say goodbye to Ryan. As we began to walk towards the bus, I turned back to see Ryan's casket gleaming beneath the sun. The rays of sunshine bounced off the ground making the scene look contrastingly peaceful. "*I love you,*" I said beneath my breath as I got into the bus that would take me away from him forever.

Chapter 10

Somehow New Year's Eve was upon me. When Ryan was alive, the four of us celebrated the same way every year: pajama party at Roger and Mahal's house. The years when Ryan had to work, the kids and I would go to the pajama party and call him when the clock struck midnight. The year before he died, Ryan was off for both New Year's Eve and New Year's Day, along with Halloween, Thanksgiving, Christmas Eve and Christmas Day - something that rarely happens in the fire service. What I originally saw as coincidence that year, I now see was a gift of time given to us by God.

I stood in my bathroom staring at the mirror. Three months had passed since his death, and I still hadn't gained back the weight I lost. My face looked hollow and my eyes were empty. I pulled my hair into a ponytail and stared at my clothing. I wore light gray sweatpants and a well-worn long-sleeved pajama top from Victoria's Secret. Ryan used to say he loved me best when I was in sweatpants and old shirts (in particular, his old shirts). I never understood his attraction to my relaxed wardrobe, but as I stared in the mirror, I found myself longing for his presence and wishing I could hear his voice trying to convince me that I looked better in pajamas than in anything else. I didn't want to go anywhere. I wanted to be home, but my kids were excited to ring in another New Year with their friends, our traditions, and a plethora of unhealthy snacks.

I looked at myself once more, *"ugh."*

I pulled out my phone to look at the photos from New Year's Eve 2015. I didn't take many pictures, but I smiled as I thumbed through the few moments I did capture that year. That night he wore red and black flannel pajama bottoms, a blue sweatshirt with the fire service Maltese embroidered on the left chest, and a hat representing Brandon's baseball team.

And then, I had an idea.

I opened Ryan's closet and grabbed that sweatshirt off the hanger on which it was being unintentionally memorialized. I took off my shirt and put on his, allowing it to swallow my small frame. It felt heavier than a standard sweatshirt with its stiff collar surrounding my neck and quartered zipper hitting my chest. I liked the weight of it on my body. It felt sturdy and strong, and I imagined that its tightly spun cotton was a hug from my husband.

When the kids and I arrived at the party, we were immediately greeted with smiles, party hats, and offers of food and drink. I felt myself ease into the celebration and allowed it to distract me from reality for a bit. Being without Ryan on New Year's Eve was nothing new to me. I welcomed several years without a kiss from him and woke up on several January 1sts without him next to me. I was fine being alone; I was used to being a third wheel amongst other couples. But as the night went on the distractions were no longer working and I found myself feeling uncomfortable in my once comfortable surroundings.

I didn't let on, though. I laughed, joked, smiled, and I think I even ate a little bit. Being on the west coast, the ball had already dropped in the middle of New York City at Times Square. On the television was the replay of the night's events with the countdown clock tucked into the corner of the screen.

"It's almost time! 5 minutes!" The kids were so excited. They loved the countdown because we would allow them to scream it to one another. Suddenly there was a lot of movement. Glasses of champagne (and sparkling apple cider for the kids) were being poured and passed around. Mahal was handing twelve grapes to each person in honor of the superstition that eating these grapes at midnight would bring good luck the following year (which didn't seem to work well for me last year). The kids were grabbing for noisemakers and lining themselves up for a front row view of the television screen. I accepted my champagne and grapes with a smile of amusement as I watched the flutter of anticipation in the room.

I backed away from the group that had formed in front of the television and prepared to watch the last few minutes of this year.

"10, 9, 8, 7, 6, 5, 4, 3, 2, 1.....HAPPY NEW YEAR!"

As soon as we hit the count of 9, I could feel the lump in my throat building. I couldn't say anything more. I couldn't count down. As everyone yelled 'Happy New Year' I searched for my kids. I needed a hug. I needed to hold someone and I needed to be held. Mahal instinctively turned towards me and wrapped me in a hug that released every tear I had been holding in.

"It feels like I'm leaving him behind."

I felt her arms hold me tighter as I cried uncontrollably into her shoulder. I don't know where my kids were or who was around us. I was lost in the realization that my husband and the life I had with him was staying in 2016. It was the end of the last year I would ever share with him. Everything about us came to a stop at the stroke of midnight. I was being forced to enter into a new year where he wouldn't exist and I still hadn't learned how to exist without him.

Chapter 11

2017

It was January 1st. A day that represents a fresh start to many but felt like a secondary death to me. I made it through the night and woke up to a New Year. I spent the day in the pajamas I wore the night before. I emptied boxes of frozen snacks onto baking sheets and considered that cooking for the day. The day had been cloudy, which I felt was an appropriate welcome into a year I didn't want to enter. But, by the time evening arrived I noticed that a majority of the clouds had cleared, exposing a softly lit sky. If I looked to my right, the sky was covered in a dark blanket of clouds, but when I looked straight ahead, pockets of light blue sky gave promise the storm wouldn't be here forever. I grabbed my phone and took a photo of the sky. In that moment, I felt God saying to me, "keep looking straight ahead. The storm is moving."

I kept my routine of sitting with God each morning. I had been reading through the Psalms, focusing on God's care for the brokenhearted when I decided to change the direction of my focus. One week into the new year, I turned my bible to the book of Job. The story of Job is known for his loss and suffering, but I wasn't necessarily looking to connect with Job's loss. In reality, the only thing Job and I shared was a similar heartache and questioning of God. Job lost his children, his wealth and his health, but not his wife. I couldn't relate to what Job lost, but I could relate to his confusion about why he was allowed to ache so greatly.

In 2016, I set my mind to fast from Diet Coke for a year. Now in 2017, I set my mind to study the book of Job for a year. I wanted to know every detail, historically and biblically, about this book of the bible. I vowed to become a self-proclaimed expert on this book. Instead, I became a devoted and humbled student of God's sovereignty and a self-appointed friend of Job. I learned Job's story was not actually about his suffering, but rather, about God, His character, and His relationship with Job.

Job, a loyal servant to God, was struck with devastation after Satan accused him of circumstantial faith. "Satan answered the Lord, 'Job has good reason to respect you. You have blessed him and made him successful in everything he does. He is so wealthy that his herds and flocks are all over the country. But if you were to destroy everything he has, I promise you that he would curse you to your face." (Job 1:9-10) God had so much faith in His relationship with Job that He allowed Satan to take away the physical blessings in Job's life to prove he was unconditionally loyal to God.

After all was taken from him, "[Jobs'] wife said to him, "Are you still holding on to your faith? Why don't you just curse God and die!" Job answered, "You sound like one of those fools on the street corner! How can we accept all the good things that God gives us and not accept the problems?" (Job 2:9-10)

He had a point. How could I accept all the good and reject all the bad? I admired Job's ability to see that trusting God meant to trust Him through all things, but as I kept reading, I discovered another aspect of Job's heart.

"What I always feared has happened to me. What I dreaded has come true. I have no peace, no quietness. I have no rest; only trouble comes." (Job 3:25-26).

I could see his heart beginning to break. His words drew me in. "I hate my own life, so I will complain freely. I am very bitter, so now I will speak. I will say to God, 'don't just say I am guilty! Tell me what you have against me. Do you enjoy hurting me? Do you enjoy ignoring me?'" (Job 10:1-3) He spoke to God so openly, I had never seen anything like it.

For several chapters, Job was essentially asking the age-old question: "why do bad things happen to good people?" His pain pushed him into feeling as though God abandoned him. Job became confused, assuming this torment was a reflection of God's feeling toward him.

Job had a group of friends who came to sit with him in his grief and they sat quietly with him for seven days. As soon as Job began to talk about his emotional torment, they began to speak in return. A majority of the book is filled with conversation between Job and his friends; however, their words were not of comfort. In fact, their words were rich with accusations that Job must've brought this destruction upon himself. They used religious explanations for his suffering, saying that bad things happen to bad people;

therefore, Job must've done something to anger God. They verbally pushed him into a corner of shame. The truth was, they knew nothing about God's faith in Job. They didn't know God described him as a "good, faithful man." They didn't know He said Job was one of a kind who respected God and refused to do evil. (Job 1:8) In reality, they didn't know God at all.

But Job did. Deep down, he knew God. His heartache forced questioning and he was saying everything I felt but didn't know I could say. I did wonder if God abandoned me. I did wonder if God was punishing me. I was confused by what had been allowed to happen. Even though I knew Job was innocent and his questions were a result of heartache, I caught myself wondering if I had done something wrong to cause this devastation in my life. I occasionally leaned into the lie that I somehow brought this heartache upon myself. I knew it wasn't true, but I also couldn't help to consider the possibility that maybe I did, in fact, do something wrong. The words of Job's friends poked at my insecurities. The hopeful side of my faith trusted that God is not a punisher, but the logical side of my brain couldn't process that fact easily.

I could feel the desperation of Job's heartache and the turbulence in his soul as he tried to cling onto the truth he knew about God: "my spirit is crushed," (Job 17:1), "O God, you have ground me down and devastated my family," (Job 16:7), "I was living quietly until he shattered me," (Job 16:12) "Depression haunts my days. ... I'm nothing more than dust and ashes." (Job 30:16,19)

"Me, too, Job," I thought to myself.

Throughout his lamenting and questioning of God, I noticed Job was able to still recognize that God was sovereign: "But as for me, I know that my Redeemer lives," (Job 19:25), "I will see him for myself. Yes, I will see him with my own eyes. I am overwhelmed at the thought!" (Job 19:27). My head knowledge knew that God was in control, but my heart was confused by that same fact. Then Job said, "I will teach you about God's power. I will not conceal anything concerning the Almighty." (Job 26:11) He was talking to his friends, but as I read those words, I felt as though he were saying them to me.

Job was everything I was: grieved, confused, desperate, and emotionally messy. There was one thing he wasn't, but I was: detached from God. I was talking to God every day, but I was struggling to connect with Him again. My heart was weary and my spiritual energy was minimal. I stopped journaling. I barely spoke. I was also afraid to be anything but positive or grateful when approaching God because I feared my disappointment might create more hardship in my life. I spent so much time trying to look for the blessing in my heartache. Well-intentioned people repeatedly sent scripture reminding me to "rejoice in my suffering." It created a fear to be honest with God. I was so busy trying to rejoice and justify why God would allow Ryan to die, I didn't allow my spirit to actually ache for my loss.

Job gave me permission to feel what I needed while still holding onto God, even if it didn't make sense. He didn't have a polished or pretty faith. He was raw, vulnerable and honest. Despite all my years reading the bible, I didn't realize we could be *that* honest with God. Job taught me that God can handle my questioning, and although I demanded answers and clarity, God's sovereignty is unconditional and answers aren't necessary for that fact to be true. Job showed me that circumstances don't dictate God's supremacy or His mercy. He demonstrated a fact about God I had been too afraid to believe: He wanted unfiltered honesty from me more than He wanted my positive and practiced religion. Before studying the book of Job closely, I only knew it to be a story of suffering. But in reality, it's about how well Job *knew* God and how well God loved Job. In the midst of crying out, Job knew God was sovereign. In the middle of devastation, Job knew God was in control. He was crushed, but he wasn't foolish. He was hurt, but he knew God was fair (Job 23:1-7). He was confused, but he knew wisdom was found in God (Job 28:23-38).

The greatest thing I took from my study of Job was God's love for him. God allowed Job the time and space for his honesty, and He stayed quiet as Job lamented. God didn't speak until He knew Job could hear Him. I imagined myself as Job, crying out to God and feeling as though He had gone silent. I believed God left me to flail about in my grief and confusion, but He never did. He was waiting until I could hear Him. He didn't wait until I perfected my prayers or cleaned up my attitude. He only waited until I could hear Him, and then He spoke. Job showed me how to have a relationship with God instead of having an expectation of Him.

"I want to be like Job." I closed my eyes and asked God to make me like his servant, and my new spiritual bestie, Job.

I opened my new planner. I was barely into January when

the rest of the year had already filled itself with events and memorials. I was overwhelmed and the year just started. I related to Job's cry, "I constantly feel upset. And my suffering has only just begun" (Job 30:27).

Memorials in Sacramento (California Firefighters Memorial), Colorado Springs (Fallen Firefighter Memorial), and Emmitsburg (National Fallen Firefighters Memorial) had already been scheduled for later that year. Just before that run around the country, Ryan was going to be memorialized at the newly dedicated "Courtyard of Courage" at our alma mater, Saugus High School.

More events and memorials were already scheduled and scattered throughout 2017: Vandenberg Air Force Base (now Vandenberg Space Force Base) memorialized Ryan on the Atlas V rocket. During a tour of the facilities the day before the launch, I was told he was the first non-industry civilian to have his name on a rocket.

The Los Angeles Kings of the NHL honored Ryan as the "Hero of the Game." The Los Angeles Dodgers of the MLB honored Ryan during Firefighter Appreciation Night.

A golf tournament, The Ryan Osler Memorial Classic, was planned and orchestrated by Missy Carter, a woman whose firefighter father was also killed in the line of duty.

In the midst of these planned events were two big milestones for my children: Brandon would be graduating from elementary school and Amanda would be starting high school. Two major transitions and milestones without their Daddy.

And then there was the first anniversary of Ryan's death. I

would be forced to walk through the memory of the days leading up to the accident and relive the worst moments of my life.

§

The calendar carried on without regard of my heart. Countless moments that occupied the corner of each day during that first year of loss left me in moments of deep grief, dark thoughts and crying out to God. I lost track of the sleepless nights and the endless number of tears I cried. But one thing I can count: the number of pennies I received when I needed to know God was near.

When God spoke to Job, He "spoke to him out of a storm" (Job 38:1). How it sounded or what it looked like, we have no idea. But it doesn't matter what it might've sounded or looked like to us because that communication was meant for Job.

Almost immediately after Ryan died, God started showing me signs that He was near. At first it was big, obvious signs, which I believe were meant for an audience greater than me. Things like Stuart Rose Air Conditioning and other coincidences made obvious to those watching our family.

But then there were the private moments spoken to my children in ways that they would know it was God. One of my favorites being the night before they returned to school days after everyone but us went back to their normal lives.

The three of us were in a daze, unsure how to process the stillness in our home following two weeks of noise and warmth. We decided we would go to dinner at our family's favorite restaurant, Islands. Before heading out, I realized I hadn't retrieved the mail in several days. I placed a large stack of mail on our table. There were bills proving that life goes on and there were cards proving that our life had changed. I slowly opened each card, smiling with gratitude for the love sent with every pen stroke. As I opened the last card, a small folded envelope bounced onto the table.

"Oh my gosh, guys. Come look at this."

The kids ran over to the table. "What!! Who?? How did they know??"

The three of us stared at the little blue card. On it were three surfers riding a huge wave and in the bottom left corner was a palm tree with the word "Islands" next to it. It was a gift card to the restaurant. The slump that the kids felt earlier was gone. Excitement and awe consumed their little bodies. My slump was gone, also.

But in between the public and private coincidences from God was the communication meant just for me. Shortly after Ryan died, I began noticing pennies around me. They were never in abundance and I didn't come across them on a regular basis.

I picked up every penny I found and tossed them into a small dish kept on my bathroom counter. They were sweet little surprises that lifted my heart in the moment, but it wasn't until months passed after Ryan's death that I realized the pattern of my penny-finding. Like Job, I needed God to speak to me out of a storm, but instead of words, He dropped in as pennies at my feet.

I was running late one morning. Trying to get the kids ready for school seemed unusually chaotic. I remember feeling stressed and overwhelmed just to get out the door. Dropping the kids off at two different schools and trying to make use of my day off work, I planned to run errands immediately after drop off. I arrived at the market and was noticeably irritated at everything from the slow-paced cars in the parking lot to the shopping carts that were stuck together that morning. I rummaged through my purse looking for my grocery list - not there. This was my big shopping trip, meaning I had a page full of things I needed to buy and the only thing I could remember writing on the list was milk. I left the shopping cart in the middle of the produce section and scolded myself for making a list with old-fashioned pen and paper. I drove home with a scowl on my face. Defeated, I pulled into my garage, slowly got out of the car and walked into the house to find my list, except it wasn't on the table. It wasn't on the kitchen counter. It wasn't in the spot where I kept my purse. "*Where the hell is it??*" I screamed into silent oblivion. I was empty. I had no energy left. As I headed back to my car, my eyes glanced up at the sign Ryan hung above the garage door when we first bought our house: "Always Kiss Me Goodbye." I glared at the memory of purchasing that sign and forming a rule between us: "we will never leave the house without saying 'I love you' or giving a kiss goodbye - no matter what." With that memory in mind, I angrily opened the garage door and returned to my car to look through my purse again. After dumping everything into the passenger seat, it was still nowhere to be found. I cried as I put my purse back together.

I was so overwhelmed. Everything felt more difficult. The smallest disruption felt like the world was crumbling below my feet. I leaned my head against the steering wheel and sobbed. I wanted my normal life back. I wanted to call my husband and ask him what we needed from the market. I wanted to hear him tell me that we needed more coffee or listen to him lecture me on keeping an archaic method of list making. I lifted my head and slammed my hands on the steering wheel. With my car door and the garage door open to my neighborhood, I yelled at the top of my lungs, "I HATE THIS!"

In that moment, I decided to quit. I couldn't go on like this. I leaned back in the driver seat and closed my eyes. *"Please, God, I can't do this anymore. I don't want to do this anymore. I don't want to be strong. I don't want to be faithful. I don't want to be anything but done. Please don't make me do this life."* I sat there until my crying stopped and my heartbeat slowed.

I turned my left leg towards the door to get out of the car and go back inside the house. I would go to the market tomorrow, I decided. As I lifted my foot to step out of my car, I noticed the shiniest penny I had ever seen. I stared at it for a moment. It was laying on the ground directly beneath me. It wasn't there when I first pulled into the garage. It was so shiny I would've definitely seen it when I first got out and when I got back into my car. I don't know when it showed up.

But there it was. I took a picture of it because I knew in that moment these pennies were more than just sweet surprises for my heart. They were direct communication from God to me. My perspective completely changed when I saw that penny outside my car door. Like a flashback scene in a movie, I could suddenly see all the ways in which God had been with me, including the ways in which He went before me. I could see His timing when I completed the Grief Recovery Method nine months before Ryan died; He knew I would need those tools in the days, months and years ahead. I saw His care in the way He protected me as I received news of Ryan's death; He made sure I wasn't driving and I wasn't alone. I reflected on the rarity of Ryan being home for every major holiday the year before as a gift of time from God, allowing us to create and cement those memories as a family. I thought about our last date together and the way in which God protected our conversation and our time together, ensuring we enjoyed each other's presence one last time. I realized God's provision by allowing Ryan's accident to occur as it did because He could see there was no financial arrangement or life insurance policy in place for us should he have died off duty.

I stared at that penny and realized God had been here all along. He was with me on the days I struggled. He was quiet on the days I raised my voice. He was next to me on the days I cried uncontrollably and questioned His presence and His plan. More than anything, He was patient with me. He waited until I could hear him. He waited until His voice was all I could hear. After that moment, I purchased a special jar to keep my "pennies from heaven." The jar has since overflowed and although I don't recall the memory attached to each penny, I know that every single one of them were given to me in moments when I needed something that only God could provide; moments when God spoke to me through the storm.

§

December 2017

I have never been one to have a "word of the year," a "scripture of the year" or a "life verse." I'm also one who doesn't make New Year's resolutions or wish when blowing out birthday candles. It's not for any reason other than I can't memorize scripture, I don't stick to resolutions, and I can't focus on wishing while people are watching and waiting for a piece of cake. But on December 31, 2017, I felt ambitious. I was going to have a "life verse," or at minimum, a scripture of the year. Not only was I not sure which scripture, I wasn't sure as to why I wanted 2018 to be the year I attempt finding such a thing. Despite knowing where to look (the bible), I didn't know how to look. I thought to myself, *'how do people find their yearly scriptures or words?' Do I Google popular words for 2018? Do I ask someone what their "scripture of the year" is going to be?'*

I didn't have a clue how to go about finding my scripture of the year, so I started thumbing through my bible. The pages softly whispered with every flick of my finger. I was waiting for the "ah-ha!" moment when a scripture would highlight itself and speak into my heart. Instead, I skimmed the pages. I looked over my previously highlighted scriptures, I went to the verses most commonly known, and I waited for inspiration.

Nothing.

I set my bible down with a thud onto my desk. I was already failing at the 2018 goal I set for myself and I was still in 2017. I mindlessly picked up my phone and opened my favorite search engine: Pinterest. I began scrolling, admiring the delicious meals with recipes attached and outfit inspirations for places I would most likely never travel.

And then a white square with black words forced my fingers to stop scrolling. There were no decorations on this squared off piece of internet, just black font. Bold, black font. I stopped to read the words that glared at me beneath my fingertips.

"As for me, I will always have hope." (NIV)

Beneath the bold font was small script I had to squint to read, "Psalm 71:14."

I traded my phone for my bible and opened it to the book of Psalms. *'Does the scripture truly read this way or is this a creative paraphrase?'*

In my well-worn bible, pages of the Psalms are colored with highlighter and words that have spoken to me in the past have been underlined for emphasis; however, Psalm 71:14 was untouched. "As for me, I will always have hope; I will praise you more and more."

Aside from the last half of scripture left off by the creator of that Pinterest square, the words on my screen were the same in my bible. How many times had I read these words before? Had I ever read them?

I stared at the untouched page in my bible. *'This is it; this is my verse for the year. I will always have hope.'*

By December 31, 2017, I had already lived fifteen months as a widowed mother of two. In 2017 specifically, I endured three different memorials across the country in which my late husband's name was permanently etched into memory. I heard his name announced and saw his photo on screens as he was honored in various ways. My children and I had gone on our family trip to Hawaii that was planned (and paid for) by my husband before he died. My son graduated from elementary school and I sobbed desperately wishing his dad could be there for that moment. We walked through our first Father's Day and his first earthly birthday.

Most tenderly, I walked through the first anniversary of his death. I stared at the calendar recalling every moment from the night of September 19th through the morning of September 21st: our last text messages, our last phone call, our last hug, our last 'I love you,' our last memories. And yet, through it all, I held onto hope.

Chapter 12

September 2017

It was a gift that had been given to me but I had no desire to use it. *"I don't want to go to the spa,"* I thought to myself as I stared at the certificate.

"It'll be good for you! I'll go with you." Mahal was trying to convince me that a day at the spa was what I needed. The first anniversary of Ryan's death was approaching and I felt anything but relaxed. She booked our appointments and before I knew it, I was putting on a heavy blue robe, sipping cold cucumber water and sharing a whispered conversation with Mahal in the spa's tranquil arboretum. We were taken into separate rooms for our massages and I prepared my body to receive fifty minutes of relaxation.

"Hello," the masseuse's gentle voice surprised me. Laying with my face down on the massage table, I mumbled a greeting in return and said nothing more. The room was dimly lit, infused with an aroma of lavender and citrus, while soft music filled the quiet air. I felt the masseuse's presence on my right as she began. I've had massages before, but for some reason I couldn't fully relax. When she reached my lower back after massaging my shoulders, I quietly burst into tears. With my face hidden beneath the table, I allowed my tears to fall to the ground, but I couldn't hide my crying for long. I sniffled. She stopped.

"Are you okay? Is that too much pressure?"

Poor thing thought she was hurting me.

"No, no, no. It's perfect, thank you." It was too much pressure. But not the pressure of her hands; it was the pressure of her touch. Nobody's hands had been so intimately on my skin in a year. I realized in that moment not only did I miss Ryan's touch, but I wondered if I would ever be intimately touched again.

§

February 2018

I didn't want to say it out loud. It felt uncomfortable, and quite frankly, it felt wrong. But I couldn't stop thinking about it. It had been a year and a half since Ryan died when I realized I missed being loved by a man. I missed being someone's girl. I wanted to be loved and I had love to give, but I didn't want to admit it. I wasn't afraid of judgment as much as I was afraid of eager matchmakers in my social circle. I was also afraid that if I said it out loud it would somehow indicate that I wanted to date, and dating was something I had no desire to do. The idea of dating horrified me. I heard too many stories of creeps and weirdos, and I collected enough of my own firsthand experiences with men who shouldn't have been contacting me to determine there was nothing desirable in the dating pool.

'At my age, if they're single, there's something wrong with them.

If they've never been married, there's something wrong with them. If they don't have kids, there's something wrong with them."

There was not a man on earth who stood a chance with me. Not because I thought highly of myself but because I had already deemed every single man to be strange, weird, creepy or bad. I never dated. Starting a relationship with Ryan when I was fifteen and marrying him when I was twenty didn't leave much of a time frame to experience dating. I didn't know life without him, which meant I actually didn't know what I liked in a man because what I liked was my husband. Who I wanted was my husband. Who I needed was my husband. Despite knowing I wanted to be loved, I couldn't fathom the thought of ever being attracted to another man. The idea of intimacy with someone else put knots in my stomach. To put it bluntly, the idea of another man made me sick.

It was a quiet night and both of the children were asleep when I decided to see what was out there. Out of sheer curiosity, I pulled out my phone and hesitantly typed in the address of a popular dating website. Not a Christian dating website, but not a 'hook-up' website either. One of those "I'm here to find love but I'm not ready to pay for a membership yet" kind of websites. I had to create a profile before getting a sneak peek into the dating world, so I set up a new email account, gave myself a fake name and jumped in.

I scrolled through the suggested profiles and my heart sank. I felt disgusted. It didn't matter how physically attractive the eligible bachelors appeared to be, I felt my stomach turn at the sight of each one. I exited out of the dating site as quickly as I could; I laid down on the couch and cried. All I wanted was my husband. I wanted the man who was familiar with my flaws, acquainted with my body and intimate with my heart.

It wasn't long after that night when I realized that although I hadn't been saying it out loud, God had been listening to my heart the whole time.

"Ok, fine. You already know, anyway. I'll write it down."

I went to my closet and grabbed a small journal. It was slightly larger than my hand and its fabric cover was teal in color and decorated with a beautiful floral motif. I opened to the first page and began to write.

The desires of my heart
02/15/2018

Loves God, has relationship with God
Sees me the way God sees me
Loves me the way God loves me
Wants to protect my heart
Not only let me love Ryan, but help me honor him
Love my children as his
Loves me and my kids with the understanding of what we lost
Full of grace (I'll need it)
Loves my heart
Encourages my ideas
Handy!!!!
Drama free (please!)
Established but flexible to be here in my home

Loves me for me
NO DRINKING (please)
Handsome
Encourages me to be active
Laughs with me
Makes me feel pretty
Makes me feel safe
Physical strength
Leadership qualities without being bossy
Stature (I want to feel dainty)
Kindness but not a pushover
No in-law drama (please)
Can have kids, but no younger than 9 years old
Not a stranger, but not someone I already know (friend of a friend)
No criminal record – none! Not even as a kid

I looked over my list, closed my journal, tucked it away, and never looked at it again. I laughed at myself as I put the cap back on my pen. "Good luck with that one, God," I said with a touch of cynicism in my tone.

I decided to tell my closest friends and my cousin about "the list." Each time I shared about it, I laughed at my petty requests. But I secretly felt settled in knowing I had been honest with God because I knew He didn't find me petty.

"I'm not worried about it," I would tell my friends. "I know God has someone picked out for me and the kids and He'll let me know when it's time."

But I wasn't just saying that. I believed it, wholeheartedly. I knew God had someone for me, I didn't need to look for him. I didn't need to date. I didn't need to wonder about each potential interaction I would have with members of the opposite sex. I trusted that God would let me know when it was time to open my heart again.

Three months later, I received a private message on Instagram:

May 22, 2018

"Hi Jennifer! We haven't exactly met, but I know you through VCFD. My husband is Bob Ameche. I have a question for you. I co-host an annual Women's gathering at Hume Lake during the Firefighters for Christ retreat. We usually have about 120 firefighter wives attend. I was wondering if you would pray about being our guest speaker next year. Our theme will be Hope. I know you would be a tremendous blessing to the ladies. The conference is March 28-31 with the Ladies Tea on the morning of the 29th. You can call or text me if you want more info. Lori Ameche"

Without hesitation, I responded:

"Hi Lori! Thank you so much for thinking of me...I would be incredibly honored to speak about hope! Since Ryan's passing I have said that God would never waste my tears and if He allows me, I will shout about His goodness and grace from every mountain top I can find. Thank you so much for asking me...I would be absolutely honored to be a part of something so incredible!"

I didn't know Lori, but I knew her husband, Bob. He was a chaplain with our department. His contagious smile and compassionate eyes were the picture of comfort during the planning of Ryan's funeral. He sat in my home and walked me through what would take place in the days to come. He stood in front of thousands and invited us to honor Ryan's life. Bob represented the closing of a chapter in my life. He represented an ending. When I thought of Bob, I thought of Ryan's funeral. But years after ceremoniously bringing honor and closure to the life I once knew, Bob (and his wife, Lori) would represent the opening of a new chapter I didn't know was being written.

Chapter 13

January 2019

"Something big is going to happen this year, I can feel it," I said to my cousin, Katie, while shoving french fries into my mouth. "I just don't know what it is." I kept eating and she began dreaming.

"Maybe this is the year of your book!" She was one of many encouraging me to write.

"Maybe," I mumbled in between bites. "Maybe this talk at Hume is the beginning of something that's coming."

During a breakfast date with my friend, Felicia, I said the same thing: "something big is going to happen this year. I just don't know what it is."

She also began dreaming of a book and imagining me as a host for a widows' retreat. "Oh, this is fun," she said as her eyes slipped into a dreamlike trance.

I told Mahal the same: "something big is happening this year, but I don't know what." Together we started imagining a best-selling novel or selling out speaking engagements.

I couldn't explain the feeling, but I felt deep in my soul that

God was moving and He was doing something big.

§

I had just under a year to prepare my talk for the Women's Tea with Firefighter's for Christ at Hume Lake Christian Camp in central California. Naturally, I waited until two months before the event to begin preparing. The theme of the tea was 'hope,' and after meeting with Lori and Teri (also in charge of the event), I could see that their desire was for me to somehow inspire the idea of having hope despite circumstances without scaring anyone by my loss.

Each morning I met with God and asked for His guidance and wisdom on this topic. 'Hope' felt so generic, but I started working on it anyway. I wrote and rehearsed for countless hours. Mahal was my test audience one night and despite her applause and approval, I wasn't pleased with what I'd written.

I continued to pray. *'It doesn't feel done, God. What is it missing?'*

Before long, it was the month of March. Hume was only three weeks away. March was also the two-and-a-half-year mark of Ryan's death. People started to get curious about when I would begin dating. My standard answer became: "I'm not interested in dating. God will let me know if or when it's time." As the inquirer would listen to my explanation, I would catch their eyes glance down at my wedding ring.

I tried to take it off a year earlier, but as soon as I put it in a box, I took it out and placed it back on my finger. I legally became single the moment Ryan died, but my heart still felt married. I wasn't ready for the world to visibly see that I was no longer a wife, but my heart was inching closer towards letting the world know I wanted to be loved, even if I didn't want to date.

I took to my blog, "Faith and Fire," and shared an open letter:

March 5, 2019

To the one I haven't met,

I first have to tell you that I never planned on loving you.

I had a husband. A wonderful husband.

And he loved me with every ounce of his being.

He would've stopped at nothing to give me everything.

He was my future. And I promised to love him forever.

I never imagined you while I was dreaming about my future.

In all honesty, I'm scared to meet you.

I don't know who you are, but I already know what I need from you.

I need you to understand that loving me involves loving my late husband.

What you love about me is the product of what I shared with him.

He is the father of my children and I search their mannerisms for hints of him each day. For my kids, I will never stop talking about him.

I won't erase him from our hearts or allow us to live as though he didn't. His pictures will still be visible, his name will still be said. His birthday will be celebrated and his death will be honored.

Milestones will touch my family throughout the years, and my heart will cry each time, wishing he could see his children or hear the cry of his first grandchild.

Please don't ask me to stop loving him.

And please don't assume I will stop missing him.

I need you to know that there will be places within my heart that you cannot possess. It's not because I don't trust you nor is it because I can't love you. But because those pieces of my heart will forever belong to the story that was written before you entered this chapter.

I need you to know that I realize you are different. I understand that your love for me won't look the same. I need your patience as I try to remember what it's like to be loved, especially when it's coming from an unfamiliar heart.

I know this is a lot to ask of you.

I know you are probably scared to love me, wondering if you'll ever compare to the memory of the man I loved first. The truth is, my late husband left something for me to share with someone like you.

Because of his love, I see the world differently. And because of his death, I live each day passionately. I will cherish every moment given with you. I will pay attention to the small things that are embedded in your character. I will enjoy the minutes in between moments and the precious seconds between minutes.

I will honor your heart, value your time, and embrace your touch.

I will not take our days together for granted and I will always search for ways to let you know that I am holding your place in my heart, the same as I am holding his.

I don't know who you are yet. But if we ever meet, please love all of me. The broken pieces, the healed wounds, and the visible scars on my heart.

I'm not damaged. And I'm not hopeless. I'm tender. And I'm scared.

Like delicate pottery pieced together after shattering, so is my heart in your hands. But if you are willing to gently hold it and protect it as best as you can, then I am willing to release my grip and allow my hands to begin writing our story.

Can't wait to meet you. Xoxo

Five days later, I laid in the center of my bed and cried. *'How is anybody going to love me, God? Is it even possible?'* I sobbed. I allowed my heart to explode through the tears landing on my pillow. *'Will anybody be able to love me as I am? Will anybody love my kids like they deserve to be loved?'* I cried harder as I thought about my kids asleep in their rooms. There was no mistaking the fact that I wanted to be loved, but the idea of my children being unloved or unfairly tolerated shattered my spirit. *'Will anybody be able to love us, God? Why would you allow love to be taken away from us?'* I cried until there was nothing left. I closed my eyes and felt my body relax. I imagined curling into God's lap. In my mind, He is a bright light with a soft presence. I can feel the warmth of His glow when I imagine laying down my head. My breathing was soothed into a slow rhythm. *'If it's just me and You, God, I'm ok with that.'* I kept my eyes closed. *'If it's just You and me forever, I'm ok with that. All I want is You.'* I could feel myself drifting towards sleep. *'Nobody will ever love me like You do, anyway. So, if it's just us, I'm ok with that.'* I fell asleep knowing that every word I spoke was true. I didn't want anyone more than I wanted God.

§

One week before Hume, God rewrote everything I had prepared for the Women's Tea. He showed me the message He wanted to be delivered, and in obedience, I changed all that I had prepared. While rewriting, I pieced together why God showed Psalm 71:14 to me over a year earlier. On New Year's Eve of 2017, I didn't know why God showed that scripture to me, but now, in March of 2019, it made perfect sense. I was being asked to speak about hope, and He had given me the scripture to use. I didn't have time to tell Lori and Teri that I changed the structure of my talk. I didn't have time to practice it with an audience. I wrote, I prayed, and I practiced into my bathroom mirror.

It was March 21st; the two-and-a-half-year mark of Ryan's death and six days before I was to arrive at Hume Lake. I woke up that morning, thankful I wasn't going into work, and planned to spend the day rehearsing my newly revised talk as soon as I dropped the kids off at school.

I stood at the bathroom counter with my printed, and heavily edited, talk. A page fell from the counter, and as I bent down to pick it up, my left hand struck the countertop with a force strong enough to make me stop in mid-movement and make sure the diamond was still in my wedding ring. As I stood up, I stretched out my hand and admired the sparkle I had been wearing for the last eighteen years.

I loved my wedding ring. The center stone was a heart-shaped diamond Ryan bought for me after we graduated from high school. I rarely wore it because it was a solitaire diamond on a gold band, obviously designed to be an engagement ring, and I was only seventeen. But I wouldn't have to wait long to wear it because two years after graduation we announced that we were going to get married. He took that heart-shaped diamond and had it placed in an engagement ring with three princess cut diamonds tiered on each side of it. The original set came with a thin gold wedding band to match the shape of the engagement ring, but Ryan wanted more for me. He kept the tiered shape, but had a thicker band made with princess cut diamonds to match those of the engagement ring. It was beautiful. Just before our wedding, Ryan took my engagement ring and had it soldered to the wedding band, making it one ring. I hadn't seen it again until he put it on my finger after vowing to love me until death do us part.

Shortly after Ryan died, I added a band to wear with my wedding ring. It was a dainty eternity band with black diamonds and four red rubies in the center. It illustrated the 'thin red line,' which represents the fire service, and in particular, fallen firefighters.

As I stared at my hand, I felt a nudge from within to take off my wedding ring. I tried ignoring it, but couldn't, so I removed my ring and kept the black band on my finger. I placed my wedding ring on the countertop just in case I needed to quickly return it to its normal place on my hand, but I didn't feel that urgency this time. Instead, I grabbed my step-stool and reached for a box in my closet that holds treasures and trinkets Ryan had given to me, along with a ring box keeping safe his gold and diamond encrusted wedding ring.

I opened the small black box, removed his wedding ring and held it in my hand. I wore his ring around my neck for a year after he died. The gold felt heavy as I wore it, but now it felt light in my hands. I placed it back in the box and laid my ring on top of it. Had it not been for the height of that heart-shaped diamond, my ring would've fit perfectly inside his. The lid of the ring box closed with a loud snap as I tucked it away. I returned the treasure chest of sentiment to my closet and shut the door. I didn't feel the heaviness or the sense of betrayal I felt the first time I took off my wedding ring. My hand certainly felt different and my thumb was fidgeting with the black band I was wearing, but the ache was no longer there.

God nudged me and I felt Him. He told me it was time and I answered His call. I was getting better at noticing when He was trying to get my attention. I had no idea this moment with God was about more than the ring; He was making sure I could feel Him.

Chapter 14

I was seated in the chair of my hairdresser for my routine cut and color when she began teasing about the upcoming firefighter's retreat. "Oooh, Jenn, maybe this is where you're going to meet your future husband!" I laughed at the thought, and she continued with hers: "you never know! A camp full of firemen? You might be able to have your pick!"

In the days leading up to the retreat, the prospect of meeting my future husband became an inside joke between me and my friends. "Right, could you imagine? Just what I need – another firefighter." We all laughed at the idea and carried on with our lives.

The day came when it was time for Katie and I to travel four hours north to Hume Lake. We originally planned to leave earlier in the day, but school schedules and mom-duties prevented us from that goal. With a bag full of snacks, we hopped into our rental car and got on the road just before 4pm. There is rarely a quiet moment when Katie and I are together, and this road trip proved no different. As we drove, we talked about everything from our childhood to our children to our future. As we began our incline into Sequoia National Park, our conversation didn't stop, but it became softer.

Surrounded by trees of enormous size, we were in awe of their grandeur. As we drove, there was a break in the trees and we caught a glimpse of the sun setting behind us.

"Pull over!"

I did as I was told and pulled the car onto the side of the road. We jumped out and stood in the gentle rays of the sun falling behind us. In front of us was a field of flowers settled beneath a mountain of trees. It felt like magic. We were taking pictures and growing frustrated with the phone's inability to capture the beauty we were witnessing, so we turned the camera and began taking selfies instead. I hadn't realized my phone lost service when we entered the Sequoias and now that we were in a clearing, a flood of text and voice messages came through at once.

One message in particular was from Lori checking on us and wondering about our arrival time. I sent a quick text letting her know that we were on our way and should be arriving soon. Katie and I continued our climb up the mountain, but stopped again when we reached a clearing near the top. It was just after 7pm and the sun was peeking through dark clouds, casting a heavenly glow on the valley beneath us.

"Pull over!"

More pictures, less impressed with the phone's camera.

As soon as we entered into the forest, the sky grew very dark. There were huge snow banks lining the road acting as protection for the trees towering above us. Driving into the forest felt as though we entered into another world: cold, dark, icy. The complete opposite of where we had just been.

I felt my hands grip the steering wheel as I slowed our pace to that of a motorized crawl. Our conversation went silent. Katie checked her phone, "we have no service."

My mind immediately began racing with thoughts of everything that could go wrong knowing we couldn't call for help. There wasn't another car on the road. It was just us, creeping through the mountains on an icy road, praying for signs of life. Without cellular signal, the map on my phone stopped loading. The directions to Hume Lake Christian Camp were still on the screen, but the map itself could no longer load.

"I think I see lights up ahead. Can you see them?" Katie was acting as my navigator while I didn't take my eyes off the road directly in front of me.

I quickly glanced up, "yeah, I see them."

"Do you think that's it?"

"I don't know. I hope so."

We continued on in silence, although both of our minds were loud with prayer. It was officially night by the time we entered into the camp. We couldn't see more than a few feet ahead of the car's headlights but to our left we could see what looked like a 'welcome' building with lights still on. After parking and gaining a better visual of our surroundings, we headed in and were immediately greeted by a friendly, but tired, smile.

"Hi! You must be Jennifer," she said. Initially flattered she knew my name, I smiled as she continued, "the woman who was expecting you will be happy to know you've arrived. She was worried about you because it's so late. I'll find a way to let her know you made it safely."

The flattery was gone and replaced by embarrassment. I pulled out my phone to look at the text I sent to Lori hours earlier; it was never delivered. *'Of course she didn't get it. There's no service up here,'* I reminded myself.

"I'm so sorry. We left later than we planned and I didn't communicate that to Lori." I kept looking at my phone, too embarrassed to make eye contact.

"No worries, we're just glad you made it safely."

As she worked to get us checked in, another employee of the camp gathered her things to leave. "Good night, thank you," I said in an effort to rebuild their first impression of me.

After giving us the key to our cabin, along with an explanation of how to locate it, Katie and I sheepishly made our way back to the car.

"I saw a sign that says the office closes at 6:00," Katie said.

I glanced at my phone. It was almost 8pm. I brought my eyes to Katie's, "that means they stayed there until we arrived."

I was grateful, but also mortified. I had been given several months to prepare for this weekend and yet I somehow wasn't prepared to arrive when I should have that day. I feared the worry I created as a result of my tardiness would make Firefighters for Christ regret inviting me.

Chapter 15

March 28, 2019

I woke up the next morning to find Katie already awake. She greeted me as soon as she saw that my eyes were open, "good morning, cousin."

I smiled in her direction and reached for my phone to check the time. It was early; the woman at the desk the night before told us breakfast would be served at 8am, and building a reputation of tardiness was not something I wanted to continue. As I climbed out of bed, Katie opened the blinds, allowing a warm morning glow into our room. I stared out the window as I convinced my body to wake up by stretching my limbs.

"Wow," I whispered. "It's crazy to be here knowing that Ryan was here, and I'm here to talk about losing him."

Before arriving, I already had so much emotion about being there. It was bittersweet to know that I would be speaking about my loss and my faith in the very campground Ryan worked hard to save.

In 2015, Ryan was involved in the firefighting efforts to protect the camp from the dangers of the Rough Fire. He came home after two weeks on the fire, exhausted but in awe of the campgrounds. In particular, he told me about a small brown church he came across while trekking through the forest and brush. He took photos of it to show me upon his return home.

"It was just there! In the middle of nowhere! This tiny little church, like a dollhouse but smaller!" He knew I would appreciate this treasure he found. He mentioned the employees of Hume Lake Christian Camp had offered the firefighters an opportunity to bring their families to camp the following summer as a 'thank you' for working hard to protect it. He talked about going back. He talked about taking the kids to this "really cool camp."

We had no idea we would never be able to go as a family. He died the following year and I never thought about Hume Lake again, until I was invited to be there.

As Katie and I hurried to get ready for breakfast, there was a knock at our door. Startled, we looked at each other knowing we weren't expecting anyone at that hour. Felicia was going to be joining us in Hume, but she wasn't due to arrive until the afternoon.

We opened the door and found familiar faces smiling back at us, Bob and Lori Ameche. The apologies couldn't fall out of my mouth fast enough. I felt terrible that I didn't think to communicate with Lori that we left my house later than anticipated. Her soft voice assured me they were glad we were safe, but also told me they were going to send someone to look for us if we didn't arrive by 8pm. Having no phones in the cabins and no service on our personal devices, the only way Lori knew we arrived safely was to go back to the welcome center and pray for good news.

Bob and Lori left us to finish getting ready and we quickly made our way to the dining hall.

We could hear the buzz of conversation as we filled our plates in an adjacent room. With plates full, we entered into the Ponderosa Dining room and stopped almost immediately to take it all in. Across the room were floor to ceiling windows showcasing the beauty of the lake and its neighboring trees. The ceiling was so high it forced me to stretch my neck while looking upwards. The tables and chairs occupying the room, along with the loud buzz of chatter, signaled to us that we were late for breakfast.

Lori spotted us and waved us over to her table. Seated beside her was Teri, and again, I couldn't stop my mouth from apologizing. As Katie and I ate, Lori and Teri told us about the man who would be speaking during the meeting that morning. He was from Northern Ireland and apparently, his accent made some words difficult to understand.

"Ok, when he says *'par,'* he's actually saying *'power,'*" Lori giggled as she gave examples of words we may not understand.

Katie and I quickly finished our breakfast and followed the crowd towards the small chapel where the meeting was being held. When we entered, we decided to tuck ourselves into a small corner of the seating area since we weren't sure what to expect and we felt a bit like intruders on a club meeting. As more people filed into the building, a man began playing the guitar and worship music was being sung. This wasn't a meeting like I expected, this was church! With that awareness, Katie and I immersed ourselves into the music and prepared to soak in the worship.

Phil, the gentleman from Northern Ireland, began to speak, and I realized why Lori prepared us ahead of time. I could not understand him. He spoke fast and his accent was thick, which forced me to concentrate heavily on what he was saying.

When the meeting ended, we were told there was an hour until lunch was being served. Katie and I decided to go back to our cabin because I wanted to change into a different top for lunch. From there, we decided we needed to get in touch with our families. We hadn't been able to connect with them since arriving and we both wanted to let everybody know we made it safely. I remembered when Ryan was at Hume, his Captain purchased access to WiFi so the guys could check in with their families. I mentioned this to Katie and we began the hunt to purchase WiFi.

We first walked towards the gift shop at the entrance of camp. We were told that WiFi was not accessible there, but the coffee shop at the other side of camp would have it, as well as the dining hall and surrounding area.

"Oh, let's go to the coffee shop," Katie requested. We headed in the opposite direction and practically skipped our way across gravel and grass only to find that the coffee shop was closed.

Much to our disappointment, we walked back towards the entrance in the direction of the dining hall. As we walked, our attention was effortlessly drawn towards the lake on our left. Katie stopped to pull out her phone and take photos of the scenery, verbally 'ooh'ing' and 'ahh-ing' with each click of the camera.

As she stopped, I continued walking a few steps ahead of her. I felt a warm sensation come over me. My hands were clammy and my heart was racing. My body felt nervous and my fingertips began to tingle. '*What the heck,*' I silently thought to myself. Katie was walking to catch up to me but her focus was still on the lake. Confused as to why I was feeling this way, I continued walking towards the dining hall in silent need of water and a seat. I'm not prone to panic attacks, but this feeling inside was familiar. My body felt like it did the day Ryan died when my limbs felt numb and my heart was racing because my soul was in shock.

As we walked, I saw two men out of the corner of my eye. I couldn't see their faces or hear their voices. I could only see that one was wearing a red jacket. They were also walking in the direction of the dining hall and as our steps continued, our paths intersected.

Upon hearing their Irish accent as they drew near, my cousin immediately engaged them in conversation. Not only is she the epitome of a 'people-person,' but visiting Ireland was a dream for her and her husband, so she took the opportunity to talk about everything Irish with her new friends.

A circle formed as their conversation continued. I was still shaky inside. I wanted to sit down but I couldn't see a nearby bench. Had there been a tree stump I would've plopped myself onto it, but there was not a seat in sight. The only thing close to me was the man in the red jacket. I felt his jacket lightly brush against my shoulder as I tried to look beyond him. Shivers electrified my body as a result of our outerwear making contact. I needed to sit down. Instead, I heard his voice pointed directly at me. He introduced himself and when I looked up to meet his eyes, the shakiness in my body intensified. He was tall, handsome and had bright, piercing blue eyes that seemed to be staring into me. I shook his hand and lowered my head. I couldn't remember his name when he said it, but being just over five feet in height next to his gigantic stature, the lanyard he was wearing with his name badge attached was perfectly placed at my eye level.

'*Michael Bolton.*' Normally, I would've said something about the familiarity of his famous name (as most would), but my wit was not present at that moment. I couldn't think straight. My heart was racing and my phone was on the verge of slipping through my fingers. My body felt nervous and I tried to quietly soothe myself. It wasn't working.

I heard Katie mention we were trying to find WiFi so we could check in with our families. She made it clear she was trying to let her husband know she was safe and I mentioned I needed to reach my kids. I nervously focused on my phone, trying to find the WiFi option as if it were my first time ever using it.

The man in the red jacket spoke directly to me, "here, I've already purchased the Wifi, do you want to connect to my hotspot?" His accent filled my ears.

"No, no thank you. I'll figure it out."

"Here," he opened the settings on his phone to share the name of his hotspot with me. I didn't immediately make an effort, but I did notice his hotspot name: '*bolty5113*.' "Go ahead and try to connect."

My fingers fumbled with the phone. I tried connecting, no luck. With the phone still in my hand, his fingers lightly tapped my screen in an effort to connect my phone to his. Nothing. I made a joke about being too short to reach the invisible rays of WiFi and I reached my arm up to the sky in playful effort. I heard his laugh and my heart raced.

The man in the red jacket asked how Katie and I were connected to the fire service. Katie paused, allowing me to answer, but my entire vocabulary was stuck in my throat. I said nothing, so she spoke up: "Jennifer is here because she's speaking at the women's tea tomorrow, and I'm here as her emotional support."

I nodded in approval of her explanation. I lifted my gaze from the phone and looked at the other gentleman in our small circle, "I'm a widow."

I was shocked at my blunt need to declare that information. I had never blurted that out loud. Being a widow was a topic I approached tenderly, especially with those I'd never met before as it typically made others uncomfortable, leaving them unsure what to say or how to go forward in conversation. But here I was - practically shouting it to two men who didn't ask for my relationship status.

Once my phone connected to WiFi, I excused myself from the conversation to contact my children. I walked towards the lake, as far away from the dining hall as I could get without leaving the campground or losing connection to the outside world.

My body was trembling as though I were coming down from an intense sugar high. I turned to face the dining hall, watching the man in the red jacket and unsure what I experienced while in his presence. My thoughts were interrupted when Katie suggested taking photos in front of the lake; I agreed, nervously smiling in each photo while looking for the man in the red jacket in between poses.

§

The dining hall was lively with the noise of conversation and the clinking of forks and knives against lunch plates. Katie and I were seated at a table with Lori and Teri, their husbands, and a couple we hadn't met, Joe and Melinda. Felicia was supposed to be arriving soon, so although I was enjoying lunch, I was keeping an eye on the time.

Aside from those two Irishmen I forcefully invited into my personal life, only a handful of people knew my story before I arrived at Hume Lake; Joe and Melinda were not one of them. I was careful not to give away my story because it was a vital part of the talk I prepared for the women's tea. In conversation with Joe and Melinda, I explained that Ryan had been to Hume and discovered the little brown church during his trek through the mountains. I mentioned I hoped to see it while I was there.

Joe was quite matter-of-fact when he said, "oh, it's way in there. You'll never get to it. The ground is wet and the snow is mush." I nodded with a sad understanding I would not get to see the little brown church that my late husband had been excited to share with me.

I excused myself from the table and made my way towards the salad bar near the exit doors of the dining hall. As I filled my plate with leafy greens, I saw a tall figure approach. He was suddenly beside me. His Irish accent said something to me about the array of vegetables and salad toppings, but I could only offer a nervous laugh. I walked away from the salad bar and left him standing there to fill his plate.

I returned to the table to find Katie engulfed in conversation and I heard my phone signal that I received a text message. It was from a friend who was in on the joke that I was going to meet my future husband at this retreat.

"Having fun?"

"I am! I speak tomorrow morning so I'm not nervous yet"

"Did you find ur [sic] *husband yet?"*

"He's from Ireland, yes."

Chapter 16

After lunch, Katie and I went for a walk around the lake. It's difficult to describe the majesty that is Hume Lake. It's nothing unusual with its water, trees and sounds of nature, but there *is* something different about it. It feels different. Maybe it's the disconnect from the outside world and the stillness that is forced upon its visitors. Whatever it is, Hume Lake feels otherworldly. We walked a slow pace as we soaked in every ounce of gentle nature around us. We came to a bridge whose backdrop was an unexpected waterfall. The sound of rushing water into the lake mesmerized me and held my attention for a while.

"Jennifer!" My cousin called out to me, snapping me back into reality. I saw her phone pointed in my direction and I automatically smiled for the camera. We posed ourselves for photos on the bridge in the front of the waterfall and continued on our walk around the lake.

We came upon a clearing that offered an elevated view of the landscape. I walked towards the edge of the rock and stood staring at the water framed by trees. Despite being born and raised in Southern California, my heart has never been drawn to the beach. The crisp, clean mountain air with the sound of wind brushing through trees has always spoken to my soul. I stared out towards the horizon with my hands in my pockets and my eyes desperately trying to memorize the picture of my soul's love language.

We eventually reached what appeared to be the halfway point around the lake. We paused and sat on a bench made of tree trunk and admired the glittery reflection of the sun landing on the water. We stared in silence at the landscape surrounding us. From where we stood, we could see the dining hall and the large grass area that had been my escape from the man in the red jacket.

I don't know what was going through Katie's mind as she watched the sunlight dance on the water, but the only thing on my mind was that man in the red jacket. I focused my attention in the direction of the dining hall wondering if I might be able to spot him; he was the only one wearing such a bold color. Well, the only one I noticed, anyway. I was confused by what I experienced, but more confusing was what I felt. In the two and a half years since becoming a widow, there was not a man I found attractive neither did I have a desire to explore the idea of dating. But suddenly, there was a man with whom I spent less than ten minutes, shared practically zero conversation, and yet, something about him was pulling at my heart. I didn't know anything about him other than his name. I didn't know if he was married or had a girlfriend; I didn't know if he was there with anyone other than his friend. I knew nothing except that I felt something and it terrified me.

By the time Katie and I made our way back, Felicia arrived and we spotted her in the gift shop. Excited to see her and relieved that she made it safely during daylight, we immediately unloaded her things into our shared cabin and slowly walked around the campground soaking in its nature while heading towards the dining hall for dinner.

Not only is the lake remarkable, but the food served by Hume Lake Christian Camp was equally as divine. Katie and I began to look forward to each meal with anticipation, and after hours on the road, Felicia was just as excited to enter the dining hall. We lined up amongst the other 'campers,' and I secretly tried to locate the man in the red jacket. However, I couldn't spot him. I refocused my attention on the conversation between Katie and Felicia and settled into the idea that I wasn't going to see him.

Lori and Teri were kind to let us know that another gathering would be taking place in the same chapel as the one earlier that morning. Although Katie and Felicia seemed enthused by the idea of nighttime worship, I was not. I wanted to worship, there was no doubt about that, but I was distracted and I knew my focus wouldn't be on the worship that night, it would be on my curiosity about the man in the red jacket being in the same room. I knew I needed a night of quiet preparation and sufficient sleep before I was scheduled to speak in the morning. I needed to reset my mind and regain my focus. I asked the girls if they minded that we skip the meeting and go to our cabin for the night. I explained that I wanted to refine my talk, even though it was fully prepared. They both understood and agreed, so after dinner while everyone walked in the direction of the chapel, we took an opposite route and retreated to our cabin.

§

The morning arrived rather quickly and the three of us eagerly got ready for the Women's Tea. I felt my nerves kicking in as I did my hair and make-up, and as soon as I was ready, I asked Katie and Felicia if we could pray. The three of us huddled into a circle with Katie sitting on the edge of the bed while Felicia and I pulled over two chairs. We grabbed each other's hands, lowered our heads, and Katie began to pray. When she finished her plea to God, Felicia's voice continued in prayer. I felt the warmth of love flowing through my body as though it were physically radiating from their hands being connected to mine. And then, it was my turn to pray.

Tears fell from my eyes before words came from my mouth. *"Thank you, God,"* I said quietly. *"Thank you for trusting me. Thank you for allowing me to be here, in this place, sharing about You."*

My tears spoke for me more than my words did. I was truly in awe that God would specifically bring me here, the very place my husband served, to share about hope. I felt privileged to be trusted with such an important message and I felt loved to be doing it in this place. Over the two and a half years since Ryan died, my relationship with God dipped into low valleys but eventually reached mountain tops. I returned to journaling and the pages began to fill with words of praise for each day I could see His hand in my life. I was no longer dreading my days; instead, I couldn't wait to talk to Him and discover where He was leading me. I heard Him through the laughter of my children and I could feel warmth return to our home. Although there were days I fiercely longed for Ryan's physical presence and moments I cried wishing I could hear his voice, I no longer wanted to quit. I could see hope for the future, even if I didn't know what it looked like. As a result, I made a promise to God that I would do whatever He asked of me. I no longer found myself questioning His reasoning. Instead, I was seeking His voice without reservation.

We picked up our heads, looked at each other with freshly dampened eyes and squeezed our hands in a silent communication of support.

When we arrived at the chapel in which the tea was being held, I immediately took notice of the love that had been poured into the room. Each table was delicately set with tea cups and saucers, a small floral arrangement, tealight candles sitting in pink votives and a gift box on each plate. My cousin and I owned a small business, Petunia Diaries, which allowed me to donate cards I designed to be placed at each table setting for the purpose of my talk. Having never been to this particular event, I did not know how it would be presented or decorated, and yet, the cards I designed with its floral border perfectly matched the tables. The room felt fancy and feminine, I loved every detail. In the back of the room were two tables beautifully decorated with scones, cakes, muffins, and matching decor, along with tea and coffee options. The effort made by Firefighters for Christ to give a beautiful morning to the women of the fire service was beyond my expectation.

Back at our table, I had a plate full of tasty goods, but I

couldn't eat a thing. I tried pretending that my insides weren't shaking with nerves, but my untouched plate said otherwise. I broke off a piece of my scone in an effort to eat when I was told I needed to head towards the back of the room to be fitted for my microphone. From there, I was encouraged to take what I needed and prepare it on the podium before speaking. I stood on the elevated stage shuffling the pages of my talk as though they weren't already in order, set my bible on the podium, and took a moment to look around the room. Women were filling their plates, talking with each other, and settling into their chosen seats.

"Let this be yours, God," I whispered. *"Thank you for choosing me."*

When I returned to our table, Lori faced me and said, "at 10:40, I'll introduce you and just come on up."

I smiled so big my cheeks vibrated. I stared again at my plate of untouched food: strawberries, pineapple, grapes, and two scones. I have no idea who I thought I was feeding when I grabbed these items because it certainly wasn't going to be me.

As I tried to take the focus off my nerves, I noticed the floral arrangement had a card sticking out from the center. I looked closer and saw scripture was printed on the card. When I saw which verse had been chosen for our table, my breath was taken away: *"why are you cast down, O my soul, and why are you in turmoil within me? Hope in God, for I shall again praise Him, my salvation and my God. Psalm 42:11"* My bible was resting on the podium, but I didn't need to open it. I knew this verse had been already circled and highlighted and my writing was next to it: *"Ryan, 9/21/16."* I read that scripture after Ryan died and it spoke clearly to me. I specifically underlined the word 'again' because I hoped I would one day praise God again. As well, it felt like a hug from God being words found in Psalm 42, a number that held meaning to me as it was Ryan's station number.

I felt my nerves settle after seeing this love note from God, but Lori's voice on the microphone found my nerves again when she introduced me at exactly 10:40am.

§

When my talk was over, I made my way back to the table to find my cousin waiting for me with open arms. She hugged me tightly, said I did well, and patted my leg as she turned her attention back to the front of the room where Lori was closing out the morning. My body was involuntarily shaking on the verge of convulsing. Katie turned to me and asked if I was okay to which I responded with an equally shaky voice, "y-y-y-yeah, I, I think my adrenaline is coming down or something." I picked up that bit of scone I had broken off an hour earlier and forced myself to eat it. I needed food. I continued to force feed myself and eventually, my body stopped quivering.

From the tea, we were dismissed to the dining hall as lunch was going to be served any moment. Grabbing my bag, I shoved my bible and notes in it as I made my way out the door. My heart was elated with how my talk appeared to have been received by the women and I was overflowing with gratitude that God would allow me to do something like that for Him.

As we stood in line waiting to enter the dining hall, I became lost in conversation with women I hadn't met prior to the tea. My body had gone back to its normal relaxed state and I felt hunger returning to my belly. I had forgotten all about the man in the red jacket. I happily filled a plate of food and I intentionally planned to consume every bit of it. Katie, Felicia and I sat at a table near the front of the room and I tried to be as polite as possible to have conversation while shoving food in my mouth.

I felt my bag shift on the back of the chair, but I paid no attention as I assumed it was somebody closely passing by our table. I kept eating and didn't bother to look up from my plate.

"Well, Jenn, how'd your talk go this morning?" It was a man's voice with an Irish accent.

With food still in my mouth, I looked up in the direction of the voice. There he was standing on my right side with a plate of food and a slight bend of his torso to signal he was waiting for me to answer. He wasn't wearing his red jacket. Instead, he was wearing a light blue sweater which illuminated his eyes, causing me to look away.

I quickly swallowed my food, touched my napkin to my lips and said, "it was good, thanks. Enjoy your lunch." I went back to eating. He said nothing more and walked to the table behind ours.

My nerves returned, practically shouting at me as I did everything to ignore them. My hunger was gone, but I kept eating. The conversation at our table continued uninterrupted but I was no longer participating. My heart was racing again and the only thing I could hear was the way he said my name.

Shortly after my interaction with the inquisitive Irishman, I was approached by Joe, the gentleman who initially told me I would never be able to reach the little brown church. Again matter-of-fact, he said, "meet us back here at two o'clock. We're taking you to the little brown church."

§

Joe wasn't exaggerating when he said the little brown church was deep in the woods and would be a hike through mushy snow and muddy terrain. Katie, Felicia, Joe's wife Melinda, and I did our best to keep up with his pace.

"Oh, Jennifer! Look!" Katie was pointing at a sign ahead of us: "Lil Brown."

I smiled and stood next to it as Katie took a photo. Further ahead was another sign, this one without words, only a symbol of a chapel and an arrow encouraging us to keep going. And then, I saw it. Ryan was right. Perched on a rock, it was no bigger than a small dollhouse. I felt a smile on my face and tears fill my eyes. Joe was first to approach the little brown church; he opened its doors and reached his hand inside to pull out a small tin. As he opened the tin, folded pieces of paper with prayers written on each one fluttered at his fingertips.

"Anybody bring a pen?" he called out.

"No," I said as I searched my jacket pockets for a pen I knew didn't exist, "oh! But there's one in here!" Inside the chapel, I saw a pen waiting for the next person.

I didn't have any paper with me, but Joe encouraged me to find a blank spot on one of the other pages and write. I opened a few of the folded pieces of paper, looking for an empty space while reading words written by strangers before me. Some signed their names, others did not. The prayers were different, but similar. All were there seeking answers from God.

Inside the church was a larger piece of paper; it was a flyer of some sort, but the bottom was empty. I checked the ink of the pen, leaned myself over a rock, and wrote:

"Ryan, to walk where you walked and see what you've seen...I miss you more than words. I love you. VCFD, Rough Fire 2015."

I could've written a prayer request to God, and I wondered if I should've after I folded the paper and placed it back inside the chapel. But in that moment, all I could think of was Ryan. I imagined him walking through the brush and stumbling upon this little brown church. I closed my eyes and saw his smile as he dug into the pocket of his yellow brush jacket in search of his phone. My heart overflowed with the idea that my husband thought of me in the middle of fighting a fire and finding a symbol of faith. I kept my eyes closed trying to somehow force Ryan back to this place. I missed him and although that chapel was full of prayers for God, I wanted people to open that flyer, read that there was a man who saw that chapel and helped save that camp, and he was mine until God called him home.

I turned my back to the chapel and stared at the enormity of the world in front of me. Trees blanketed the horizon as far as my eyes could see. Big, white clouds rested on top of snowcapped mountains. The sky was bright blue and the breeze was a crisp chill broken up by the trees surrounding us. I closed my eyes again feeling the air's movement on my face. *"I am Yours, God."* I paused as a stronger wind crossed my path. *"Take me wherever You want me to go. Use me however You want. I will follow You anywhere and everywhere. I am Yours."*

I didn't need to write my prayer and leave it in the little brown church. I left my prayer on the side of a mountain in the hands of God. A prayer nobody would read and nobody would squeeze next to on a piece of paper. A prayer between me and God, and a promise that I would allow Him to take me anywhere.

Chapter 17

After our visit to the little brown church, Katie, Felicia and I went back to our cabin to rest before dinner. The day had been full of excitement and emotion, but we wouldn't have long to recoup before we needed to line up at the dining hall once again. More people arrived for the remainder of the weekend, and once dinner concluded there was a nighttime worship service taking place in a chapel larger than the one we met in before.

There was a proper stage themed as a 50's diner with a checkered floor and a neon guitar with the words "Let's Rock" glowing above the stage. There were hundreds of seats in comparison to the staggered bench-type seating in the smaller building. It felt as though we entered into a theater rather than a chapel. The girls found seats to the left of the stage and I found myself looking for the man in the red jacket. Suddenly, the lights dimmed, music started to play, and we consumed ourselves with worship. I lost myself in the music; swaying my body and clapping my hands, I allowed my voice to sing along despite being fiercely out of tune.

The emcee introduced an ice-breaker game to the audience. He asked for volunteers to come to the stage without telling them what they would be doing. It was evident that within this large gathering of brave firefighters, none were brave enough for this. Slowly, a handful of men approached the stage. We all clapped in encouraging support as each one stood and walked forward, but my clapping slowed and my cheering turned into a silent smile when I saw the man in the red jacket appear across the room. He stood up and walked towards the stage. In an attempt to be discreet, I watched him. Everyone was still clapping and cheering, but I was stuck. I held my hands together and placed them in front of my mouth, hiding my smile. I could finally look at him without his eyes on me. His smile was big and contagious; his entire face lit up when he laughed. His presence was undeniable as he lined up alongside the other men and I couldn't take my eyes off him.

It was a donut eating contest, and I can't remember whether or not he won, but I do remember watching him walk off the stage and allowing my eyes to follow the path he took back to his seat. The service carried on and although I was attentive to the lesson, my eyes occasionally wandered in the direction of the man in the red jacket. I couldn't see him once he sat down, but that didn't stop me from trying to look.

When the service ended, we were told that dessert was being hosted in the dining hall. Everyone stood to exit the chapel and I saw the man in the red jacket walking towards the exit doors. I very slowly put on my jacket, dragging out our exit from the building. I didn't want to cross paths with that donut-eating Irish firefighter, and it worked.

§

Saturday morning greeted us with a clear blue sky and cool temperatures in the fifties. Hume Lake was putting on a muster, a competition of teams comprised of men and women with physical tasks to be completed and bragging rights to the winners. Bundled in my cold-weather jacket, all-weather boots, a beanie, and sunglasses, I grabbed a hot cup of coffee and followed Katie and Felicia towards the area of the muster. We came upon firetrucks in place, hose being laid out, and large buckets of water waiting for its participants. We didn't know who volunteered themselves for this event, but we were looking forward to our roles as spectators.

We walked slowly along the setup and decided on a spot close to the last event so we could see the finisher. I looked further to my left towards the starting point and noticed a tall man in a black t-shirt and gray bottoms. He was at the furthest distance from where we stood, but there was no denying that it was him.

Spotting a patch of sunshine in front of the area where he was, I called out to the girls, "let's stand over here, where the sun is - I'm cold." In agreement, Katie and Felicia followed me to the starting event of the muster. He was in a group with three other men and their event was focused on teamwork and communication. Standing with each foot on parallel planks of wood with rope attached, the team had to communicate walking together with their feet on the wood using the rope to pull and move the planks. The man in the red jacket was at the front, wrapping the rope around his wrists and preparing to move with his team.

Thankful my stare was hidden by sunglasses, I brought to my lips the warm cup I'd been holding and slowly sipped the steaming hot coffee as I pretended to be interested in the outcome of the muster.

"Go!" A loud shout from the speakers announced the start of each event. I watched the tall Irish firefighter pull up on the ropes. His arms showcased an indisputable strength and it was no longer the coffee making me warm.

Before the first event ended, a woman and her husband approached and placed themselves directly in between me and the man I was watching. I could no longer see him, and instead became focused on the conversation being shared with this sweet couple. Katie and Felicia walked over to let me know the muster ended. I missed the entire event, and when I looked around, I saw that I missed the exit of each participant, also.

§

The last evening service took place that night in the large chapel. We returned to the left side of the stage and as we settled into our seats, I began looking for the man in the red jacket. He wasn't in the same area that he was the night before. Out of fear I would be too obvious, I stopped looking for him and allowed myself to fall into the depths of worship. I closed my eyes, focused on the lyrics being sung and the words of the message. By the end of the service, I had almost forgotten about the man in the red jacket. Until I caught sight of him out of the corner of my eye when he stood to leave the chapel.

Thinking my plan was foolproof the night before, I slowly put on my coat and we followed behind the few remaining people towards the exit. Assuming he was already outside, I felt my heart stop when I saw him walking near the door. Pretending I lost something in my jacket pocket, I stopped walking, which allowed him to exit. When I looked up, he was nowhere in sight; my plan was successful. However, as soon as we were outside, I saw that my plan had failed.

The man in the red jacket was stopped in front of the door. I quickly looked away and nearly crashed into the back of Katie because she stopped abruptly. I put my hands up to break my stride into her body, but she didn't even notice. I could hear her voice talking, and then I heard his. I poked my head around and slowly removed myself from the protection of her back. He looked at me and smiled. I returned the smile and let their conversation carry on. She introduced Felicia to him and his friend, Chris; I stood smiling, but silent.

The conversation turned to the discovery of six deer that he and Chris saw while walking around the lake earlier that day. He opened his phone to show photos he took of the deer and when he directly turned his phone to me, I could only say, "wow!"

Another man approached the five of us. He began telling the Irish firefighters which restaurants they should try on their way to the airport the following day. Leaving from Hume Lake in the direction of the Los Angeles International Airport, Michael and Chris would drive through Santa Clarita, the town in which I live. It was the perfect opportunity for me to chime in and offer something to the conversation. I didn't. After living in Santa Clarita for my entire life, I suddenly forgot every restaurant to ever exist in that town. Instead, I awkwardly stood there listening to the conversation until it ended.

As the girls and I turned away from the chapel in pursuit of our final night of dessert, I noticed the Irish firefighters were walking in the other direction. Katie hollered out to them and asked if they were heading in for the night. The man in the red jacket mentioned they were going to pack their things because they were leaving early in the morning but they might return to the dining hall. I watched him as he spoke and he offered a smile when he caught my stare. I shyly smiled at him and turned to walk away, glancing back as I walked. He was still looking my direction, and if there had been a light shining on me, he would've seen how intensely his smile made me blush.

§

Katie, Felicia and I decided we were going to leave in the morning before the final service being offered. We woke early, packed our things and went to the dining hall for our last meal at Hume Lake. The room was fairly quiet; either we were there earlier than the rest or some of the guests had already left. We ate breakfast while chatting with some of the women we'd met, and I visited the coffee station one last time. As I was walked back to our table, my eye caught movement to my right. It wasn't a red jacket; it was that blue sweater that made his eyes a brilliant blue. He was leaving, but stopped at the door and locked eyes with mine. My heart stopped. He was going back to Northern Ireland and I didn't know if I would ever see him again. We hadn't said more than a handful of words to each other over a three-day period but I couldn't stop thinking about him each day I was there. His presence held something over my heart and

I knew those interactions had to have meant something, but I wasn't sure what.

He looked at me and held my gaze. He raised his hand to wave and his lips looked as though he was going to say something to me, but I quickly offered two words that told him there was nothing more to say: "travel safely!" He thanked me with a smile, lowered his hand and pushed open the door to leave. I didn't stop him to get his contact information. I didn't watch him leave. I didn't look to see which car he got into. Instead, I returned to the table with my coffee, and I let him go with the hope I would forget about him.

Chapter 18

The drive home from Hume Lake was long and relaxed. My cousin and I talked throughout the entire four-hour drive, but never once about the man in the red jacket. There was no need to mention what I experienced because I was never going to see him or talk to him again. I was home by Sunday afternoon and back into my normal routine of life. Katie, Felicia and I immediately began a group text desperately trying to hang onto the youthful and spiritual freedom we experienced while at Hume Lake.

April 2, 2019

By Tuesday morning, our text thread was hours long, rich with inside jokes, the moments that impacted us most, and our vow to return next year. But one thing I left out of our text thread: I couldn't stop thinking about the man in the red jacket. And because I couldn't stop thinking about him, I did what any normal female would do: I stalked him on social media. During my lunch break at work, I typed "Michael Bolton" into

Instagram's search bar. I was soon staring at a long list of fan pages for the globally famous musical artist, Michael Bolton. I started scrolling. The profile images were so small, it wasn't immediately obvious which account might've been his. Until I came across something I had seen before: "*bolty5113.*"

I placed the phone onto my desk, sat back in my chair and stared at the screen. "*That's him.*" I didn't need to open his profile for confirmation. His Instagram handle was the same as the name of the hotspot on his phone, which I remembered seeing when he tried to help me connect to WiFi days earlier. I habitually tucked my hair behind my ears as I leaned forward and stared at his small profile picture. My shaky fingers hovered over the screen. I lightly tapped on his name.

It was him, and I quietly praised God for the fact that his profile was open to the public. Very carefully I scrolled through his photos. My hands were trembling as my fingertips brushed over the still images of his life. I prepared myself to be heartbroken as I anticipated finding a photo of him and a romantic partner; however, the only ladies he shared about were his two young daughters.

Without any warning, an idea popped into my head: "*I should send him a message.*" I heard myself with that thought and knew it was completely out of character for me. I'm not the girl who does that. I couldn't even speak to him, who did I think I was to send him a direct message through a social media app? Never mind the fact that if I were to send him a message, he would obviously know I was looking for him. Despite these thoughts, I still wanted to send him a message.

Staring at my phone, I reached beyond it and picked up the phone on my desk. With nervous hands, I called my cousin.

"Hey, so remember those Irish guys we met? I found one of them on Instagram. Remember the tall one? I was thinking I should send him a message because it'd be cool to stay in touch with someone over there because you said that going to Ireland is, like, your dream vacation, so I was thinking it would be a good idea to stay connected so we have friends over there…"

I didn't take a breath, I kept repeating my words, and I rambled until she interrupted: "yeah! Send him a message! Wait, let me find his profile."

As soon as she found his account, I told her I needed to add him as a 'friend' on Instagram, otherwise he might not see a message from me. I then suggested we both add him as a 'friend' at the same time. Thankfully, she agreed. We counted down from three and simultaneously pressed the blue "follow" button beneath his photo.

"Ok, I'll send him a message, but what do I say? I don't want to sound weird."

"I dunno, just say hi, he'll remember you."

It took nearly twenty minutes for me to put together a friendly three-sentence message, and it took even longer for me to send it:

"Hey! It's Jenn from the FFC retreat. The couple times we all met up we didn't have a chance to exchange contact info and we thought it was so awesome to meet so many people from Ireland! I hope you made it home safely and that the Tommy's burger wasn't a problem on the

plane for you and Chris!"

I read it to my cousin before sending it.

"Come on, just send it! What's the big deal?" My cousin was growing impatient with my hesitancy.

I still hadn't told her about what I experienced over the weekend or the fact that I hadn't been able to stop thinking about him. With the deepest inhale, I closed my eyes and hit 'send.' I don't remember exhaling, but I remember my cousin being excited we now had a connection in Ireland. A friendly connection, I emphasized. I sat back in my chair and kept the screen on my phone open to the message I sent. Katie and I talked about her dream trip to Ireland and continued with normal conversation.

Until I saw those little dots appear on my screen.

"Oh my God, Katie! He already saw my message! He's responding. Oh my God! I can't be in this screen! It'll look like I'm waiting for an answer! Oh my God, he's responding already??" Sheer panic took over my body.

I heard my cousin laugh, followed by a low and slow statement, "ohhh my gosh, you like him."

I immediately lowered the tone of my voice. "What? No, I don't! Give me a break."

But she continued to giggle and playfully taunt me, "yes, you do. You like him. I knew it! I could totally see it at camp."

"What do you mean you could see it? See what?" I was genuinely curious because I thought I had been extremely discreet.

"It makes sense now why you weren't talking when we were

around him! And I think he likes you. He was definitely into you."

"No, he wasn't. Knock it off," but I allowed her to carry on with her theories because it kept me from going back into Instagram and checking my messages. After minutes of her relentless teasing, I finally admitted I did find him attractive. I confessed that my heart did weird things, and more importantly, I was scared about what I felt.

"Open his message, read it to me," my cousin was fully invested in this new communication.

"Ok, give me a second." Still at work, the office was quiet because it was the lunch hour. I didn't want anyone to hear about this, so I opened his message and quietly read it to my cousin:

"Hey Jenn... so lovely to hear from you... it was great to meet you girls... we certainly had lots of laughs! Chris and I had an absolute ball! Did you enjoy your time at Hume? Sorry to hear your husband passed, I never got the full story but I'm sure it's been a hard time for you! We thankfully got home in one piece! I'm convinced that would not have been the case if we had visited Tommy's burger lol... that chili burger on an 11 hour flight would not have been a good combination"

After some giggling and a promise that I would keep her updated on this conversation as best as I could while at work, Katie and I hung up the phone. Over the next hour, Michael and I chatted about Hume Lake and international travel, and my fingers were no longer shaking as I typed. Then he stopped my heart with words I wasn't expecting: *"did you happen to notice at camp I may have liked you? You're so pretty and very sweet..."*

My hands began to shake again, my palms were sweating and my face was flushed. My heart was racing and my smile was so big it was hurting my face. I ran to a phone in the back of the office and called my cousin.

She screamed into the phone, "I knew it!! I told you!! I knew he liked you!!"

My body began with that nervous sensation I felt five days earlier just before my path crossed with that of the man in the red jacket, but this time I understood the cause of that feeling. It was him now, and it was him then.

Chapter 19

It had been a few days, and text communication with the man in the red jacket became so regular that the eight-hour time difference felt like torture when I was forced to wait on hearing from him. Our messages to each other began to read like novels. We spilled every detail of our lives, shared about our days, and he woke me each morning with a sweet message.

But he never asked for my phone number and never suggested a video or voice call. Was he content to keep texting through Instagram? My mind started to get anxious with wonder: *why hadn't he suggested a FaceTime date?* I had become familiar with the idea of FaceTime dates as a result of my sweet friend, Katee, who met a man during her mission trip to Fiji and embarked on a long-distance relationship with him. So, even though I was not current in the technology-led dating scene, I knew FaceTime dates were a thing.

Despite immediately knowing there was something special about this man as soon as I saw him, I had no idea if he thought of me with the same intensity. As days went on, our conversations drew us into each other, but I had come to the realization that he may not want to be anything further than an Instagram pen-pal. Who could blame him? I was some random American girl he met while on a trip in California and I had refused to talk to him despite every effort he made.

I convinced myself that I was alone in this feeling and I imagined he was filling his evenings with dates and real-life women. He never said he was; in fact, his messages made it seem as though I were the only one he was thinking about. My insecurity and uncertainty about the dating world spoke louder than his obviously flirtatious texts.

I couldn't handle it anymore. It was clear that I was going to have to initiate a FaceTime date.

Sunday, April 7, 2019

Michael: *"I'm not sure of the coming back thing at the moment... but hoping we can work a visit out!"*

Me: "If it weren't for the fact that I'm already doing small traveling without my kids, I'd be extremely tempted to put a stamp in my passport. You just might have to visit me by video instead."

"A video call sounds good, maybe during the week some evening? x"

"I would love that, just tell me when!"

My eyes widened in disbelief. I couldn't believe how easily that worked!

"I will give you a video call my early morning time? Maybe my Thursday morning, your Wednesday night?"

"Perfect! What time did you have in mind?

"I'll try for 6am... (10pm US)? xx"

"I'm excited! That's not too early for you?"

"I can cope. You're definitely worth an early start. Will be nice to have a chat! x"

I immediately panicked and called my cousin, who was loving every moment of this.

As the days passed and our FaceTime date drew nearer, I realized I didn't actually know how to use FaceTime. I sent a text to Katee.

"Help!! I don't know how to FaceTime, what do I do? Do I have to use my phone number? How does this work? What do I wear?? Do I look like I'm on a date? Help me!"

Despite being unable to see her, I knew she was laughing as she responded to my text. She told me that Michael and I did, in fact, need to exchange phone numbers. My mind started panicking: *"why didn't he ask for my phone number? Was I supposed to ask?"* Thankfully, Michael handled that dilemma the following day and we exchanged phone numbers.

And then the day came.

Wednesday, April 10, 2019

I don't think I've ever put the kids to bed so timely and so quickly. I made sure they were in bed, doors were closed, and they had everything they needed so they wouldn't have to come knocking on my door. I hated being secretive with them, but I wasn't ready to tell them I met somebody. I needed to feel this out first. I needed to make sure he was safe, and I needed to see if this was even worthy of telling my children – he lived in another country, after all.

After going back and forth with my cousin about how I should dress for this FaceTime date, I decided I needed to show up as me and who I really am at 10pm.

Pajamas. No makeup. Hair in a bun. If he didn't like this version of me, there was no need to go any further.

I sat down at my computer at 9:45pm. I opened it up, prepared my desk area to receive a phone call, and tried to find a comfortable position in my chair. But then I stopped. I clasped my hands together and rested my forehead against them. I closed my eyes, let out a deep breath, and prayed.

"God, I need you. Right now. I need you. Please guide this conversation. Please expose in Michael anything that is not of You. Expose things in his character that I need to know about. Show me who he is. Direct our conversation and protect me throughout. And help me to understand his accent so he feels we can communicate. I love you. I trust you. I need you."

I prayed like that for the entirety of time leading up to our FaceTime date. I opened my eyes when I heard my computer make an unfamiliar sound. It was him. He was calling. I sat up in my chair and with a hesitant hand, I clicked on the green circle begging for my attention. Seeing only myself on the screen, I nervously smiled in anticipation.

Almost instantly, Michael appeared on my computer screen. He was wearing a light blue t-shirt which showcased his piercing blue eyes. He was more handsome than I remembered. Even having stalked his Instagram page for hours, this live version of him was more than my heart expected.

"Heyyyyy," he said through his smile; his voice a different tone in my ears. I realized that I hadn't paid attention to his voice or his accent during our brief interactions at Hume. I couldn't wipe the smile from my face. It felt permanent, as though if I received bad news, I would be inappropriately smiling. Our conversation was light and easy. There was no awkward silence or lack of things to talk about.

"There's a couple things you need to know about me," I said as I dared to test the waters of tolerance. "I can't cook, I decorate for Christmas on November 3rd, and I have a rule that whenever either of us leaves the house, we don't leave without a kiss goodbye."

He laughed, but I couldn't tell if he was laughing because he thought I was joking or because he thought I was being ridiculous.

"Well, I love to cook, you're free to decorate whenever you want, and your rule sounds like a privilege."

I didn't realize I had been holding my breath until he finished his sentence and I exhaled a sigh of relief.

Michael went on to share that he noticed me before we actually met at Hume. During that first meeting where Katie and I tucked ourselves away so as not to intrude, Michael's eye caught sight of me. "I was instantly curious about you," he said. "I couldn't tell if you were there with another firefighter or if you were there as a firefighter."

I laughed, "me? A firefighter?"

"Well, I couldn't figure out why you were there so I was

going through the options," he said. "All I knew was that you were all I saw. I told Chris I needed to visit the bathroom but I was really just wanting to see who you were. You didn't notice me looking at you as I walked past?"

"I honestly didn't. I must've been focused on worship," I teased.

Michael shared that not only did he find himself attracted to me, but he couldn't stop thinking about me after noticing I was there. As he spoke, I felt my mind return to the memory of what I physically felt just before our paths crossed. *Had God arranged for the two of us to notice only each other that weekend?*

Throughout our week of texting and learning about each other, I was slowly checking things off my not-so-imaginary list of future husband characteristics I desired. As he spoke, I continued checking my list.

He helped his friend install wiring in his house. Handy. Check.

We were making each other laugh. Check.

Complimented my hair despite it being a mess. Makes me feel pretty. Check.

His youngest daughter turns ten in three days. Kids older than nine. Check.

I didn't have my list in front of me, but I knew there was one huge box I needed to be able to check off. And so far, I didn't see it as being possible.

"I hope you don't mind, but I looked up Ryan's accident. I wanted to know what happened, so I looked it up." His voice was soft as he delivered this information to me.

"I don't mind," I reassured him.

"He worked for Ventura County Fire Department?"

I smiled with pride as I nodded in confirmation.

"I know a guy from Ventura County. I wonder if you know him?" Michael was still talking about this guy he knew from our department as I prepared myself to hear an unfamiliar name. There were over four hundred members of personnel on the department and I knew only a handful of them.

"Jeremy..."

I cocked my head in curiosity. *'He's not gonna say the name I think he's gonna say, is he? Of course he's not. What are the chances?'* I was too curious. I didn't let him finish. "Bower? Jeremy Bower?"

"Yes! Do you know him?"

It took a couple seconds for my thoughts to come together and form an answer: "yes! Yes, I know Jeremy Bower! He took down my Christmas lights a couple months ago! He is the one who gets things taken care of around the house that need to be fixed! Ryan worked with him. Yes, I know Jeremy!"

Michael's face lit up for reasons different than mine. Michael didn't know about my list. He didn't realize that the last box on my list had just been checked: *'not a stranger, but not someone I already know (friend of a friend).'*

Michael went on to tell me that Jeremy went to Northern Ireland with Firefighters for Christ in 2011 and Michael hosted him during his time there. Jeremy went to work with Michael, he met Michael's daughters, Michael showed him around Belfast, and they stayed in contact for a while afterwards.

I sat in amazement knowing about my list, knowing about my prayer before our first FaceTime date, and realizing that God had been crossing our paths years before our paths would actually cross. Now knowing God had been orchestrating this all along, I found myself relaxed as our conversation continued.

Two and a half hours after we said hello, we were forced to say goodbye as Michael had to leave for his shift at the station in Belfast. As I stared at my now lifeless computer screen, I sat in silence with a smile on my face. I knew my cousin stayed awake hoping to hear every detail of our call.

My phone lit up. It was a notification on Instagram. Being 12:45am, I knew it could only be one person, and it was.

"Just so sweet talking to you...you're such a gem. Now my heart is a little sorer when again I'm reminded you're so far away."

"Thank you for waking up early to talk to me. I believe in miracles, so I'm secretly hoping there's one in store for us."

"It was very much my pleasure! Enjoyed our chat...lovely we connected so well. Yes I'm a miracle believer too so let's see what happens! All things are very possible. x"

I exited the app and called my cousin. She was wide awake and ready to receive everything I had to tell her. I began pouring out the details of our conversation.

"Jennifer, go pull out your list."

I went to my closet and placed myself in front of the hiding space holding my journal. Still giddy, I pulled it out, opened to the first page, and began reading my list to my cousin. We sat in silence until I began to cry.

"He's your list," she said through tears that matched mine. We both were silent. I sat on the floor of my closet with my back pressed against the door and I laid the journal to rest on my legs. "I don't know what to do," I finally whispered.

"Pray," she answered.

We hung up the phone and I did exactly as she said. I prayed. I prayed God would take Michael away.

Chapter 20

The idea of dating was not a surprise to my children, but until now, it was just an idea. Several months before meeting the man in the red jacket, the kids and I sat at the kitchen table discussing the possibility of someone new coming into our lives. It was a lighthearted conversation. Amanda was gentle and reassuring as she shared that she didn't want me to be alone, and Brandon carried us into laughter as he made an attempt to detail the name of this imaginary man. For so long it was just an idea, until it wasn't.

"If there was going to be someone new in our lives, what three things would you want him to be?" My daughter was seated in the passenger seat of my car. I kept my eyes focused on the road as I drove, desperately wanting to look at her face.

She paused and then said, "no drinking. Like, no drinking at all. Umm, he has to be nice and funny. And he has to love us like his own."

I kept driving, silently thanking God for putting on her heart the things I knew she needed and hoped she wanted.

She caught my smile and started teasing me about the

weekend I spent in Las Vegas days earlier. "Why, did you meet someone in Vegas?"

I laughed at her suggestion, which prompted her to continue, "oooh mom, who'd you meet in Vegas? Hmm?"

"Well, I didn't meet anyone in Vegas," I paused when I felt her energy shift from cheery to serious, "but I did meet somebody." The car fell silent.

I broke the awkward silence, "his name is Michael and I met him at Hume Lake."

"Is he nice?"

"He's really nice, baby. He lives in Ireland," I could feel the whip of her head turn in my direction.

"Ireland??"

As we approached her friend's house, I told her about the man in the red jacket and how I had grown to know him over the last few weeks.

"I didn't want to tell you until I knew he was safe - for all of us." I parked the car and turned my body towards her. "I don't know what this is going to look like or how this is going to work out, but I did meet someone and I really like him."

She smiled at me, "well, when do I get to talk to him?"

"Whenever you want, baby," I put my hand over hers and squeezed. She was only fifteen years old and had been forced to mature beyond her years. She smiled at me before opening the car door and hopping out.

"Love you, mama!"

It was early evening in California, which meant it was the middle of the night in Belfast, Northern Ireland. I sent Michael a text letting him know I told my daughter about him. Hours later, when he woke and read my text, he responded immediately, *"how did that go?"*

Before I could answer via text, he was calling via FaceTime. Amanda was still awake, so I quickly ran upstairs into my bathroom and sat on the floor next to the tub as though it were sheltering my voice from being heard.

It was just past five o'clock in the morning for him, and his would-be sleepy eyes were wide awake with curiosity, "well? How did it go?"

I whispered the details of the conversation I had with her and he nodded in silence with each word. I heard a gentle knock on my bedroom door. Before I could answer, Amanda appeared in the doorway. I was crouched down on the floor, holding the phone in front of me with Michael's face on the screen waiting in anticipation for me to say something. I felt like a teenage girl caught on the phone with her boyfriend when I should've been in bed.

"Hi baby, are you ok?" She walked towards me. "I'm talking to Michael right now," I said with uncertainty about what I should do in that moment.

Her soft voice asked, "can I talk to him?"

Knowing Michael was still in bed and barely awake, I glanced at the screen for an answer. I hadn't noticed that when he heard her come in, he had gotten up from bed and put on a t-shirt. He nodded in approval when he saw that I wasn't sure what to do. I got up from the floor, sat on the edge of the tub and Amanda sat beside me. I held my phone up for her to see

Michael for the first time.

"Hi Amanda," his voice was rich with kindness.

Hers was youthful and gentle, "hi."

Michael engaged Amanda in conversation about school and friends and then he broke the ice by acknowledging the elephant in the room, "this must be weird for you, huh?"

She nodded and giggled in nervous response. He continued to talk with her and I watched her body relax. After a few minutes, she said goodbye to Michael and left my room. Still on the phone, Michael and I stared at each other in amazement over what took place. It wasn't how I planned to introduce the idea to my kids nor was it how I planned for them to 'meet' him for the first time.

We quickly hung up our call so I could check in with Amanda. She was getting ready for bed when I poked my head into her room, "hi baby, are you ok?"

"Yeah, he's really nice and funny. I like him," she smiled as she spoke. I hugged her tightly and wondered what this meant for the three of us.

§

The next morning, Amanda and I were in her room talking in detail about the man in the red jacket. I was planning to talk with Brandon about him, but was first making sure she was comfortable with everything that took place the night before.

Suddenly, Brandon burst through the door.

"You love somebody??"

I smiled at his interpretation of what he'd overheard. I didn't tell Amanda that I loved Michael, but Brandon heard love in the way I was speaking of him. Amanda giggled at Brandon's intrusion. I invited him to sit next to me on her bed.

"Buddy, if someone comes into our lives, what three things would you want him to be?"

He looked towards the ceiling as his mind began to calculate what he would like to see in a man being brought into our lives.

"No drinking. He has to be nice and he has to have a job."

"That's a good list," I answered. With that, I told him about the man in the red jacket I met while at Hume Lake. Brandon was quiet, allowing me to speak openly about Michael.

"Brandon, I talked to him last night and he's really nice and funny," Amanda reassured him.

"When do I get to talk to him?"

"Whenever you're ready, buddy." There was a pause in the conversation.

Brandon broke the silence by saying, "you sent him a message on Instagram? Can I see it?"

I knew he wasn't asking to see the message I sent; he was asking to see Michael's social media profile. Both kids scrolled through his Instagram account, studying those little squares trying to learn about him through photographs. They both followed him from their personal accounts, and from there, we went on about our morning.

Not much later, I received a text from Michael with a screenshot of the notifications he received that both kids were now connected to him on Instagram.

"I take it they both know?" Michael knew I was waiting to tell my son after making sure Amanda was settled with the idea, so

he was surprised to see Brandon's name on his phone.

When Michael called a bit later, I went to my room to privately share what transpired that morning, but it wasn't long before both children walked in and placed themselves onto my bed. They sat facing me and didn't say anything, but I could see what they were wanting to ask.

"Do you want to talk to Michael?" It was a repeat of the night before; I was doing my best to interpret Michael's body language through the screen while keeping my eyes on my kids. I could see that he was preparing himself to meet my son by the way he shifted in his seat and straightened his posture. Brandon crawled across the bed and placed himself beside me. With a nervous smile and a giant wave, Brandon met the man in the red jacket.

"Heyyy Brandon," for the first time Michael's Irish accent filled my room. Prior to this, his voice was restricted to my headphones in order to keep his presence silent from my kids. Just as he did with Amanda, Michael engaged Brandon in conversation about video games and sports, particularly soccer.

Amanda then propped herself next to Brandon so she could say hello to Michael. I felt my heart surge as I watched the three of them interact. I laughed as a result of their laughter, and I relaxed as a result of their comfort. When they finished talking with Michael, they handed the phone back to me and left my room talking to themselves about Michael's accent and the words they couldn't understand. After my door closed, I looked at that handsome Irishman on the other side of the screen and both of us smiled with wide eyes and a feeling of disbelief. I smiled when he said, "they're great. Great kids, I can't wait to meet them."

The truth was, I didn't know if he would. I didn't know what this meant for all of us - my kids, Michael's daughters, our families. There was so much at stake and so much to consider. From the moment I met the man in the red jacket, I knew he had a purpose in my life but I didn't know what that purpose was going to be.

§

As I sat alone with God that night, I confessed that I didn't want to fall in love with this man, although I feared it was already too late. *"There is no possibility of this working out, God. I can't see it happening."* An ocean separated us, we each had children that needed us, we had lives established and in motion. And yet, despite every obstacle set before us, I knew deep in my soul this was no mistake. God brought Michael and I together. I didn't know how it was going to work, but I believed it would and I wasn't the only one who felt that way.

Michael felt it, as well. Having never touched beyond a handshake, never embraced, and never kissed, we both felt and believed our souls were meant to connect. By the time I started telling the people in my life about him, without having any idea how our separate lives were going to blend into one, he was already shopping for a ring.

Chapter 21

I woke one morning to a text, *"are you free the first week of July?"* My partially closed eyes worked frantically with my fingers to open the calendar on my phone. Almost as soon as I said yes, the man in the red jacket said he wanted to come back to California. A week later, I received another text, *"I'm coming to see you, ticket is booked!"*

As the days went on, Michael and I felt that our visit in July was incredibly far away.

"Is it weird that I miss you even though I've never held you?"

I sighed when I read his text. "No, it's not weird at all because I feel the same. How is that even possible?"

"I'm not sure. But I don't think I can wait until July to hold you."

He looked over his work schedule with hope he might be able to come to California a couple of weeks earlier. Being a firefighter, he was able to pick up extra shifts, swap them for days off and collect them to be used all at once. He worked tirelessly, but it paid off when he said, *"I can be there June 21st."*

This was ten days earlier than he originally planned, which meant I needed to stop delaying the news about him and have the conversations I was dreading with the people in my life, including my parents and Ryan's family.

The first person to learn about the man in the red jacket (outside of my children, Felicia, and Katie) was my little brother, John. We were on a trip in New York with my dad when John and I found ourselves in a Starbucks in the middle of Times Square late one night. Over hot chocolate and a chai tea latte, I said, "so I have something to tell you, but you can't tell mom and dad."

He raised his eyebrows in anticipation of the juicy gossip that was about to land on his ears. In a low, deep voice he said, "ok, I'm listening."

"I met someone."

He took a sip of his hot chocolate as I began telling a very condensed version of how I met the man in the red jacket.

"Ok, here's the thing: he lives in Ireland." The hot chocolate he had been sipping throughout my story nearly made an appearance on the table.

"Ireland? Like, he's from Ireland or he lives in Ireland," his confusion was understandable. Even I felt confused as I shared about our geographic conundrum.

"He lives in Ireland. Northern Ireland, specifically. Like, he's there right now."

John playfully shook his head as he let out a deep breath.

"I have no idea how this is going to work, but..."

He cut me off, "do you like him? He's a good guy?"

"Yeah, I really do. I don't know how to explain it, but like, I think this is it."

"Well, I can't wait to meet him."

I brought the plastic lid of the Starbucks cup to my lips as I took a sip of my latte and watched my brother's eyes. I felt instant relief having shared about Michael with him. Even if he didn't understand it, my brother supported me and trusted my intuition. Each time I felt my nerves rise at the thought of having difficult conversations, I remembered this one with my brother and the confidence he had in me.

Over the course of the following month, I had individual discussions with several people, but the conversations that weighed heaviest on my heart were those with Ryan's mom and his sisters. If I could've avoided it, I would've. I would've rather been labeled a coward than have to face those who became my family through Ryan's time on earth, but they didn't deserve my cowardice. I wasn't as fearful of their reactions as I was of losing each of them. We weren't strangers or even in-laws; they had known me since I was fifteen years old. We were family. I cried as I told Ryan's mom. I tried so hard to place myself in her shoes having to hear about her son's wife finding love with someone new. I worried she might think I forgot about her son, something my heart and my soul could never do. I was scared I'd lose my Osler family over this. I desperately wanted to remain an Osler and I was scared this news of second love would mean I would no longer belong and I would have to forfeit my place in their family.

I don't pretend to know what they felt when their ears heard and their minds processed what I shared with each of them. The only thing I know is that although it couldn't have been easy, it was welcomed and I was assured that I will always be an Osler.

When it came to telling my parents, I was uneasy but not for the same reasons I had been apprehensive to tell Ryan's family. I repeatedly practiced what I was going to say to them, but the more I practiced, the more ridiculous it sounded.

Sitting at my parents' kitchen table with my children in attendance, I said with a shake in my voice, "well, we have something exciting to share." My parents didn't take their eyes off me. "I met someone!"

I didn't give them a chance to react, I carried on with my rehearsed speech about the man in the red jacket. I rattled off the geographic problem that was me and Michael, and they were quiet as they listened.

"Ireland?" They didn't smile.

"Yes, he's in Northern Ireland."

"So, you met him online?"

"No, no. We met in person when I was at Hume Lake in March. He's a firefighter in Northern Ireland; that's why he was at the retreat."

I could see their minds calculating my story. And then it hit me: my parents had been leisurely invested in a popular reality show, "90 Day Fiancé." This television show circled around couples in which the non-US citizen in the relationship applies for a visa and has to marry an American citizen within ninety days. Realizing they were imagining I was being scammed by a foreign man, I reminded them about his career as a firefighter, as well as his secondary job as an HVAC engineer. I assured them that he was well established on his own and wasn't in need of any American money.

As though I could read their minds, I said, "we don't know what this looks like for either of us. All we know is that we both feel something and he's coming out here so we can spend some time together and see where this goes."

The discussion ended on that note and I was thanking God that another conversation was over.

§

It was Monday morning and a couple of days had passed since telling my family, Ryan's family, and Roger and Mahal, about the man in the red jacket. While my news wasn't being turned away, it also wasn't being eagerly received. I didn't expect it to be received with celebration, but I was beginning to question if what I was feeling for Michael was wrong as a result of everyone's hesitancy. I started to wonder if I had been misled by emotion and I knew upcoming talks with church leadership would try to convince me that being misled is exactly what happened.

I wasn't at work that morning. I dropped the kids at school and returned home to the chores awaiting my attention. I couldn't focus on what needed to be done; my thoughts were scattered and my mind was distant. I sat down on the hearth that stretched across the length of my family room and thumbed through the messages on my phone. Exasperated, I silenced my phone and placed it face down beside me. I lowered my head into my hands and exhaled as though I were trying to empty my soul onto the floor beneath my feet.

After three years of practice, I had become used to talking with God throughout each day. I spoke to Him as if I were speaking to a friend who ran errands and did chores with me.

From big decisions (*"should I cut back my hours at work, God?"*) to small wonders (*"should I wear my hair up today, Father?"*), my heart was trained to talk with God about it first – whatever it was. He was my co-parent, my counsel, my advisor, and my closest friend. I had become so dependent on His direction that I didn't dare take a step without His reassurance that it was safe to do so. When decisions were met with a peaceful feeling, I knew God was behind it. If a decision ever felt confusing or left me feeling unsettled, I walked away from it.

I felt no confusion when it came to Michael; nothing about his presence in my life felt unnerving or alarming. I could see our future together even if I couldn't see its possibility. But I needed more than this safe and peaceful feeling. I needed divine clarity and obvious direction. I was on the verge of demanding God show himself to me by way of a burning bush as he did to Moses.

"God," I paused. My voice wouldn't allow another word. I tried again, "God," and instead, I burst into uncontrollable tears. I allowed my body to release everything it had been holding. Within the walls of my home, I allowed my crying to become sobbing and my voice transformed into wailing. My body moved in rhythm with my tears as my shoulders tried to lower themselves to the ground with their heaviness.

"I can't do this, God. I have no idea what I'm doing. I need you to be clear. RIGHT NOW." I was yelling. My voice echoed throughout my home. "BE CLEAR! NOW!" I continued to cry until my breathing slowed. "God, I trust you. I have trusted you with everything and I trust you now. I need to know if this thing with Michael is of You."

With my eyes closed, I took a deep breath, and entered into conversation with Him: "God, if this is not from You, I need You to take it NOW. I need You to stop it NOW. Show me, make it obvious to me! Expose something through Michael, not through outside opinions, show me through *him* that this is not from You. Expose something, show me something! I'm ok with it! I'm fine with it! If Michael's only purpose was to show me that I am capable of opening my heart again, fine. If his only purpose is to show me that You hear my heart and I shouldn't settle for anything less than what I desire, fine. But You need to make it clear to me NOW."

My heart wanted Michael. I wanted this to work. I wanted to keep this feeling in my life, but I desired God's will more than my own. I wanted nothing more than I wanted God. I wanted to follow His lead more than I wanted to figure it out on my own. I was too afraid to make decisions by myself. I was scared of stepping out of alignment with God. If He didn't approve, then I didn't want it. I wanted to be obedient more than I wanted to be fulfilled. I was severely dependent on God, so much so that if He were a physical man in my life, some might refer to my extreme dependency on Him as an unhealthy addiction.

I continued, "...but, if this is from You, make it clear to me. I need You to be obvious. I need You to be clear and make it known. If this is from You, I will do whatever You ask me to do with it. I will continue to have the hard conversations. I will lay the foundation and do the ground work. I will do whatever You ask of me if this is truly from You. I don't want this to be about me. I *need* this to be about You. I love you. I trust you. I need you." With my eyes closed, I exhaled until my lungs were emptied. I sat in silence, allowing my words to hang in the air.

The sound of my doorbell and my dog's subsequent barking jolted me back to reality. I found myself irritated, *"who would come to my door in the middle of a Monday morning?"* Annoyed, I tiptoed to the front door, gently using my fingertips to balance as I peered through the small peep-hole. A woman was walking towards her car, and as I opened the door, I quickly glanced over my porch to find a large bouquet of red and white roses waiting for me.

I had never seen such a lavish floral arrangement; the roses were perfectly shaped, vibrant in color, and enveloped by greenery that spilled over as though its purpose was to decorate the outside of the vase. It was the most beautiful arrangement I had ever seen and most certainly the most extravagant I had ever received.

"Watch out, Lily," I warned the dog as I attempted to walk the flowers into the house. I couldn't see over the large display of roses and was forced to trust my familiarity with the layout of the house.

I didn't have a clue who would send such flowers until it hit me: *"Mother's Day wasn't long ago; these are probably from the department."* The fire department had been so good to remember me for each birthday, anniversary and holiday, so this was a safe assumption.

I reached for the card and didn't read the note attached; instead, I searched for the name of the sender. I dropped to my knees. My hand tightly gripped the card and shook with the vibration of my sobbing. My arms felt weak and I couldn't bring myself to stand. I laid myself down on the ground; my tears turned into a smile and my crying turned into laughter.

I looked at the card again: *"Love, Michael xx"*

I clutched the card to my chest and closed my eyes. The flowers were from Michael, but the timing was from God. I asked Him to be clear, and He was. I asked Him to do it now, and He did. I whispered, "okay, God. I hear you. I'll keep going."

Chapter 22

Meeting Michael in the way that I did was considered unbiblical according to the doctrine of the religious organization of which I was a member. I knew this ahead of time; I had known this about the church for the entirety of time I had been attending. This group is known for believing they are the one true church of God. Therefore, single men and women were to date, court, and marry only those within its congregations. Additionally, one-on-one dates were not advised, therefore, dates were chaperoned, and prior to becoming a couple, consultation from leadership was "strongly encouraged."

Long before I met Michael, I publicly declared to my friends, "my future husband is not in this church."

I was met with, "oh no, of course not! There's nobody here." The local church I had been a member of for eighteen years was full of families; there were no single men, and the ones that were single were college-age boys.

"No. I mean, he is not part of this church at all." I knew I didn't want to marry a man who belonged to this organization. In my time of fasting and prayer before Ryan died, I discovered a lot about God that wasn't being taught in the church and a lot about their doctrine that isn't taught in the bible.

In that time before, and after, Ryan died, I learned how to listen to God. My relationship with Him had become personal, deep, and spiritually rooted. I had already seen the way that leadership and other members of the church casually ignored my stories about God communicating with me through pennies. I'd heard that my social media was being closely watched to ensure I didn't lead people astray and my excitement about a spiritual connection with God wasn't matched by leadership. But my soul knew better. Deep within my heart, I knew I didn't actually belong in this place, and I knew God didn't have a future for me within it. But I stayed. I stayed because it was all I knew. I stayed because my friends were there. I stayed because I was comfortable, but I had one foot out the door long before Michael walked through mine.

The time came to meet with leadership and let them know about the man in the red jacket. I wanted to have these conversations for two reasons: I wasn't interested in keeping a secret and I wasn't going to hide him when he came to visit. I arranged to meet with several people (some in official leadership positions, some in socially high positions) to tell them about Michael and the story God had been writing.

The first was Amy, the one who originally placed a bible in my hands almost two decades earlier. I sent a text asking if we could meet for lunch and we decided on a quaint spot for a light meal. The small restaurant is hidden amongst various businesses inside a well-worn shopping center. After we welcomed each other with a hug, we walked through the restaurant towards the back and decided to seat ourselves outside at a small bistro table. We ordered lunch during our casual small-talk and then I took over the conversation.

"Well, I have something exciting to share," I began.

She shifted in her chair, leaning forward in anticipation. Her smile was big, but stiff. I realized, she wasn't smiling with excitement, she was smiling in fear. I also realized she most likely already knew what I was about to say; word travels fast in church communities.

"I met someone," I paused to watch her body language. I knew she wasn't going to like this conversation. I knew it wasn't going to go well. But I hoped she would hear the details of God and consider there may be other ways God would bring people together outside of their congregation.

I continued with my story about Michael. I explained in detail the feeling in my soul prior to our meeting. I told her about my 'list,' including my specific age request of his children and the ages of Michael's daughters. I told her about the flowers arriving in the middle of my prayer. I told her about Michael and Jeremy and how fitting it was that a man coming into my life would have a connection to Ryan and the department that had been caring for me since he died. I told her about my conversation with the kids and their response to the idea of Michael. I told her about the mornings I would wake up to find texts from Michael with encouragement from scripture. I told her about the way we would pray together at the end of each FaceTime call. I told her everything.

Her face was frozen; her smile was stuck throughout the entirety of my speech.

"Wow," she finally said. "That, uh, was a lot." I could tell she was not thrilled about this information, which I anticipated, but I hoped after being my friend for almost twenty years, she would know that I am faithful to God and not reckless with the world. I felt my eyes squint as I studied her face and waited for her opinion.

"I mean, that all sounds great, but how can you be certain this is from God?"

"I haven't made a single decision without first going to God. I've looked for Him in every way, even if that meant walking away from Michael. I've never been afraid to give him up if that's what God wanted me to do."

"Well, yeah," she paused while collecting the words she knew I wouldn't want to hear, "but this could also be of Satan, too. Sometimes Satan comes through looking like God, but really, it's not."

She had a valid point. The enemy is cunning and capable of deceiving the most intentional hearts. However, since the time of my fasting, and especially after Ryan died, I was afraid to breathe outside of God, and Amy was a witness to that. She had a front row seat to my grief and my faith after Ryan died; not only that, she saw my journey of faith closer than most in my life since the day she invited me to church. She saw my years of doubt and the time I walked away from God in my early twenties. She saw my prideful defiance and she witnessed my humble submission as I entered my thirties. I assumed she knew my faith was beyond religious obedience; it had become necessary for me to live. She often complimented my faith when it came to trusting God, but now, she was unsure about that same trust.

I let her talk because I understood the majority of her words were due to fear. This was uncharted territory and a shock to her heart; I didn't want to minimize that. I believed Amy was truly concerned for me, but I also had a clear understanding of the church's doctrine and stance on dating. The only thing I wanted was for her to hear me and consider the idea that maybe the church had it wrong about who, what, when, where and how God would move to bring people together.

"I mean, have you considered going to a 'singles' event? Because at least at those...." her voice trailed off.

I glared at her. "No. I will not go to a 'singles' event. Don't ask me that again." My words were fierce because I had already made it known to my friends that I would never attend a 'singles' event with the church. I also didn't want to be invited on 'encouragement dates,' a popular concept within the organization in which single adult men take single adult women on dates as recommended by their disciplers for the purpose of spiritually stimulating the women. While I can appreciate the kindness of this concept, I found forced dates to be awkward and misleading, as well, these dates were not a place I wanted to give my energy or spend time away from my children. I didn't want church leadership meddling in choosing a suitor they felt appropriate. I had seen it too many times with young couples groomed to date each other, only to marry and then suffer hardships because they weren't encouraged to naturally select their partners. The result: forcing a connection that sometimes never existed. I spoke loudly and openly about the fact that I was waiting on God to reveal who He chose for me and my children. Apparently, everyone assumed I was joking.

God knew I wasn't.

Highly discouraged after my time with Amy, I arranged for my next conversation. This time with leadership: the women's ministry leader, Sandra. I've always enjoyed her company and I wasn't overly worried about our upcoming conversation. We met in a trendy, healthy restaurant and jumped right into discussion. There was no point in small talk because I had no doubt she already heard, and had been warned, about the new addition in my life.

Just as I did with everyone before her, I shared the story of how Michael and I met and God's detailed hand in it all. When I finished, her expression was a little more receptive than Amy's had been, and she didn't immediately brush it off. However, she did proceed to tell me that the way in which Michael and I met was not "how [they] have always done things."

Sandra explained to me that "typically, when a brother is interested in a sister or vice versa, we let their disciplers know and we meet with each of them to make sure they are in line with scripture." I stared at her in disbelief.

She could see that I wasn't responsive to their dating traditions, so she asked about Michael's upcoming visit. I explained that he would be staying with Felicia and her husband, Will, both members of the church.

"I wouldn't recommend that you see him every day while

he's here," she said. Again, I stared at her in disbelief. "I also wouldn't recommend Face Timing him every day. That much contact with each other can lead to temptation."

I felt my eyebrows gather in confusion. I was 39 years old and being spoken to as if I were a teenager with hormones gone wild. "Sandra, how am I supposed to get to know him if I don't talk to him?"

During my eighteen years in the church, I sat with many women whose marriages failed or were failing as a result of the toxic dating rituals within the church. Marriages had either been orchestrated and developed by leaders, and dating couples were not allowed to be alone or talk frequently. The restrictions placed on these couples resulted in two strangers marrying for the sake of purity.

Early in my years of observing the church's dating rules, I was grateful to be married and would not have the invasion of church in my romantic life, as I had seen being done to others. I recognized its unhealthy dating practices, which is why I knew my story with Michael was going to cause a problem - especially because I wasn't going to back down.

She avoided my question and instead asked, "would he be open to a bible study while he's here?" The church has its own study series for the purpose of training new disciples of their doctrine. According to their belief system, Michael was not a 'true' Christian until he went through their series of studies and deemed worthy of baptism by leadership. It didn't matter that Michael had given his life to Christ years before we met; if it wasn't done within their organization, they didn't consider it a saving faith.

"No," I said. I didn't give further explanation for my answer. I knew the purpose behind those studies: to teach unknowing, unsaved people about the 'true church' and convince already-saved Christians that they are not part of the church and they are not, in fact, saved by God's grace.

My meeting with Sandra left me feeling unheard, mistrusted and unresolved. I requested a second meeting for another day. This time with a witness.

As I drove to Mahal's house, I prayed God would be present. I asked Him to fill my mouth with the words He wanted me to say. I begged Him for clarity and guidance, and I asked that He remove any selfish intentions I had and replace it with His will and His wisdom. I didn't want anything I said to be of my own motive; I wanted God to direct the conversation and replace my words with His.

Mahal, Sandra, and myself sat at a table each visibly stiff in preparation for this conversation. I don't remember how it started, but I do remember Sandra asking, "did I say something that bothered you?"

"Yes, actually, at one point you said that this is the way it's always been done, and I don't think that's okay. Who are we to put God in a box and tell Him that He can only work within one group of people? Nothing about faith is linear. None of our stories should look the same or appear to be on the same path."

I continued with my deeply felt convictions that what the church was teaching about God was incorrect, and as I spoke, Sandra's eyes never left mine. I have always respected Sandra, and in this conversation, I felt she had mutual respect for me. She didn't interrupt me. She didn't argue with me. She allowed me to continue speaking about non-linear faith and my conviction that all of our stories should look and sound different. She sat quietly as I spoke confidently; I had never been so bold in my entire Christian life.

When I finished, she looked at Mahal. "What do you think of this?"

Roger and Mahal were a well-respected couple in the church, and aside from Katie, Felicia and Amy, they were two of the closest people to me who had personally witnessed my relationship with God over the years.

Mahal smiled, kept her eyes on Sandra, and said, "I trust Jennifer's faith. She's not reckless."

As I watched Mahal, I felt my heart fill with gratitude and I let out an exhale I didn't know I was holding in. I wasn't reckless. I hadn't been reckless. From the moment I learned of Ryan's death, I made myself dependent on God, even when it was difficult. I fought hard for my faith and Mahal's words were the acknowledgment I didn't realize I needed. If it weren't for the serious tone of the conversation, I would've leapt across the table and wrapped her in a hug.

Sandra looked at me and smiled, "Well, I can't wait to meet him." The three of us grabbed each other's hands as Sandra began to pray. She thanked God for the time we had together, she prayed for my heart and Michael's safety as he traveled. I felt her squeeze my hand as she mentioned Michael's name, and I believed I was going to make a positive change in the church.

Days later, Amy invited me to her home for a conversation between her, myself and Daniel. Sitting in their backyard, Daniel smiled and said, "I've heard about your story, but I haven't heard it from you yet."

After leaving my meeting with Sandra convinced positive change was coming, I assumed this conversation was going to be eye-opening for Daniel and beneficial for the church. It felt like an invitation for my thoughts on potential doctrine modification. As I finished sharing about Michael and the many ways God had been showing Himself to me, my smile was big and natural. Daniel wasn't smiling. It was the same look he had on his face the day he gave Ryan and I an ultimatum about studying the bible. He looked away as he sucked in a breath and then launched into all the reasons why this couldn't have been from God. He asked if Michael would be willing to go to the church in Belfast. I didn't answer. My heart was equally broken and angered to know Michael was being judged before ever being received simply because, in their eyes, he belonged to the wrong church.

I listened to be polite, but as soon as he was done talking, I said, "Daniel, if you can't see God in this, then you're not actually looking for Him."

I understood how shocking and fast this felt to those who were learning about Michael for the first time, and it wasn't praise or approval I was seeking. I recognized this would make many feel uncomfortable and create questioning of my judgment. I appreciated their concern for my well-being, but I was also aware of the staunch belief system implemented by the religious organization. I knew their doctrine well because I studied it for 18 years. It wasn't their worry that frustrated me. It was the "no chance, "no way" denial by leadership that was disheartening. I watched as couples who wanted to be together were encouraged to separate because one was a true Christian (aka: church disciple) and one was not (aka: a Christian belonging to another church). I watched as someone close to me was rebuked and shamed for going on a double-date with her church boyfriend and a 'worldly' couple without first getting permission from their disciplers. I was a witness to marriages falling apart because leadership believed it was a good match, but the couples were afraid to disagree. My frustration wasn't with their concern for me, it was with their doctrine.

§

I walked into the quiet café and found Felicia waiting for me. As though the walls were going to repeat whatever was said, I whispered an apology for being late. She smiled knowing that tardiness was, unfortunately, a common practice of mine.

"I was on the phone with Michael before he starts his shift," I explained while trying to put my phone back into my purse.

Felicia and I were in the habit of getting together every week; we usually spent our time talking about God and the bible, but lately, our conversations had been about the man in the red jacket and the reception I'd been receiving about his presence in my life.

As it normally did, our conversation organically turned to the topic of God, specifically, the signs He was delivering each time I prayed for His guidance.

"Tell me what you've been noticing," she prompted. She took a bite of her lunch and continued, "tell me about what's happening with leadership. What are they saying about all this?"

"Honestly," I took a sip of water, "it's frustrating. It feels like the only way they'll trust my faith is if they have control of it. They're not even willing to consider anything different." I paused. "I've talked to God every day about this and I haven't made any decisions without going to Him first, you know that. If He wants it to stop, He will. I've asked Him to. I don't want anything that's not His. "

She nodded in agreement.

For the entirety of time Michael and I had been communicating, Katie and Felicia (both faithful and Godly women) had been intimately involved. I took screenshots of every text conversation Michael and I had and shared those with Katie. I poured the details of our verbal conversations onto Felicia's ears. I didn't censor or hide anything from either of them. I did this for the sake of maintaining honesty and alignment with God. Even after sharing with church leadership about the transparency I was maintaining to ensure honesty of tongue and purity of heart, it didn't matter. In their eyes, this relationship couldn't have been of God because they weren't participants in its fruition.

"The church is looking for my obedience, but I'm obedient to God first."

I took a bite of my sandwich, which gave Felicia the chance to answer. "You know, it's a lot like Job and his friends, the ones who thought they had all the answers."

I nodded in agreement. She continued, "Job was so transparent, so honest, and they cut him down with their head knowledge. I mean, they were trying to blame Job's hardships on him. They had no idea how God felt about his situation, but they acted like they knew the cause of it. That kind of arrogance is dangerous. As soon as we start thinking we know as much as God does, we actually lose sight of Him." Felicia paused as she contemplated her own words. "The interesting thing is that despite their head knowledge about God, it was Job who actually knew Him."

"And, the thing is," I mumbled as I swallowed my bite, "people forget God was actually annoyed by Job's friends and their unwillingness to step out of their heads."

"And," Felicia said, "they were twisting truths about God to maintain their narrative that Job was in the wrong."

I studied the book of Job for a year after Ryan died. I admired Job's raw emotional, spiritual honesty and I was bothered by the arrogance of his 'know-it-all' friends. They weren't listening to Job at all. A lot of what Job's friends said about God was true, but they were turning that spiritual truth into worldly accusations, which became a deep misrepresentation of God.

I continued with my thoughts, "the church is basically saying that God can only work within this one group of people and I just don't believe that to be the God I know of the bible. God used people from all over to accomplish His plans! Jews, Gentiles, Romans - everyone! God can do anything He wants with anyone He wants..."

"And at any time He wants," Felicia finished my sentence.

"Yeah." I paused and stared out the window just over Felicia's shoulders. "Who are we to limit God and think we know His plans? They haven't even met Michael yet and they're already throwing stones at him."

Felicia slowly shook her head as she finished the bite in her mouth. I was proud of the way I had been handling conversations with the religious leaders. I had been speaking with confidence because prior to each meeting, I asked God to do the talking and He did. Every time.

"You know what's interesting about Job's friends," she said, "is that they weren't the ones God spoke to and they weren't the ones He agreed with."

"I know," I agreed, "it was Job."

Felicia nodded while sipping her water.

At the end of Job's lamenting, God spoke to him through a storm (Job 38). He reminded Job of His power and sovereignty, and Job responded in humble submission. God then spoke to Job's friends, "I am angry with you and your two friends because you did not tell the truth about me, as my servant Job did." (Job 42:7). He continued, "You have not spoken the truth about me, as my servant Job has." (Job 42:8) God then restored Job's health and "gave him twice as much as he had before." (Job 42:10)

"Here's the thing," I said, "I know all of this is shocking. I'm not denying anyone that, but the only ones to completely deny the coincidences are the ones who claim to know God. They're not even willing to explore the possibility of it all. I don't get it."

"Well, you know I won't stop you," Felicia chuckled as she spoke. "I'm in this battle with you." She knew I was going up against a religious system that had been in place for forty years. She was battling that system for reasons outside of mine and we both lowered our eyes to the table knowing it wouldn't be easy.

"Anyway," I said lifting my eyes and energy back up, "I can't believe Michael is going to be here soon." My smile naturally grew each time I said his name.

Felicia and I spoke excitedly about what his arrival would be like, plans we had for the time he was in California, and how we anticipated it would go when Michael would meet my parents for the first time.

We were lost in our imaginations when Felicia said, "if you got married again, would you keep your last name or would you change it? Have you thought about that?"

"Oh yes, I've thought about that, even before I met Michael. I'm definitely going to keep Osler and hyphenate with whatever my new married name would be."

"I like that," Felicia said. "Imagine if you marry Michael? Wouldn't that be wild?"

I smiled, "yeah, it would." I felt my expression change. My eyes locked in on Felicia, whose eyes were glittering in a dreamy state.

"Felicia," my tone dropped and she looked at me, "if I marry Michael, my initials would be J.O.B. My initials would be Job."

Chapter 23

As well as I'm known for my tardiness, I'm known for getting lost and having zero sense of direction. It was finally June 21st and Michael was flying into the Los Angeles International airport that evening. I couldn't sleep the night before; my mind was racing with a mixture of excitement, nerves, and fear. Over the course of nearly three months, Michael and I spent so much time together (albeit virtually) that I felt as though I had known him my entire life. We missed being together despite sharing only minutes in each other's presence. We had already forsaken anyone else in our future; we knew that what we had was "it."

Yet, I was so nervous to meet him again. I wasn't sure if the comfort I felt through a screen would be the same as being in his physical presence.

Long before this day came, I asked Katie and Felicia to go with me to the airport. Knowing my history of being late and getting lost, I knew my nerves weren't going to be helpful. I was unfamiliar with the airport and feared I would end up at the wrong terminal or somehow miss his arrival. Without hesitation, they both agreed to take me to the airport.

§

A couple of weeks prior to Michael's visit, I was standing in my kitchen when I pulled out my phone to inquire about the number of days it had been since Ryan's accident. The 21st of each month drew my attention and served as a reminder of the time that had gone by since becoming a widow. I began paying attention to dates and numbers because, along with pennies, I was finding confirmation of God's presence through numbers. He symbolically used numbers in bible times and I didn't find it a coincidence that He was using them with me now.

The number 42 is significant to me because it was the station number of Ryan's last assignment at the time of his death. I typically came across this number when I seemed to be missing Ryan more than usual. It felt like a wink from God each time that number would appear before me, as if He were letting me know He was watching. In all honesty, it still feels that way when I come across the number 42. Whether it's on a license plate, the number of my food order or the dollar amount I spend, I smile each time knowing I'm not alone. I don't think it's a coincidence that 21 (the date of Ryan's accident) when doubled is 42, which made my study of the book of Job even more notable. Job's healing and blessing occurred in the last chapter of the book, chapter 42. I could tangibly feel God's presence when I originally made that connection.

When I prepared my talk for Hume using the scripture God showed to me at the end of 2017 (Psalm 71:14), I found myself turning to the NIV Exhaustive Bible Concordance to see how many times the word 'hope' appears in the bible. 'Hope' is in the bible 167 times, but the 42nd time it appears in the bible is in Psalm 71:14. And so began my awareness of numerical confirmation and communication with God.

The number seven is another number that holds personal meaning because biblically it represents God's holy work and His perfection. It represents something being finished and complete. God loves the number seven; it's used over seven hundred times in the bible. And while both of those numbers frequently cross my path, it is the number three that often gets my attention and forces me to stop and acknowledge that God is trying to tell me something. The number three in Hebrew is *shelosh,* which means harmony, new life, and completeness. It appears in the bible 467 times, which is significantly less than the number seven, but holds an incomparable symbolic depth.

Jesus prayed three times in the garden of Gethsemane before his arrest (Matthew 26:44). Jesus was nailed to the cross during the third hour of the day in Jewish time (Mark 15:25). Darkness covered the land for three hours before Jesus died (Luke 23:44). Jesus died during the ninth hour (3:00pm) in Jewish time (Matthew 27:46). Christ resurrected in victory over death three days after his crucifixion (recorded in all four gospels). Essentially, God completed his perfect plan for humanity using the number three.

There are many other instances in scripture showcasing God's intentional symbolism with the number three. However, I find that the most profound and precious is the representation of the Holy Trinity in the number three: the Father, the Son, and the Holy Spirit. When I come across the number three, especially in the form of multiples (3:33, 33, etc.), I know it was symbolic of my communication with, and confirmation from, God.

Ryan died on the 21st of September, a number perfectly divisible by three (new life) and seven (completion), and when doubled is 42. Ryan entered into new life on the 21st. His time on earth was complete and God's holy work was just beginning.

I typed into the Google search bar on my phone: *"how many days between September 21, 2016 and June 21, 2019?"*

"1004"

"Hmph," I pouted at the screen. None of God's numbers. I had grown so dependent on His communication with me that I would've been willing to leave Michael at the airport if God told me through numbers not to pick him up. I stared at the number, entered it into my calculator and discovered the number wasn't divisible seven or three. I had a fleeting moment of doubt: either God doesn't actually use numbers with me or He wasn't part of this upcoming visit with Michael.

Disappointed, I set my phone down on the counter. *"Wait,"* I whispered to myself. I grabbed my phone again, but instead of another Google search, I opened the calendar.

June 21st, 2019 – the day Michael arrives in Los Angeles was exactly three months before the third anniversary of Ryan's death, which occurred exactly 33 months before Michael was due to arrive. Michael's arrival on June 21st would be the beginning of new life. *Shelosh.* I laughed at myself for doubting God's communication with me. For years now, God had been training my eyes to look for Him and my ears to listen for Him, and this moment was no different.

§

The airport is less than forty miles from my house, but with LA traffic, it takes an hour and a half to get there, sometimes longer. Katie and Felicia arrived at my house and my body was visibly shaking due to a rush of adrenaline. My cousin came up with an idea to wiggle out the nerves.

"Let's practice when you see Michael for the first time!"

My cousin stands beautifully tall at six feet; I stopped growing when I hit five feet, two inches. Michael, being six-foot and three-inches in height, liked to joke that when we'd meet at the airport I would likely jump into his arms. Katie was now offering the chance for me to practice that jump. Through a fit of giggles, Katie got in position to receive me, Felicia was ready to break Katie's fall if I knocked her over, and my daughter was recording the whole thing on my phone.

Katie prepared her stance, lowered her voice, and said, "oh my gosh, Jennifer!" I squealed and ran to her, jumping into her arms. She effortlessly twirled me around while the sound of laughter filled my home.

Before I knew it, it was time to go. I don't actually remember the drive to the airport. I can't remember if we talked during the drive, I don't remember arriving, and I can't recall walking into the terminal. But I do remember the vibration within my body as I waited for him.

We arrived a half hour before his plane was scheduled to land and we didn't know exactly where he would be coming out of the terminal. The three of us parked ourselves near a corridor that appeared to be an exit for passengers and did our best to be patient as we waited. Katie and Felicia had their phones pointed in my direction, ready to capture every minute of the reunion between me and Michael.

My eyes were bouncing between the corridor in front of me and the phone in my hands, as I continually refreshed the FlightAware website for information on Michael's flight. I couldn't stand still but I also couldn't move, so I gently swayed my hips from left to right as I waited.

"Jenn," Felicia said with a steady voice.

I looked at her, but she was focused on the ground. I followed her gaze which was pointed in my direction. Directly in front of me, laying perfectly at my feet was a penny so shiny, I don't know how I missed it. It reminded me of the penny I found on the day in my garage when I wanted to give up. I bent down to pick it up. My eyes were filled with tears, which clouded my vision and made it difficult for me to see the year on the penny. I wiped my eyes and brought it close to my face.

2018.

The year I wrote the list of my heart's desires. The year I surrendered my heart to God. The year I put all my trust in God that He had a future planned for me and my children. There was God, using pennies and numbers to let me know He was near, again. I tucked that shiny penny into my pocket and almost instantly my phone alerted me of a text.

"Just landed!"

My hands were shaking. His plane landed fifteen minutes earlier than scheduled. My smile was ridiculously big and my two precious friends were equally thrilled.

As people began filing out of the corridor, Felicia had the idea to confirm that we were waiting in the correct spot. I didn't take my eyes off the crowd of people entering into Los Angeles. I was afraid to blink out of fear that I would miss his entrance into the baggage claim area. I could hear Felicia's gentle voice in the background, "excuse me, did you just come in from Dublin?" I didn't turn to look her direction, but suddenly she was in front of me. "This is not where they're going to come out. I think it's down there." She pointed to my left; I broke my stare to look in that direction.

We walked toward the area Felicia was told would be the entrance for Dublin passengers and planted ourselves in a new spot. More people were entering into the baggage area; this time they were coming down an escalator and we could see each face through the glass doors that separated overseas visitors from Los Angeles natives. Instead of a corridor, I now had my eyes glued to the escalator in front of me. I heard Katie's voice confirming with people that they were coming in from Dublin.

"Ok, we're in the right place," she said. I nodded in acknowledgment and didn't take my eyes off the steady flow of people appearing before me. I studied the escalator as if I was going to be quizzed on how many people walked through the doors. It felt as though the entire plane had disembarked and he was nowhere to be seen.

Until he was.

I saw his blue t-shirt and then I saw him bend down to get a better look into the baggage claim area. We made eye contact and my smile took over my face. I felt my heart surge and my lungs gasp. A warm sensation came over me and my spirit jumped in anticipation; my body had gone through this before. It was the same as I experienced at Hume three months earlier. I didn't know what it was then, but it was so clear to me now. My soul had been trying to tell me that he was the one my heart desired and my spirit was responding to the divine orchestration of our meeting.

Like a magnet, I was pulled towards him, walking quickly, ignoring the crowd around me. I entered into the area behind the glass doors to meet him at the base of the escalator. Just as practiced, I jumped into his arms, wrapped my legs around him, threw my arms around his neck and buried my face into his shoulder. I could feel the strength of his arms around me, pulling me close to him.

I felt tears coming to my eyes. Instead of crying, I brought my head off his shoulder, met his eyes with mine, and kissed him. I held his face in my hand, the stubble of his beard was rough against my palm. Our smiles broke our kiss. I felt him move one of his arms from my waist and hold the back of my head. I rested my head on his shoulder as he held with me a protective, yet gentle, hug. It was the kind of embrace that cradled my heart, not just my body. I couldn't believe how natural and comfortable it felt to be in his arms. Three months earlier, I couldn't form a word in his presence, and now I couldn't form a future without him.

He was the first to say something, "well, how are ya?" I answered with a smile. He laughed and brought his forehead to mine. "Are you alright?"

With my forehead resting against his, I nodded. I don't

know if he knew that tears were on the verge, but he seemed to know I needed to be quiet in that moment. He smiled gently and returned his hand to the back of my head. It was the most tender touch. It was simultaneously protective and nurturing; the kind of touch I hadn't felt in a very long time.

Eventually I climbed down from the tree-top that was Michael and allowed him to release me back to reality. Overdue hugs were shared between Michael, Katie, and Felicia, and I stood to the side watching his every move. When I last saw him at Hume Lake, I couldn't focus on his mannerisms, but here in the middle of a busy airport I was memorizing every detail of his movement.

He excused himself to the restroom and I immediately turned to Katie and Felicia. I began to cry through my smile, "he's the one. This is it. He's the one!" They didn't think I was crazy; they didn't tell me slow down. They didn't tell me anything that I had been hearing from others during the last month. Instead, my cousin took photos of me in that moment and Felicia met me with tears.

Like paparazzi, Katie and Felicia kept their phones pointed at me and the man in the red jacket. Katie captured our kiss as we waited for his luggage; in the midst of a sea of moving people, we were frozen in time. Felicia secretly took video as we walked from the airport towards the car, capturing our first moments hand in hand, stepping into the real world.

Being in his presence was exhilarating. With Katie at the steering wheel and Felicia in the passenger seat, Michael fit himself into the backseat next to me.

"I can't believe you're here," I said through a smile that showcased all my teeth. He wrapped his arm around me, bringing me into the center of the seat directly beside him. Chatter, laughter, and several "this is crazy" statements filled the car during the hour-long drive from the airport to my house.

When we finally arrived, both of my kids were waiting at the front door. As though they met him before, they greeted him with hugs and welcomed him into our home. Michael promptly unloaded a bag of sweets he brought to Amanda and Brandon from Northern Ireland, along with Irish Rugby jerseys and hats, and a bottle of perfume for me. After an exchange of gifts, I could see the kids had reached a social limit and needed space to process this new presence in our home. With arms full of goodies, they retreated to their bedrooms.

Katie, Felicia, Michael and I settled into the family room. I curled myself into the nook of Michael's body; comfortably nestled beside him with my head resting against his chest. He draped his arm over me, securing my body next to his. I felt my eyes getting heavy. I hadn't slept well the night before in anticipation of this day, and as the nighttime hours carried on, I felt myself drifting in and out of consciousness. The three of them continued to talk while I closed my eyes to excuse myself from conversation.

I held onto his arm that was laying across me and allowed myself to sink further into the nook of his body. I could feel the vibration of his voice as Katie and Felicia fawned over the accent I had been hearing every day for the last three months. I felt safe, a feeling I hadn't experienced in nearly three years. I was comfortable and at ease in his embrace, something I believed I would never feel with anyone. Warm tears began to flood my eyes; I kept them closed in an effort to keep them from falling. I became overwhelmed at the realization that I was safely in the arms of a man who loved me. I could feel love radiating from him, as though his heart were beating for the sole purpose of loving me. And then, he gently kissed the top of my head. I couldn't hold back any longer; tears moved slowly down my cheek. I took a deep breath, curled myself tighter into him, and fell asleep. My soul could finally rest.

Chapter 24

Michael had given himself two tasks to complete during his visit: ask for the permission of my children to propose to their mother and ask for the permission of my father to marry his daughter. Although we couldn't explain it, we knew within days after our first FaceTime date that not only did we want to get married, we believed we were meant to be married. It didn't make sense to either of us, but it never felt confusing or alarming. We trusted that God brought us together and would make clear His plan for our families. While some would assume we'd wait to marry until our geographical dilemma was solved, we didn't feel the need to delay marriage. We could see there wasn't a quick or clear answer to our predicament, so, we decided, "why wait? Let's see what God does."

Michael was at my house when I ran upstairs to grab something from my bedroom. My phone alerted that I received a text from him: *"stay upstairs for a bit."*

I immediately responded, *"why?"*

He didn't answer, but I soon heard his voice, although I couldn't make out the words. His voice was low and soft. I tried to listen, but felt bad about eavesdropping, so I stepped away from the bedroom door and waited to be told when I could make my way downstairs.

I heard another voice. It was my daughter's. All at once I pieced it together: he was talking to my kids about proposing to me.

ding

"You can come downstairs"

I did my best to pretend I had no idea why I had to stay in my room, but after locking eyes with each of them, they realized I knew exactly what had taken place at our kitchen table.

Two days before Michael was set to leave Los Angeles, we were at my parents' house for a Fourth of July BBQ. This was Michael's first time experiencing our American holiday, so my mom pulled out the stops to make it spectacular for him. She lined the fence with American flags, planted red, white and blue pinwheels into the ground, and made every classic American food typically consumed on the Fourth. Katie and her family joined us that day, and while we were splashing around in my parents' pool, I noticed Michael hadn't yet jumped in. I looked towards the house where I saw my dad sitting in a chair facing away from all of us. I quietly swam to the opposite side of the pool and noticed he was intently focused on Michael who was sitting across from him. I swam towards my cousin. Reading my mind by way of my eyes, she swam past me and looked towards the house.

"It's happening," she mouthed silently.

I felt my stomach begin to turn while her smile began to widen. A large splash of water interrupted our moment.

"Did you see my cannon ball, mom?" My son was bouncing in and out of the water creating ripples and waves that thrilled his sister and their cousins. I broke my stare with Katie and joined the game being played by the kids in the water.

I didn't look back towards the house. I didn't know how long they had been talking. I didn't know how it was going. I didn't know it was over until I heard an Irish accent holler that he, also, was a human cannonball.

§

Later that evening, Felicia and her family joined us at my home along with Katie, her husband and their children. Kids were running wild in the backyard while music and laughter between the six of us filled the inside of my house that was typically quiet. Michael and Felicia's husband, Will, were talking when I overheard Michael sharing his affinity for fast cars and adrenaline-pumping speed.

"I would absolutely get an American muscle car and fly it down the road." I turned around to see his eyes sparkling with the idea of pushing a classic car to its limits.

"I'll be putting you in a Prius," I teased as I interjected myself into their conversation. "You're not getting a fast car." Michael made a sound that was a blend of scoffing and laughing. "You think I'm joking," I answered. I've always enjoyed a bit of playful banter, so I smiled as I spoke, knowing I was partially joking about his need for speed and my need for safety. But his smile didn't match mine.

In fact, he wasn't smiling at all. He didn't take his eyes off the screen of his phone when he said, "you think you can tell me what to do?"

Under the assumption we were engaging in lighthearted banter, I allowed my response to have a sarcastic bite when I said, "you think I can't?" From the kitchen, Felicia let out a quick, sharp laugh. I took her laughter as a sign of encouragement, so, I kept going. My sarcasm was rich as I continued to tell him about the car he would be driving if he was going to be in my future.

Michael didn't laugh. I walked towards him, wrapped my arms around his broad shoulders and kissed his cheek. His body stiffened; he acknowledged my presence by continuing to scroll through a long list of American muscle cars for sale. Annoyed because I was ignored, I removed my arms and backed away from him. As the rest of the night went on, he avoided me as though I were carrying a disease that was lethal by touch. His movements were exaggerated in an effort to showcase that he was purposely avoiding contact with me. Instead of recognizing that he clearly didn't want to interact with me, I hunted him down and forced him to acknowledge me.

"What is going on with you?" I demanded as I cornered him in a hallway. He tried to walk past me, but I moved my body to block his exit. "What the hell is this?"

He lowered his voice, "I don't want to talk about it right now. Move out of the way."

I didn't respect that boundary and I continued to push: "what's wrong with you? Why are you acting like this? Are you seriously mad because I said you can't have a fast car?"

He didn't answer. I stepped aside to let him exit my interrogation, but as I did, I made the decision to ramp up my pride and become the one who was now going to ignore him. I didn't know what made him so angry. I had no idea what shifted in, what I assumed was, our playful banter. We spent the rest of the night avoiding each other until our friends left and the house became quiet.

He sat on the couch and I placed myself directly beside him. It was the same spot where he held me close that first night and sitting there had become an invitation to fall safely into his arms. I expected to be received with open arms, but he didn't welcome me in. He didn't adjust his body in an effort to allow mine to melt into his. Instead, he stood up, walked towards the front door, and walked out.

I sat on the couch in confusion and waited a few minutes for his return, but he didn't come back. I tried calling his phone. No answer. I tried again. No answer. My third attempt went straight to voicemail. He made it clear: he didn't want to speak to me.

"Ok, fine," I thought to myself, *"but you don't get to ignore me."* I sent him a text message: "where are you?"

His response came quickly: *"I'm leaving tomorrow. I'm changing my flight."*

My heart sprinted into a panic. He wasn't supposed to leave for another couple of days; in fact, we had just discussed the possibility of extending his trip. I tried calling him again. No answer.

I ran to my room and burst into tears. I called again, this time he answered. Through sobs, I begged him not to leave. "I don't understand why you're doing this," I cried.

His voice was empty when he said, "I found a flight that

leaves tomorrow. I'm going home."

Anger replaced tears as I felt my temper begin to surface.

"You don't get to do this," I said. "You don't just get to leave. Why are you doing this?"

He wasn't speaking. The only thing I could hear on the other end of the phone was the sound of his movement as he walked. We weren't connected to each other's locations on our phones; I didn't know where he was or how far he had walked from the house. Suddenly, the phone went silent. I looked down at the screen: "*call ended*."

My mind raced with thoughts: *he fell and hit his head, a car approached and he was attacked, he went into cardiac arrest, he's seizing and choking, he's dead.* All of those scenarios made more sense to my traumatized heart than the idea that he would deliberately end the call without saying goodbye.

I heard the front door open. A mixture of relief and resentment coursed through my body. I asked him to come upstairs so we could speak privately. He cautiously approached. My bedroom was the one area of the house he never entered into. I watched his eyes search the room with discretion. I was too heated to consider the fact that he stepped into an intimate space I once shared with another man. I was too hurt to realize his imagination might've been placing Ryan and I in this room together. He sat down on the upholstered bench at the foot of my bed. I stood in front of him, crossing my arms and looking down as he lowered his head.

I should've taken this moment to shift my mood and lower my guard. Instead, I couldn't stop my mouth from spilling the thoughts in my head: "did you hang up on me? You left this house without saying goodbye? You wouldn't answer my calls? You're threatening to leave? Why? Why are you acting like this?"

He said nothing. I waited for an answer, my silence demanding acknowledgment. After a torturous minute of reticence, I lowered myself to the ground and knelt in front of him. I placed my hands on his forearms and my heart softened when I felt his skin beneath my fingertips.

"What happened tonight?" My voice was no longer harsh.

I saw him hesitate to answer, but he finally said, "is that what our marriage is going to be like? You're going to tell me what I can and can't do?"

My mind hurried back to the memory of my uninvited commentary that took place hours earlier. "Babe, I was teasing!" I smiled thinking my three-word explanation would ease this tension between us and he would wrap me in his arms as we both apologized for our behavior. Having not learned my lesson, I playfully continued, "I mean, I would prefer you *not* be in a fast car...but..." My voice trailed off as soon as I saw that my explanation did not do what I assumed it would. The tension was still there and my playfulness was not being received. My mind revisited a different kind of memory, *"Ryan would've laughed with me by now."* I removed my hands from Michael's arms and sat on the floor in front of him in a posture of defeat.

"I don't appreciate you making me feel like I'm not going to have a say in our marriage," he finally admitted. "Especially in front of other people."

I didn't apologize. I should've, but I didn't. I felt annoyance rise (along with pride) as he wasn't responding in the way I felt he should. I believed my soft voice, playful response, and gentle touch should've been enough; after all, it was enough for Ryan. I stared at him and awaited his apology for walking out of the house without saying goodbye. I waited for him to apologize for instilling fear into my heart and threatening to leave. He didn't. He stared at me with no signs of backing down and my pride kept me from rising above. He wasn't going to apologize and I wasn't going to surrender.

It took a moment for me to realize what actually happened. When teasing Michael, I assumed he and I shared a level of understanding between us. I approached our three-month relationship with the assumption our familiarity with each other was the same as what Ryan and I built in twenty-one years. I assumed he knew I was joking. I assumed he knew my body language. I assumed he knew me well enough to know I wouldn't actually tell him what he can and can't buy. Those assumptions stemmed from an underlying belief I didn't know I had: I assumed any future relationship would operate the same as the one before it. I didn't know anything outside of my marriage with Ryan. I didn't know how to be romantically involved with anyone else. Without realizing it, I infused the relationship patterns and emotional behaviors I shared with Ryan into this new relationship.

Being so young when we started dating, Ryan and I grew into adulthood together. By the time he died, we had worked through the kinks in our relationship and had an understanding of each other. Michael and I didn't have that yet, and just as I was bringing my patterns and behaviors into this relationship, Michael was doing the same. His youth taught him that the easiest way to avoid conflict is to run away from it, and his past relationships taught him to build a wall of protection around his heart. So, that's what he did.

We sat in silence until I couldn't bear it another minute.

"Are you really going to leave tomorrow?" I finally asked.

"I want to," he answered. I nodded in disappointment.

"Do you love me?" My voice was low as I felt defeat settling in.

"Of course I do. That's a strange question to ask."

"Then why would you leave? We can't run away from problems, that's not how relationships work," I spoke as though I were an expert despite my own flawed patterns.

We continued circling around each other with accusations of disrespect and abandonment, neither one of us actually knowing how to move forward, and for a moment, I wasn't sure if we could. I had been so fixated on the excitement of his presence and the gift of his love that I hadn't even considered the possibility of having to relearn communication styles and rebuild relationship patterns. *'Am I willing to start over?'* I looked up at him. His bright blue eyes appeared dull. I thought about the day we met when those same eyes nearly stopped my heart with their brilliance. *'Am I willing to relearn everything?'* My mind felt fatigued at the thought. He stared as if he were waiting for me to answer my own inquisition.

Instead of answering, I propped myself onto my knees and knelt in front of him. The truth of it was that neither of us wanted to be in this situation. I didn't want my marriage with Ryan to end; he was the one whose hand I was supposed to hold as we wobbled down the street in old age. Michael didn't marry the mother of his daughters with the idea that one day they would no longer be married. Both of us had different plans for our marriages, and none of those plans included one another.

As I inched closer towards Michael, I noticed he kept his body stiff in an effort to emotionally protect himself. We had two choices: start over or quit. I decided I *was* willing to start over. I *was* willing to relearn everything. I *was* willing to accept that so much of what I assumed about our relationship was wrong.

"I don't want you to leave," I whispered. He kept his arms folded across his lap. I moved in closer. "I also don't want it to be like this." He pulled his gaze away from me. "We have to figure out how to do this." He refused to meet my eyes. "I'm sorry I embarrassed you." He still wouldn't look at me, but I felt his posture relax. "Please don't ever walk out on me like that, and don't threaten to leave when things get hard. We're not going to quit just because it gets hard."

He finally looked at me. I knew it would take time to break down walls and build trust that I was not going to quit on him – no matter how hard it gets. I knew this wasn't going to be a one-time thing; I knew we were going to go through this again. I could see how our individual history of relationships and trauma were going to affect the way in which we communicate. I could see that our past was going to force us into revising our future.

I reflected back on that night I cried out to God wondering if anybody would be able to love me with my battered and blemished heart, but I hadn't stopped to think about the man coming into my life. His heart would be also torn and scarred. I wondered if Michael ever questioned someone's ability to love him as he is now - emotionally bruised and relationally leery.

Creating a life together was going to require more forgiveness than I realized and more grace than I imagined. With more than two decades of relational experience, I wasn't naïve to think the blending of our lives would be easy, but I was expecting it to be only me that would require forgiveness and grace. For some reason I believed I was the only one who would require gentle and merciful love. I foolishly assumed I would be the only one with trauma and heartache, and whomever would come into my life would have to learn how to love me.

But God brought this man into my life who had his own history of heartache, loss and trauma. Just as I hoped God would place my delicate heart in the hands of someone willing to love me gently, God placed Michael's fragile heart in my hands trusting I would love him tenderly, and yet, I entered into this with an agenda to love him in my own way.

I looked at Michael as he stared at the ground. I glanced behind him and took in our surroundings: a bedside table whose drawers still held Ryan's belongings, a pillow that used to cradle his head on top of a mattress that absorbed his body, and a frame holding the photo Amanda took the night he left home. In addition to the tangible signs of Ryan, this space was drenched with his memory. Michael was never supposed to be in this room; hell, he was never supposed to be in my life, and I was never supposed to be in his. But there we were - two broken hearts, two separate lives, and two people assuming this relationship would be just like the last. I felt a wave of sympathy billowing inside me. I didn't want to be loved in the way Michael loved the woman before me. I wanted him to love me for *me;* I wanted him to discover my quirks, study my heart and learn my needs. What a fool I was to assume he wouldn't want the same from me. I allowed myself to use his respect for Ryan's memory as permission to love him as I loved Ryan, forgoing the reality that he needs to be loved differently. He carries different heartache, different history, and different experiences - requiring a completely different love.

Neither of us planned to love someone new. Neither of us planned to overhaul everything we've learned about relationships. But then and there, I decided that no matter how unplanned his presence was in my life, I was willing to unlearn everything and relearn him. There, at the foot of the bed I once shared with another man, I vowed to myself that I would love this man differently. The lessons I learned throughout my years as a wife would follow me into this relationship, but the patterns I had grown to know would stay with the memory of the man I first learned.

I leaned towards Michael, kissed his cheek, stood and walked out of my bedroom. I waited downstairs for a few minutes despite desperately wanting to call his name and ask why he didn't follow me out. Eventually, the floor croaked as he stepped out of my room. I leaned against the kitchen counter in an attempt to look unbothered.

He slowly walked towards me, then grabbed my arm and

pulled me into a hug. "I don't want to fight. I'm not going home tomorrow," he said.

"Good," I whispered in relief. I felt his arms tighten around me as we stood in the middle of the kitchen. I rested my head against his chest, focusing on the sound of his beating heart while promising God I would start over and discover this heart He brought to mine.

Chapter 25

My passport was soon going to expire and it didn't have a single stamp in it. I held it in my hands, which were shaking due to nerves. Without looking at me, the immigration officer at the Dublin airport extended his hand towards me.

"Hello," I said as I held out my passport.

Still looking down, he grabbed it from me and asked, "where ye' travelin'?" His accent sounded much different than Michael's and I had to lean in to make sure I heard him correctly.

"Um, I'm going to Belfast." I felt rattled; he was doing his job well.

"What's the reason for yer visit?"

"Oh, um, I'm visiting my boyfriend." Boyfriend? I realized I hadn't ever referred to Michael in such a way.

"Does he live in Belfast?"

"Yes."

"How long are ye stayin'?"

"One week."

"Do ye' have yer return ticket?"

My fingers fumbled; I wasn't prepared for this. As fast

as I could with noodles for fingers, I opened the booking confirmation on my phone to show the return date on my ticket.

"Are ye' goin' anywhere else?"

"No."

He briefly looked up at me and almost immediately a loud thud came from his side of the glass partition. "There ye' go," he said as he handed my passport back to me.

It was the first time I traveled internationally, and I did it on my own. I felt a sense of pride as I exited immigration controls. Knowing that Michael was waiting just beyond the doors of the baggage claim area, I found myself pacing as I waited for my suitcase to appear. It had been two months since we last saw each other and yet the walls separating us in the airport felt to be a greater barrier than the ocean normally between us.

"I'm through! Just waiting on my luggage," I texted.

"Great babe! I'm here waiting."

I couldn't wait to be in his arms again, and although I was thrilled to see Michael's country and hometown, there was a purpose behind this trip and it was more important than the sights I would see and the places I would visit. I was here to meet Michael's daughters.

I had spoken with Sarah and Evie several times via FaceTime whenever they were with Michael. Their youthful spirit lit up the air each time their faces were on the screen of my phone. Being ten and eleven years old, their voices were full of girlish energy, along with the sweetest sounding accents. I was excited to meet them, and I was equally as nervous. I had never experienced something like this before. All the children in my life were either related to me or related to my friends. I was either someone's Auntie Nen or someone's Jenn-Jenn; I had never been a child's 'Jennifer.'

My luggage bounced onto the moving belt and I tried to run towards it as casually as possible. I must've appeared too eager to leave the airport because two men stopped me just before the exit door.

"What do ye' have in yer case?"

"Oh, umm, just my clothes and some candies."

"Mind if we run it through?"

I didn't know there was a customs checkpoint beyond baggage claim. I watched as my fellow passengers walked by without being stopped.

"Yeah, of course." I let go of my suitcase (which I struggled to get off the luggage carousel), watched one of the men pick it up with ease and place it onto another conveyor belt. I began to convince myself I was not going to be let into Ireland because of the chocolates I tucked into my sweaters. Once my suitcase made it through, the other gentleman removed it from the belt and propped up the handle for me.

"Enjoy yer visit."

I thanked them both and quickly headed for the door. I needed to get to the Irishman waiting for me and I didn't want another person to slow me down.

§

It was late Sunday morning and we were on our way to pick up the girls. "We'll collect them after church and take them back to my apartment."

I wasn't sure if it was the anticipation of meeting his daughters or the fact I still wasn't used to being in a car on the opposite side of the road, but my stomach was in knots. We pulled into the parking lot of the church and waited in the car until we saw its congregants begin to leave. I opened the door, felt the cool air against my face and thanked God for the excuse to keep my hands in my coat pockets, allowing my nervous energy to fidget with the inner lining.

Two girls came bouncing our direction; their curls moving with them in perfect harmony and their smiles matching mine - apprehensive. They ran straight to Michael, covering him in hugs while I stood to the side watching this interaction for the first time.

In photos and videos Michael shared with me, I could see that the girls were tall, but having them in front of me I could now feel their height. They both towered over me, and when Sarah let go of her dad to hug me, I was lost in her stature.

"Hi Sarah!" Her hug, although quick, felt as though we met before. We broke our embrace and Evie stuck her arm out towards me.

"This is for you," she said while squinting her eyes in protection from the sun. I took hold of the business card she handed to me, but when I looked at it, I saw that it was not a business card at all. On the front read the words, "He fills my life with good things - Psalm 103:5." On the back of the card were handwritten words: "To Jennifer, From Evie + Sarah."

I couldn't hide my smile. I noticed a heart was drawn to replace the ordinary tittle I was used to seeing above the 'i' in my name. I ran my fingertips across the heart. "Thank you, Evie," I said gently, "this is really nice. I love it."

A female voice came from behind, "the girls picked that out themselves for you." It was the girls' mum. We had never spoken before, but I thought about her so often that I had to hold myself back from hugging her as though we were friends. She introduced herself to me and I did my best to mute my nerves as I did the same. From the moment Michael and I began to entertain the idea that we might be something more than Instagram pen-pals, the girls and their mum became permanent fixtures on my heart, as well as my prayer list.

Being a single mom of two children myself, I knew I was entering into sacred space. The protection of a mother is strong, fierce, and unwavering. I desperately wanted to tell her that I understood the desire to protect our young. I knew the unspoken code between mothers and I would always respect our common interest: her daughters. But I didn't say any of that. Instead, I followed the lead of Michael and his daughters, said goodbye to her, and got back into the car.

The car was loud with chatter; everyone's nerves seemed to be elevated, creating a buzz of our voices. We arrived at Michael's apartment; it was cozy with two small bedrooms, a bathroom, and the kitchen and living space blending into one room. The girls quickly occupied what appeared to be their usual placement on the sofa and I took that as my cue to present them with the gifts I brought.

The rest of our time during my visit was sweetly filled with pockets of awkward interactions as we learned how to be in each other's presence. They flooded me with stories and I could sense their nervousness as they spoke. I imagined myself in their position; despite their parents being apart since their toddler years, I understood that my presence could potentially generate fear, uncertainty, and resentment.

The only experience I had with divorce was spending every other Easter bored in church without my cousin, Katie, and being jealous of the kids at school who got two Christmases every year. I didn't know how to go about this, but I knew I wanted to make sure the girls felt comfortable *with* me. As well, I wanted them to feel seen and respected *by* me. I wanted them to know I understood my boundaries, I was sympathetic to their wonders, and I was willing to be as patient as necessary until they felt safe with me.

For weeks before meeting the girls, I begged God to pour wisdom onto me as I entered into this situation with zero knowledge of how to exist within it. This was my first time in their presence, but for so long, they had already occupied my heart.

Chapter 26

It was September 19th and Michael was returning to Los Angeles. I was on the phone with my cousin when she asked, "does it feel weird that Michael is flying in on the anniversary of the day Ryan left?"

September 19th is the most tender day on the calendar for me. Although it was not the day Ryan died, it was the day he left home, thus becoming the anniversary of the last time I saw him. In the three years since he died, my grief physically responded to this day. Fatigue would take over my body, weighing me down as I remembered watching him drive away. My movements were slower and my brain was foggier; over all, I felt empty. As expected, I felt it again that morning.

"It is weird, ya know? Like, I'm so excited to see Michael, but my body doesn't match that feeling."

I knew I was thrilled to see Michael; especially because he told me he had something planned for us in a couple days. As the day went on, I did my best to sift through the duality of happiness and grief. I didn't need anyone to drive me to the airport that evening, so I used the time to talk with God. I still couldn't see how this new relationship was going to work, but I had no doubt in my mind it would.

Then, Ryan appeared in my thoughts. I glanced at the time on my car's dash, it was 5:30pm. My mind flashed back to 5:30pm on that day three years ago. I was at work, finishing up with patients and preparing to begin my commute home unaware that I would be driving home to my husband for the last time. My mind flooded with images and I found myself caught up in memories when the traffic around my car began to move. I snapped back to my present surroundings and looked up just in time to see an airplane flying above me in preparation to land at the airport.

I exited the freeway and felt a rush of excitement as I thought about the much-needed hug I would be getting from Michael. Now familiar with where passengers would be entering into Los Angeles, I quickly found my waiting spot, and just as before, my heart fluttered when I saw him descend the airport escalator. His smile was unlike any I had ever seen. He nearly jumped over the people in front of him and wrapped me in a hug that could've suffocated a grown man. I studied his face as we waited for his luggage; he was beaming.

As we stood beside the seemingly endless rotation of suitcases and bags, I noticed something on the ground a couple of feet in front of me. I dropped my arm from Michael's waist and took a step forward. A smile quietly appeared on my face as I realized what it was: a penny. It wasn't shiny; it had clearly gone through many exchanges of hands, and within the minutes we had been standing there, several people stepped over it without notice.

It was there for me. A bit of heavenly communication to let me know that on the anniversary of the day love left my home, new love was being ushered in, and God was the composer of it all.

§

Michael was staying at my parents' house during this second visit. I was so grateful to them for not only opening up their home, but for opening their hearts and joining us in the belief that this wild love story was, in my dad's words, "ordained by someone above."

A week before he arrived, Michael told me to leave September 22nd open. He told me that he had plans for us and I needed to pack a bathing suit and my passport. 'Confused' doesn't begin to describe the bewilderment I felt at this request. Were we going to Canada for the day? Mexico? Why would I need my passport? Did he think I would need it to travel into another state? *'That must be it,'* I thought to myself, *'he must not realize that we can travel into any state in the country without a passport.'*

I knew we would be gone for the day and Michael arranged for Katie to come to my house and stay with the kids. The night before, Michael told me that he would be at my house at seven o'clock in the morning and we were to leave promptly at 8:30am.

I asked what I should plan to wear for the day and his response was, "I'll let you know in the morning."

My alarm went off at 5:30am, giving myself time to get ready for the day at a pace that didn't feel rushed. Michael arrived precisely at 7:00am; he greeted me with a hug and handed me a card.

He said, "when you open this, you'll find out where we're going."

I opened the envelope to find a card with one of my favorite scenes on the front: Hume Lake with two red Adirondack chairs facing the serene water bordered by large pine trees.

I looked at him in surprise, "we're going to Hume??"

I could feel my eyes burning with tears that were begging for release. I read his handwritten words as my heart nearly escaped my body. He was taking me back to Hume. The place where we first met. The landscape of God's creation that held a mixture of my emotions. His smile was hidden behind his phone as he captured my surprise on camera. Inside the card, he explained that I didn't need my bathing suit or my passport, which was news I was glad to hear. I was dressed in pajamas and a robe, and now that I knew where we were going, Michael instructed me to return upstairs to finish getting ready while he was going to make breakfast.

Amanda popped into my room as I was getting dressed. "Hi baby," I said as she entered. She woke up to the smell of bacon on the stove and asked if I knew where I was going that day. I told her and she gave me a sleepy smile as she watched me curl my hair.

I came downstairs to breakfast waiting for me, and soon it was time to leave. Brandon was still asleep, so I went upstairs to wake him up and let him know I was leaving and would be gone all day. He gave me a nod of acknowledgment and wrapped his limp arms around me as he said goodbye and then returned to his bed.

Amanda walked us to the car and as she headed back inside, I reminded her that Kiki (my kids' nickname for Katie) would be arriving later that morning. She disappeared into the house as I disappeared into the passenger seat of the Chevy Camaro Michael rented for the day.

"Ok, I need you to do something and you can't ask any questions." I stared at Michael as he said these words to me: "give me your phone."

"What? But what if the kids need me?"

"They know they can contact me if they need something."

I didn't move. My phone was sitting in my hands because I was reluctant to hand it over. Within a matter of seconds, I imagined my kids coming into a variety of dangers and being unable to reach me. Michael could see the worry on my face.

"It's ok, I promise. They know how to get me." With expectation, he held out his hand and I placed my phone in his open palm. I watched as he silenced my phone, opened the center console of the car and lowered my phone into its abyss. "Alright, let's go!"

With Hume Lake being four hours away, I settled in for a long car ride and fervently prayed that God would keep my children from needing me until I returned home that night.

§

When I was at Hume Lake in March, the weather was cold and there was snow on the ground; however, in mid-September, the air was warm and there was no evidence of a lingering winter. As we entered into the campground of Hume Lake Christian Camp, my heart fluttered with the familiarity of its natural beauty and the excitement of being here again with the man in the red jacket. We parked on the far side of the lake and as soon as I stepped out of the car, I could feel the magic of Hume entering my soul. I tried to soak in the majesty of the trees as best as I could, but even my eyes couldn't capture the power that stood over our small presence.

"Ready to walk around the lake with me?" His voice caused me to whip my head back down to earth and I turned to find him eagerly waiting to escort me on a walk. "We didn't get to do this last time we were here."

I grabbed his hand and we began the walk we didn't take six months earlier. We marveled at the splendor of the trees and the way the lake reflected the light of the sun.

"Here, stop and let me take a picture of you," he posed me in front of a clearing, telling me the lake was nothing in comparison to my beauty.

We laughed as we reminisced about our first meeting when I wouldn't dare look into his eyes nor engage him in conversation. We talked about all that has taken place since then and the many ways in which we have seen God at work. We continued our walk around the lake when he mentioned we had reservations for lunch and he was feeling the ache of hunger pangs. I marched forward in an attempt to pick up the pace, but for someone who was claiming to be starving, Michael wasn't keeping up with me.

Suddenly, he stepped in front of me, picked me up with ease, began walking the opposite direction and frantically said, "what does Lily do all day?"

Granted, we had been discussing my dog, but I didn't understand why that question would be reason enough to sweep me into his arms as though it were a romantic moment.

"What?"

"What does Lily do all day?" He was laughing as he asked and carried me further away from the trail that would lead us to the campground.

Bouncing with his steps as he continued to carry me, I answered, "lay around all day?"

After a few more steps, he placed my feet on the ground and instructed me to walk back towards the bridge we had already crossed. He was laughing, which caused a giggle to escape my lips, but I had no idea what was so funny.

"What are you doing?" I asked. He laughed.

Through wide eyes and contagious chuckling, the man in the red jacket directed me towards the edge of the lake.

"What just happened? What's so funny?"

He wasn't answering me. He only smiled, laughed, and then said, "let's sit down here and enjoy the view." As we sat and I continued to study his sudden bursts of laughter, he reached for his phone. "Let's read some scripture and pray together."

Side by side, we read Psalm 71, Psalm 62, and Psalm 100. I wrapped my arm through his, leaned my head against his shoulder and closed my eyes as he began to pray. I was lost in prayer and momentarily forgot we were sitting in the midst of God's beauty. When I opened my eyes, everything appeared more magnificent.

We began our walk back towards the campground and I was now aching to find some water, but our walk was interrupted when I noticed someone with a camera not-so-secretly tucked behind a tree. I squinted my eyes for a better look. It took me a few seconds to realize that Katie was the one behind the camera.

"What are you doing here??" She only smiled. "Who has my kids??" Another toothy grin. She wrapped me in a hug and I began to cry into her shoulder. I had an idea there was an agenda to this day, but I had no idea anyone else was involved. My heart nearly exploded inside my chest.

Once I collected my emotions, the man in the red jacket swiftly grabbed my hand and continued to lead me on our walk. As I tried to piece together when my cousin arrived at Hume, and wondered who had my children, I didn't realize what I was walking towards. I felt Michael tug on my hand and lead me off the trail. Every sound that I noticed before went quiet. I couldn't hear the wind. I didn't hear the birds. There was nothing but silence as I approached what was waiting for me.

It was the same clearing at which I stopped to marvel at God's beauty six months earlier. At the time, Katie took a photo of me as I stood at the edge of this rock. I didn't know she took that photo until we got home and she sent it to me. I shared it on social media with the caption circling around my thoughts about God's plans and His timing.

And here I was again. I could've never imagined that I would be standing in the same spot six months later, but this time, the view was much different. Instead of God's beauty, I was marveling at His faithfulness.

Through tears, I watched as Michael dropped to one knee as he took my hands into his.

"I love you so much. I'm so thankful for you and for this place where we met." As he spoke, my mind was flooding with memories of our first interaction.

Like a flashback scene in a movie, I could see him so clearly in that red jacket. I could feel the rush of the Spirit-led emotion that grabbed my attention when I first saw him. I could hear that nervous giggle when he first spoke to me and I could feel the shock in my soul that kept me from speaking to him. But this time, when he spoke, there was no trembling. There was no shakiness in my voice. There was only an overflowing gratitude for God's love coming through this man on bended knee.

"Would you like to be my wife?"

"Yes, I want to, yes!" I bent down to kiss him as the words fell out of my mouth.

He pulled a small red box out of the pocket of his shorts and revealed a brilliant diamond ring. As he placed it onto my finger, he said, "my beautiful Jennifer, I love you so much and I'm so happy you want to be my wife."

He stood to wrap me in his arms, and as soon as he pulled me into him, I sobbed with gratitude. Just as my eyes stopped crying, there was another surprise waiting for me.

From behind a rock popped up my children, and as they made their way to me with smiles on their faces, Brandon said, "did you say 'yes,' mama?"

I began to cry again. I grabbed him tightly and cried into his shoulder. Through sobs, I nodded in response to his question and I felt his arms hold me tighter.

As soon as he released his grip, my daughter approached me. I embraced her with all the energy I had left, and through more tears, I whispered to her, "thank you. For everything."

Once the emotions settled, I could take in what was surrounding me. It was a beautifully decorated scene made just for me. A large blanket was laid down, decorated with pillows reading the lyrics, *"a million dreams for the world we're gonna make"* from the popular song, "A Million Dreams." Flowers and a proper picnic complete with pink lemonade and a charcuterie arrangement adorned this space that was typically barren.

Michael wrapped me in his arms and directed my attention to a detail I hadn't yet noticed. In the middle of the beautiful setting was a photo of the very thing that connected me to Hume. The little brown church. The one Ryan discovered when he was assisting the Rough Fire years earlier. The one that made him think of me and the one I now connect to him. The one that bridged me to Hume from a distance, never knowing that one day my tragedy would lead to hope in the place that would intertwine my past and my future. And the only one to witness my prayer on the side of the mountain that I would allow God to take me anywhere.

Michael showed me another detail I hadn't yet seen: my ring. Inside the ring, Michael had it engraved to say, "The Lord is so good." Back in March, my cousin took a photo of me in front of a sign on Hume's property that read those exact words from Psalm 100, verse 5.

"When I think of Hume, I think of that photo and those words," he said. I studied the small inscription inside my ring. *"The Lord is so good."*

The rest of that verse reads, *"there is no end to his faithful love. We can trust him forever and ever."*

§

After the initial excitement settled, I found myself in the midst of storytelling as Michael's crew of helpers replayed their day to me, including what caused Michael make a quick u-turn on our journey.

"I organized for everyone to drive to the other side of the lake and setup a picnic on the rock you posted on Instagram back in March. When I stopped you for a photo, I was really trying to look over to the other side of the lake to see if they made it. I saw people, so I was happy we were all set to go. I couldn't see any sign of Katie, but I did notice a few people up on the road as we got closer, and I realized it was Amanda!!"

At this point everyone began laughing as Michael continued with his story, "she had two pillows under her arms and a bag of food in her hand. She saw me and realized it was us, and she panicked, but when she went back up the hill, she slipped and yelped! That's why I had to hurry up and turn you around and try to distract you!"

I was told the reason I couldn't have my phone was because Michael didn't want me to know the location of my children as they traveled with Katie to Hume to surprise me. To know how greatly he wanted to surprise me with my children being present meant more than I could express. I was overwhelmed with the love and attention that had been poured into this day.

Before leaving Hume, we stopped in front of the lake. The scene looked exactly as it did on the card Michael gave to me. I noticed the two red Adirondack chairs were unoccupied, so we sat and allowed gravity to pull us into the sloping backrest of the chairs.

"Do you feel loved?"

I glanced down at the ring on my finger. My hand seemed to sparkle as the sun made the diamond look as if it were composed of glitter. I leaned against him, resting my head on his shoulder. He kissed the top of my head.

"Very," I answered softly. "Thank you for making today so special. Thank you for loving me."

He kissed my head again. "It's the easiest thing I've ever done."

§

Ten days after our engagement, I was headed back to Northern Ireland but this time, I wasn't traveling alone. Brandon was curious about the country Michael called home but the peak of his curiosity were the two girls he would now call family.

Straight from the airport, we drove to the girls' home where we packed the three kids into the car and made our way to the North Coast for a mini-holiday. For the next six days, Michael and I watched as Brandon, Sarah and Evie transitioned from awkward behavior to being comfortable in each other's presence. Their laughter spilled over into every room of the house and by the time our trip was over, they were referring to each other as siblings.

On our last night in Northern Ireland, the girls returned home to their mother while Michael, Brandon and I returned to his apartment. We settled into the couch and decided on a movie to close out our night. I expected Brandon to sit beside me knowing his little body was getting tired and he would likely fall asleep against me. But he didn't. He sat next to Michael and as the movie played, I watched his body sink into relaxation against

Michael. I stared at the two of them. Seeing my son so comfortably affectionate with another man was beyond anything I could've imagined for him. Michael caught me staring at Brandon and when I looked at him, he glanced down at my thirteen-year-old son resting against him. He smiled and motioned for me to sit closer. I felt Michael kiss the top of my head as I nestled in close to him. When the movie ended, Brandon and I retreated to Michael's bedroom for the night while Michael prepared his bed on the couch. I stopped before disappearing into the hallway and turned towards Michael.

"Thank you for that," I whispered. He stopped arranging the pillows on the couch and looked up at me.

"For what?"

"For loving him, for making him feel safe, for just, everything," I mumbled. He walked around the couch and took me into his arms. Being held against him in a gesture of protection and care caused a deep exhale to escape my lungs. I felt most at ease whenever I was in his embrace. He kissed the top of my head again.

"It's the easiest thing I've ever done."

Chapter 27

May 9, 2019 (six weeks after we met)

Michael: *Why, after our chat this morning, does my life all of a sudden feel temporary until I'm with you. Every piece of my heart is yours. I'm ready for you, my love.*

May 15, 2019

Me: *I love you more than I'll ever be able to tell you…thankful I'll have a lifetime to try.*

Michael: *I'm speechless…we're getting married. Can't wait to see you walk toward me, the day you become my wee wife. I've never looked so forward to a day in all my life. I mean that with all my heart.*

May 22, 2019

Michael: *Such great fun on the phone earlier…how full does it make our hearts when we laugh together! I'm absolutely crazy about you! I feel so loved by you! I'm very thankful for that. You're an incredible human and I know I've said it many times before, I treasure that you're mine. I can't wait to have our wedding day in NYC! It's a dream come true.*

§

September 23, 2019

I woke in the morning and immediately held my left hand above my face. It hadn't been a dream. Staring back at me was the beautiful engagement ring Michael placed on my finger the day before. I admired its sparkle and the unique design of the ring itself. Set in rose gold, the center diamond was floating in a floral halo, surrounded by a dozen glittery diamonds. It had a vintage flair, which I loved, making the ring itself look incredibly romantic.

I reached for my phone to text Michael. Before sending a message, I re-read a text he sent the night before:

"as for the rose gold colour...it reminds me of copper. I love how copper is so resilient to water... water representing the storms of life and the colour being a strong indicator that together we can face those storms."

On the way home from Hume I complimented his ring choice; he answered, "well, you actually picked it." My mind flashed back to a morning with Katie and Felicia when they were asking hypothetical questions about the ring I would choose if I were to get engaged. With each ring I selected, they were secretly sending screenshots to Michael. I didn't remember seeing this particular ring, but apparently out of all the rings I liked, this was the one Michael felt best depicted our love.

Unique, romantic, eye-catching.

* ding *

"Good morning my beautiful fiancé"

I got lost in the admiration of my ring and forgot I was supposed to be texting my new fiancé to let him know I was awake.

"Good morning my love. I've been staring at my ring, it's so beautiful, thank you."

Knowing he was awake at my parents' house, I hurried to get ready and make my way over. When I arrived, he was in the kitchen with my parents and all three of them had big smiles on their faces when I walked through the door. My mom greeted me with a hug and promptly grabbed my hand to look at the ring. "Oh wow," she said, "it's beautiful! Great job, Michael!"

The day was full of excitement as we celebrated our engagement, sharing photos and video with my parents and describing the details of the day to them.

§

Months before our engagement, Michael and I dreamt about eloping in Central Park in New York City. We daydreamed about getting married in the middle of the romantic city and celebrating our 40th birthdays in the same week. We discussed our idea with all four children and decided we would elope at the end of October, then plan a wedding celebration with family and friends in February when Sarah and Evie could travel to California. With the six of us knowing our future plans, the only ones to be surprised was everyone else.

A week after our engagement, Michael was back in Northern Ireland and I was with my parents in their home. "So," I turned my body towards them, "Michael and I decided that we want to elope in New York next month."

I braced myself for the impact of questioning and judgment

that was bound to come my way. They said nothing, so I kept going in order to fill the awkward silence. "The green card process is long, so we want to get started on that and we have to be married first."

Michael and I decided he would make an attempt to relocate to the States, but we were equally settled on the decision that we would not stand in the way of God if He said 'no' during the process. We were in contact with an immigration lawyer who was walking us through the steps of Michael becoming a legal resident of the United States. While it's true that he advised we get married sooner rather than later, his advice was simply confirmation of what we were going to do anyway.

Adding a bit of legal jargon and immigration logic to our explanation seemed to land a little easier on the ears that would hear our announcement. To them, it made legal sense as to why we were hurrying to get married. But to us, it was just an excuse to appease the masses. Michael and I carried on with our plan to elope in NYC and I contacted a wedding planner who specialized in Central Park elopements. We looked over the packages offered, decided on a location within the park and put down a deposit.

"That's it!" I said as I placed my phone in my lap. "We're officially getting married!"

I ordered three potential wedding dresses from an online boutique and when they arrived, Amanda stood in the hallway outside of my bedroom, took photos of me in each dress, and helped me to decide in which gown I would become Mrs. Bolton.

I stared at the photos and asked Amanda for her opinion as

to which one she liked best. We both agreed on the same one, and I felt good about having her opinion on the dress I would wear. This was something shared between the two of us and I deeply cherished that memory being made. Being alone with Amanda as I tried on dresses in the privacy of our home, watching her study the photos she took of me in each dress, and hearing her voice tell me which one she liked and why, was more precious to me than I can explain. My daughter chose my wedding dress; something neither of us ever imagined her having to do.

§

I reflected back on a conversation Amanda and I shared after Michael's first visit to California. I came home after dropping him off at the airport to find her sitting on the couch buried in her phone. She didn't acknowledge me when I came in; she continued to focus on the screen in her hands.

"Hey!" I said in a cheerful effort to get her to meet my eyes.

"Hey." She didn't look up.

I sat down in front of her and examined her face as she continued to ignore my presence.

"What's going on? Why are you upset?" Her cheeks began to redden, letting me know she was on the verge of tears.

"Nothing."

I stared at her until she finally glanced up at me. As soon as our eyes met, hers filled with tears. I knew I needed to take charge of the conversation, even if it meant hearing something difficult.

"Is it Michael?"

"No," she answered as tears fell. "I mean, kinda, yeah."

"Tell me what's bothering you about him."

"It's not him, he's great. It's you."

My heart stalled. I wasn't expecting that answer.

"What do you mean?"

She burst into tears. "It's you. You love him more than you love dad or, like, you don't love dad anymore."

Of all the things I assumed she'd say, it wasn't that. I quickly ran through reasons why she might feel this way. I had been really affectionate with Michael and I imagined that seeing me with a man who wasn't her father could've led her to that assumption. I did laugh and giggle in Michael's presence more than she might've witnessed (or remembered) I did with her dad. Over all, I was happier than she had witnessed in almost three years. I felt my expression soften as I grabbed her hands and held them in mine. She was only fifteen years old and life had already revealed how cruel it could be sometimes. My heart ached for the loss of her innocence.

"Baby, I could never love Michael more than I love Daddy."

She closed her eyes as more tears fell. I squeezed her hands as I continued. "I love Daddy so much and I miss him every day. Michael won't ever take away the love I have for him."

She remained silent, but opened her eyes to look at me. "Baby, the love that Daddy and I shared was for who I was when I was with him. That's his love. That's only for Dad." She looked at me as I continued, "Michael can't touch that because the love he and I share is for who I am now and what I need today. And that's completely different than the love Daddy and I shared. I will *always* love Daddy."

I watched her body language and although the tears stopped,

I could see there was still something on her mind. She wouldn't look at me as she fidgeted with her hands. Her body told me she had something to say despite her mouth refusing to do so. I asked, "are you afraid to love Michael?"

She nodded.

"Are you afraid that by loving Michael, it means you don't love dad?"

She nodded again. I wrapped her in my arms. "Daddy will always be your dad, baby. Nobody will ever replace him. Just because he's not here doesn't mean he's not yours and it doesn't mean you stop loving him. Unfortunately for us, we have to live with the difficulty of enjoying one person while missing the other. It's really hard and I struggled with that idea, too."

"Was it hard for you to love Michael?"

"The idea of it was really hard. I couldn't imagine loving somebody else." I paused, silently asking God to help me with words. "You know, I couldn't imagine loving another baby after having you. I was actually afraid I wouldn't be able to love your brother when I was pregnant with him. I thought, 'there is no way I'm going to be able to love this baby the same way I love Amanda.'" She laughed at the idea. "But the minute he was born, it was like my heart opened up or something and it was so easy to love him without taking love away from you. I loved you both equally, but, differently. I love you for who you are, and I love him for who he is."

She smiled and nodded, understanding that loving someone new doesn't replace the love that was there first. I kissed her forehead and released her back to her phone. I walked away knowing this would be the first of many conversations, many transitions and new feelings, and I prayed we would get through them all.

§

** ding! **

My phone alerted me of a text from Amy: "Hey, can I stop by?"

I was on my way to a nail appointment as I was getting ready for my upcoming trip to NYC. I hadn't shared with anyone other than my family and a handful of close friends that Michael and I were planning to elope. Despite keeping this information relatively close, I knew exactly why Amy wanted to stop by my house. Of the friends who knew about our plan to elope, a few went to church with me and were friends with Amy.

I responded that she could come by, but I had an appointment scheduled that would require this to be a quick visit. Minutes later, she appeared on my doorstep and I met her outside on the porch. We sat on the steps leading up to my front door and I avoided eye contact with her.

After some uncomfortable small talk, Amy's voice filled the space between us: "I'm concerned that you may be confused about salvation." She was referring to a post I shared on social media about Ryan being in heaven with his dad, Ralph. I felt my spirit rise in anger and defense, but I said nothing. She warned me about misleading those who follow my social media. I nodded for the sake of polite acknowledgment, knowing I wasn't going to change a thing about my post. As with dating, the church was known for believing they are the "one true church" and anyone outside of their organization was not a true Christian, thus making my claim that Ryan and his father were with God blaspheme according to their doctrine.

She managed to segue from that topic into her concerns that Michael "may not be a true Christian." I stared straight ahead as she continued her argument. "We just don't know where his heart really is, there are so many people who claim to be Christians, but really aren't."

"Amy, how can we really know that about anybody?"

"Well, if you were to date in the singles' ministry, we know that those men have been through a complete bible study and..."

I interrupted her. "Just because someone goes through a bible study doesn't mean their heart is right with God. I wouldn't call half the men in church Christians, and they went through the same studies."

She stammered for words. "Well, we don't know where Michael is with God, and..."

I interrupted her. "Michael was brought up with a rough past. He's made the same mistakes we've all made. He chose to change his lifestyle; he chose to live differently and walk with God, just like we all have. If that isn't evidence of a heart for God, then what is?"

I turned to look at her and watched as she lowered her eyes. I had been growing weary of these conversations and the assumptions being made by a self-righteous doctrine. The air fell silent. There was nothing left to say; I wasn't going to change my mind and she wasn't going to accept my decision.

Acknowledging the time and my upcoming appointment, I stood to usher Amy off my porch and into her car. We hugged, and I squeezed a bit tighter before letting go because I knew our friendship would never be the same. She was the one who brought me to church, the one who introduced me to God, and I had to wonder if she regretted being the one to place a bible in my hands.

§

The days carried on and before I knew it Sunday, October 27th was upon me. I was scheduled to take a red-eye flight to New York the following night, arriving the day before our wedding. I was hurrying to my car after assisting in the kids' class at church that morning. I saw Sandra walking my direction. She smiled brightly and waved when we made eye contact.

"Hey Jenn!" I continued walking towards the parking lot and Sandra changed her steps to walk alongside me. "I was wondering if we could get some time together this week?"

I wasn't a fool. I knew that despite not telling her about my plans in New York this week, she knew about them. After all, words travel fast in church community.

"I'm actually going to be in New York, I leave tomorrow night."

"New York! How fun! Just to go? Or..." her words trailed off as we walked.

"I'm going with my cousin; my 40th birthday is this week." It was true. I was flying to New York with my cousin and I would be celebrating my 40th birthday while there.

"Great! Well, maybe when you get back. I'd love to talk with you about your relationship and your spiritual future."

I kept walking, but felt my heart stop. My spiritual future? I already noticed that I had been pushed out of a bible study I was in with Amy and a few other women. I learned about it when the potential new church-disciple caught me one Sunday and asked if I would be at her bible study that week. When I told her I didn't know anything about it, she looked surprised and showed me the group text confirming the date and time. It was a new group chat, and I had been left out of it.

I also noticed that in the kids' Sunday school class of which I had been teaching for years, I was given an 'assistants' role - no longer teaching, no longer doing crafts. The new teacher informed me that she was 'happy to do everything,' leaving me to do nothing but observe.

The messages from the pulpit felt oddly pointed in my direction, so much so that a friend sent a text during church one Sunday: "is this about you?" On a different Sunday, a friend suggested they add my name to the sermon. I was told from friends inside the leadership meetings that people were being encouraged to discourage others from spending too much time with me. The church was making it very clear they would not tolerate my decision making, and if they couldn't keep me quiet, they would silence me from the pulpit.

But it wasn't just me receiving this isolated treatment. During Michael's first visit to California, he excitedly went to church with me, Amanda and Brandon. He knew how much I loved my church family, but he didn't know about the conversations that had been taking place before his arrival. I didn't want to tell him. I didn't want him to feel judged before stepping foot in their building. Instead, he experienced their judgment firsthand. I watched as Daniel ignored him. I saw Amy's disappointment as she greeted me and then reluctantly introduced herself to Michael. An event took place a few days later at which several people from church were attending, and I again, watched as Michael was intentionally avoided by several men who said hello to me and walked past Michael without acknowledgment. Despite that treatment, Michael was willing to try again. He attended the church in Belfast at the request of Daniel and others, where he was immediately questioned about his Christianity. He attended a second time, and a third time when I went with him during my visit to Northern Ireland. We were questioned about our relationship status while there and when I stated we were, in fact, a couple, I was met with, "oh. But I thought he's not a disciple?" I told Michael to never go back.

The church that once told me to trust God now considered me a danger to their congregants for doing that very thing. The people that once praised my faith and used it as an example of obedience now rebuked it and deemed it rebellion. The leaders who told us that God could do anything were now trying to deny the very thing He was doing, all because it didn't line up with their gospel.

I didn't stop walking as I answered Sandra, "yeah, sure," knowing that meeting was never going to happen.

As I drove away from the church parking lot, I knew it would be one of the last times I would be there. I had outgrown my religious 'home.' The church had become a place for my social engagement rather than a sanctuary for my spiritual growth. I had known this time was coming. For so long I had one foot out the door, but I had no idea the other foot would be pushed out by rejection of the faith they once praised me for having.

I felt my heart break as I kept driving. It wasn't the people I disliked. I loved Amy and Daniel dearly; they were a witness to so much in my life for almost two decades. I really enjoyed Sandra; she was fun and being in her presence made me feel loved. There were many within the congregation I had grown to love over the years, and I'll be the first to say that when Ryan died, the church served my family with great love and care. It wasn't actually the people that hurt me, it was their doctrine.

In reality, it wasn't even their fault. Like thousands of others who belong to the organization, they were victims of an unhealthy doctrine. They were doing everything they were taught and told. They were doing what they believed was right. They believed a doctrine created by a man whose moral authority was questionable, and that doctrine was then pushed into the minds of thousands. I was part of it for so long that I understood their blind obedience and felt sympathy for their entrapment. They hadn't learned how to see outside of the legalistic boundaries that had been created; therefore, it robbed them of true freedom in Christ. They were trained to see and do things one way, stripping them of the chance to witness so many miracles outside of their congregation. They built their own box in which they tried to contain God, keeping them from experiencing His true power and sovereignty.

For eighteen years I had been part of that, too. But not anymore. My spiritual future was not up for discussion because the church would no longer be part of it.

§

It was Monday morning and I was leaving for New York that night. After dropping the kids off at school, I ran out to pick up some last-minute items when I felt emotionally paralyzed while sitting in my parked car. I was frozen. I stared out the windshield as I tried to understand what was happening within me. It wasn't the jittery butterflies of excitement one would expect two days before she was to be married. It was heavier. My mind felt foggy and my thoughts were displaced. The longer I sat, the more I recognized this feeling.

"I need to grieve Ryan," I said to myself. I had been grieving Ryan since before he died when I first went through the Grief Recovery Method with Sharon facilitating my healing. I grieved the years Ryan and I lost due to hardship and separation, and I had been consistently grieving him in the three years since he was killed. I pulled out my phone and opened the 'notes' app.

"Dear Ryan," my fingers flew across the touchscreen keyboard as I poured my grieving heart into the words I wish I could've said to him. It was full of apologies for things I didn't realize until he was gone and filled with forgiveness for the moments that created insecurity. Emotion was pouring out of me that I didn't know I had been holding onto in the midst of the excitement of new life. I needed to say goodbye, again.

"...this feels so final, as if I'm being forced to recognize that you're never coming back. ... None of this would be happening if you were still here. ... I wouldn't have to look in the eyes of our children and wonder if I'm making the right decisions for them. ... I wouldn't have to find a new routine, a new normal, a new life, if you were still here. ... I will

never stop loving you. You are the reason I am who I am. ... The one who loved me first. The one who unintentionally taught me how to be a woman. The one who prepared me for this next stage in life. ... Please forgive me for moving forward. Please forgive me for falling in love when I vowed to you that I would never love another. Ryan, I will love you forever. Each day I hope I make decisions that would please you. ... This next stage of life is waiting for me. ... I love you more than you could ever know."

I drove to Felicia's house, sat in her presence, read my letter to Ryan out loud and let the emotions consume me. I sobbed for everything I couldn't express. I cried for everything that had changed. I mourned everything that was lost and I wept for everything that was new.

It was the release I didn't know I needed. Once my crying and my breathing slowed, I looked up to find Felicia watching me intently. She had been a firsthand witness to every moment I experienced in the three years since Ryan died. She sat with me countless times watching me grieve; she brought meals to my house to make sure I ate. One week after I met Michael, she sat in a park with me as I cried in fear over the awakening of my heart. She defended me to those who argued I was not following God correctly. She was getting on a plane tomorrow to meet me in New York and stand beside me as I married the man in the red jacket. And here she was again, being what I needed when I didn't know what had been necessary. Her eyes were drenched in tears like mine.

She hugged me, holding me as tight as possible until she felt my body rest. With a heavy sigh, I released our embrace and wiped my eyes. I smiled at her as I felt the invisible weight lift from my heart.

"I didn't know I needed to do that work but it makes sense," I admitted. Despite knowing how in love I had fallen with Michael and how divinely this had been arranged by God, it didn't erase the fact that none of this would be happening if Ryan were alive.

Chapter 28

Oh my gosh, we're going!" My cousin's eyebrows raised into perfect arches, her words were said through her smile, and her hands found a way to my body in a transfer of her energetic buzz onto me. She grabbed my leg and squeezed with so much excitement it caused me to jump in my seat. It was almost 11pm and we were settling into our seats on the airplane taking us to NYC. Katie was seated in between myself and her husband, Johnny, and if anybody walked by our row, it would be easy to assume that she was the one preparing to get married. I smiled back at her with tired eyes and when she turned towards her husband, I opened my phone to text the man in the red jacket.

"Getting ready to take off babe! I'll meet you in New York!"

As soon as I felt the vibration of the roaring engines, I turned off my phone, grabbed my cousin's hand, closed my eyes and prayed. My mind raced in conversation with God: praying for safety, our time in New York, the plans we made, His protection during our trip, and our marriage.

It wasn't long after take-off that I saw my cousin nestle into her husband and she drifted easily into sleep. I couldn't sleep. I tried my hardest. *"Go to sleep, Jenn. You need sleep,"* I tried to talk myself into slumber. It didn't work. I dozed in and out of consciousness during the five-hour flight, but my nerves wouldn't stay quiet long enough to give me peaceful rest. Instead, I continuously checked the flight route, wishing the pilots would increase the speed of their plane.

§

From the backseat of our driver's car, Katie's hand landed on my shoulder as she exclaimed again, "oh my gosh, we're here!" It was just after eight o'clock in the morning and we were on our way to the hotel. My stomach felt as though it were housing a thousand butterflies; my body was shaky as my bones seemed to vibrate against my skin.

We arrived at the hotel hoping by some miracle our rooms would be ready; however, being so early in the morning, the three of us were asked to checked our luggage with the bellhop instead. We happily obliged and stepped into the crisp autumn air of New York City. First on the agenda: breakfast at Rue 57 on Sixth Avenue. I replaced the butterflies in my stomach with a plate of French toast and allowed social media to see that my cousin and I were starting my 40th birthday week with mimosas.

Michael wasn't due to arrive in New York for a few more hours, so the three of us squeezed in as many sightseeing stops as possible. When the hotel receptionist called to let us know our rooms were ready, we hurriedly walked back, and I was hoping to take a quick nap before Michael arrived. As I was handed my room key, I asked the receptionist if a box of flowers had been delivered for me.

"I believe so, allow me to check."

The receptionist reappeared with a large box. "Perfect. It's my wedding bouquet," I revealed to her. I couldn't believe the thrill I felt when saying the words, 'my wedding.' It was surreal.

"How exciting! Congratulations!" Just as I thanked her, my phone alerted me of a text message.

"Hi my beautiful princess. Just landed! Hope you're having a good day. Can't wait to see you xx"

So much for that nap I needed. I quickly answered his text, then turned to my cousin with a burst of energy: "he landed!" The butterflies returned to my stomach as we ascended the floors of the hotel, first stopping at the room I would share with Michael. I took several items out of my suitcase and handed them to Katie. I wasn't going to be sharing a room with Michael that night; I would be staying with Katie and her husband in their room until I officially became Mrs. Bolton. She helped to unpack my bag, unbox my bouquet and Michael's boutonniere, and make sure I had everything I needed before leaving the room to Michael when he arrived.

As she admired my wedding bouquet, I walked to the large window on the opposite side of the room. The city was covered in a light fog, creating a dreamy mist over the trees in Central Park. The trees were full and beginning to change from lush green into vibrant shades of orange, red, and yellow. I took a photo and sent it to Michael with a text, "the view from our room babe. And! Our room number is 3902 - the two of us are 39!"

I smiled at this sweet little nod from God. At the time of our wedding, Michael and I would both be 39 years old with each of us turning forty a couple days after becoming husband and wife.

From there, Katie, Johnny and I made our way to their room where I promptly hung up my dress and made myself at home in their space. There was only one bed, so my cousin called for a cot to be delivered and that is where I'd be sleeping the night before my wedding.

* *ding!* *

"I'll be 15 mins. Are you in the lobby or the room?"

"I'll meet you in the lobby babe, you need a key for the elevator."

Ten minutes later I was seated on a couch in the lobby watching the revolving door in the same way I'd watch the Terminal 2 escalator in the Los Angeles airport.

He walked through the door and I felt my heart jump. He was wearing blue jeans, a dark blue sweater and a jacket that accentuated his broad shoulders. His face lit up when he saw me. I stood to receive his embrace, balancing on the tips of my toes so he didn't have to bend too low to reach my lips.

"Well babe, ready to get married?" His smile filled his face as his voice filled the small lobby.

"I wish it was already tomorrow," I said as I skipped towards the elevator.

§

After dropping Michael's luggage in our room, the four of us took our excitement for a walk through Central Park. Earlier that morning I received a text from our wedding coordinator, Valerie. Due to a possibility of rain, she suggested we move from the original location in the park we chose for the wedding to West Drive Boat Landing.

"I love the Boat Landing idea. Let's plan on being there instead. I'm sure Michael will love it as well."

As we walked through the stunning fall foliage of Central Park, I told Michael about the change in location.

"Honestly babe, whatever you want. I'll marry you anywhere."

The four of us continued our walk, stopping to take pictures in an effort to capture the magnificence of color surrounding us. As we approached Bethesda Fountain, we stopped in front of the Terrace to discuss where we would like to have dinner. I left the conversation when I heard a familiar song being sung by a man and a woman inside the echoic open-air halls of the terrace.

"Babe. Listen."

"...all of my doubt suddenly goes away somehow..." the woman's voice filled my ears, and then a man's voice joined her, *"...one step closer...I have died every day waiting for you..."*

It was our wedding song, "A Thousand Years." During my most recent visit to Northern Ireland, Michael and I were discussing a wedding song during our drive to the coast. We began going through several well-known love songs when "A Thousand Years" began playing. We both fell silent. Despite hearing the song countless times over the years, I hadn't really contemplated the lyrics. Michael was driving, but as the song played, I looked over to find him wiping a tear from his eye. I paid attention to the lyrics being sung around that moment: *"...I will be brave, I will not let anything take away what's standing in front of me, every breath, every hour has come to this..."*

He caught me looking at him and gave me an embarrassed grin.

"I have goosebumps," I said. "I think this is our song."

Michael nodded in agreement, "it's a great song. It's perfect."

Now, in Central Park, goosebumps covered my body beneath the warm layers of coat and sweater. As though a magnetic force was pulling us toward the terrace halls, Michael and I walked in the direction of their voices. Throughout the entirety of the song, I felt warmth rush through my body. *"I feel you, God,"* I thought to myself. *"I know you're here."*

We eventually made our way to dinner, and just as every bride most likely *doesn't* do, I ordered a giant plate of baked ziti pasta after chowing down on the warm rolls first brought to the table. Like the dream feedings moms give to their babies to ensure they sleep through the night, I sleepily ate my way through heavy carbohydrates with the same hope in mind.

A couple of hours after dinner, we received a text that Will and Felicia arrived and were checked into the hotel. We met them in the hotel bar and I tried my best to stay awake as the six of us sat in disbelief that we were in New York together. As the night came to a close, Michael kissed me goodnight to the background serenade of whistles coming from the now delirious group of friends surrounding us. I giggled in youthful embarrassment and made my way into the elevator with Katie and Johnny.

I forgot about the cot I would be sleeping on until I walked into the room ready to collapse into deep slumber. The bread, pasta, and wine did the trick and I was ready to sleep. I quickly got ready for bed and crawled onto the cot that held my pillow at eye-level to the bottom of their luxurious king-size bed. I reached for my phone to make sure my alarm was set for the morning. But instead of my alarm, I checked the email notification waiting for me. It was from the wedding coordinator.

"Hi Jennifer, if you get a chance before tomorrow, please send me a copy of your vows so we can get them printed for you."

I quickly sat up, the squeak of the cot's legs announcing my rapid movement. I opened the notes app on my phone and began to type. My cousin finished getting ready for bed and walked out to find me in the dark, my face lit up by the light coming from the screen in my hands.

She whispered, "what are you doing?"

I glanced up at her, "writing my vows."

"What? Right now?"

I nodded and returned my focus to the screen.

"Do you need me to help with anything?"

I shook my head but didn't answer out of fear that pausing to verbally decline her offer would interrupt the thoughts from my heart being sent to my head. It didn't take long for me to write my vows. Everything that came through my fingertips was a direct translation from my heart.

I turned off my phone, closed my eyes, and when I opened them again it was my wedding day.

Chapter 29

October 30th, 2019

7:09 am

G*ood morning my love"*

I had been awake for an hour, trying to get ready as quietly as I could while Katie and Johnny were still sleeping. While all of us slept, Mahal was on a red-eye flight from Los Angeles to New York and I expected her to arrive at the hotel any moment.

"Good morning my husband to be!"

"How are you baby? I can't wait to marry you today"

"I'm great!! Mahal is almost here so I'm going downstairs to meet her and have some coffee. Do you want a coffee? I can send Mahal with something for you."

Despite our entire relationship being anything but traditional, I was keeping to the tradition of not seeing each other prior to the wedding ceremony. Mahal happily delivered a latte and a croissant to Michael on my behalf and I was grateful for her willingness to act as room service immediately upon arrival.

Our wedding was scheduled for four o'clock in the afternoon, giving us plenty of time to sit down for a decent brunch without having to rush through eating. The girls and I visited while getting ready, looking up restaurants within walking distance that were known for having a good brunch. We stepped out in the city full of chatter, smiles, and empty stomachs. We walked several blocks towards a restaurant whose breakfast reviews were all the rage, but when we entered into the establishment, we quickly decided that although its pancakes may have been the best of Midtown East, it wasn't the kind of place that was going to serve the mimosas and avocado toast we imagined having. We began our trek back towards the direction of the hotel while searching for another restaurant appropriate for a bridal brunch.

"Sarabeth's? It looks like it has good reviews."

The four of us found ourselves in fits of laughter as we approached Sarabeth's and realized it was next door to our hotel. Not a block away from the hotel; not even a couple doors down. It was directly next door to the hotel. We were quickly seated and with only an hour left to eat before the hair and make-up artist was to arrive, we promptly ordered. With mimosas in hand, we raised them in a toast to the future Mr. and Mrs. Bolton.

§

"Ruby is downstairs"

It was a text from Valerie, the wedding coordinator. "Shoot, the hair and makeup girl is already there, we need to go," I announced to the table as I quickly replied to her text.

"I'm on my way now! I'm right next door to the hotel."

We each snuck one last bite and one last drink before rushing out of the restaurant and into the hotel lobby. Ruby was sweet and she followed us into my cousin's room. I changed out of my clothes into the silky white robe I purchased for myself with the word "bride" adorned with rhinestones on the back.

As Ruby began to work on my hair, there was a knock at the door which elicited a flutter of noise from my three friends. It was Johnny. Michael had given him the task of delivering a card to me as I got ready.

"Ahem, this is for you," Johnny said as he placed the card in my hands with dramatic flair.

I giggled at his performance and thanked him for the delivery. Inside the envelope was a delicately crafted card with our names and wedding date cut out amongst a filigree design. Ruby had already done my makeup, but as soon as I opened the card to find Michael's handwritten words, I feared she might have to redo the areas touched by my tears.

With my back to the room, I couldn't see, but I could hear, the buzz of the girls getting themselves ready for the wedding. My heart was full, nearly at capacity, and I was filled with immense joy. It was deeper than happiness. It was profound and internal- something I once believed I would never feel again and something I didn't want to forget feeling in that moment.

Ruby announced that she was done with her work and placed a mirror in my hands so I could see the finished product. I forced a smile. My hair looked nothing like I hoped it would despite explaining my vision to her and my lips were colored in a frosted pink I'm sure hadn't been seen in public since 1988. Ruby's services were part of the elopement package and I did not get to choose who would be doing my hair and makeup. I was at the mercy of whomever the coordinator chose for me. I could see that Ruby was proud of her work and I was not about to take that delight away from her.

I thanked her for making me feel special and headed into the bathroom as she packed up her things and left our room. As soon as I heard the door close, I came out of hiding, looked at my cousin, pointed to my hair and said, "fix this."

Katie promptly took the position of a hairstylist. She removed a large number of bobby pins Ruby placed throughout my hair and lightly brushed through the tight, crunchy curls trying her best to create the soft boho-chic hair I originally envisioned.

It was three o'clock; the wedding coordinator would be arriving in twenty minutes to take me to the ceremony site. Katie perfected my hair and gave me the look I had been hoping to achieve. I wiped the pink lipstick from my lips and put on a gloss that enhanced my natural lip color. I slipped into my dress and Katie fastened my mom's diamond necklace around my neck.

I reached for my bouquet, which was a colorful arrangement of peach, orange, and white flowers and laid it on the table that previously acted as Ruby's makeshift salon. Around the stems and over the ribbon already in place, I tied another ribbon. I ran the silky material through my fingers and tenderly touched the knot holding it in place. It was once white, but it was now an aged cream color. I smiled softly at the memory this ribbon brought to me; it was the ribbon tied around the bouquet I carried the day I married Ryan.

§

"Ok, we gotta go," Katie said as she ushered Felicia and Mahal towards the door.

Before handing my phone to them, I sent a text to the coordinator: "I won't have my phone with me, my girls are leaving to the lobby now. Call my room and I'll come down since you need a key to use the elevator." She responded that she would be arriving in five minutes. With that, I hugged each of my girls and thanked God for their presence in my life.

The room was instantly quiet. There was no longer the sound of laughter, the murmur of conversation or the noise of four women getting ready for a wedding. It was just me. I didn't even have the distraction of my phone to pull me away from the silence.

I walked towards the window overlooking Central Park. The view was breathtaking, but that wasn't what took my breath away as I looked out at the colorful trees below. Somewhere in the middle of the park, Michael was waiting for me. I involuntarily gasped as I envisioned him waiting to begin our future.

"God," I began to pray, *"thank you. I am in absolute awe of what You can do. I can't believe I'm getting ready to marry Michael. Thank you for choosing him for me. Thank you for the love you've put in our hearts for each other."* I felt myself beginning to get emotional. *"I didn't know this was possible. I didn't know what my future looked like, but You did. Thank you for being so faithful. Thank you for bringing me here to this very moment. Please don't leave me. Please protect what You have brought together. Cover us in Your protection and allow us to share of Your goodness."* I paused, and with a chuckle, I continued, *"I can't believe You didn't drop me a penny today. Can't*

say I'm not disappointed." I giggled.

I was brought back to the surroundings of my cousin's hotel room when there was a knock at the door. Assuming it was Valerie, I opened the door without first checking the peep-hole.

She gasped, "oh, you are beautiful! Are you ready to go?"

"Yes, yes, let me just grab my flowers." I had nothing more to bring with me. We walked quickly down the hall and waited to see which of the three elevators would open for us. It was the middle one. On our way down from the 45th floor we made small talk about the traffic and the preparation that was taking place for the upcoming New York City Marathon.

As we reached the lobby level, Valerie asked again, "are you ready?" I felt the elevator park itself and Valerie's exit seemed to challenge the door's slow opening. She stepped out ahead of me and I moved to follow behind her.

"Wait!" I shouted.

My eye was drawn to something resting just beyond the elevator threshold. Valerie stepped right over it. I bent down, my body blocking other hotel patrons from entering the elevator. I heard Valerie's footsteps stop. I felt the pressure of an annoyed group trying to brush past me. I didn't care. I picked it up and held it tightly in the palm of my hand.

It was a penny.

Valerie asked if I was okay and reminded me that we needed to hurry. I nodded to signal that I was okay and I picked up my pace as I followed her to the revolving door.

Once in the car, I opened my hand which had become damp as a result of the grip I was keeping on the penny. I stared at it while trying to process everything this copper-colored love note meant to me. Pennies had become my communication with God; they were the voice I needed to hear in the storm and the confirmation I needed to receive in the quiet. I looked at the year on the penny: 2016. The year Ryan died. The year my life became unrecognizable. The year I learned how to lean into God, how to listen for His voice, and how to surrender to His will. As the car continued towards Central Park, I could feel God's presence with me. An overwhelming sense of peace coursed through my veins. I was exactly where I was supposed to be and He was with me now as He had been all along.

Valerie was feverishly texting on her phone while giving me updates about our arrival time. I wasn't listening. I tucked the penny into the ribbon of my bouquet and quietly thanked God for letting me know He was near. *'A nod from God,'* I whispered to myself.

The car pulled up to our stop. Valerie, again, asked, "are you ready?"

I opened the car door and stepped out onto Central Park West and West 72nd Street. I held the bouquet in my right hand, feeling the shape of the penny beneath my thumb.

"Yeah," I answered, "we're ready."

Chapter 30

The sky was gray, making the park explode with colors of autumn. As soon as I exited the car, I heard gentle gasps coming from those passing by. Valerie quickly circled around me, making sure my dress was straight. I heard her calling someone on her phone, "she's on her way." She began to walk briskly and I did well to maintain her pace as we approached the area of the ceremony. She stopped abruptly when she turned to face me, "ok we're here. Are you ready?"

"Oh, like, right now? We're here?"

"Yeah, he is waiting for you, are you ready?"

My heart was still racing from the brisk walk into the park, but now I felt my pulse increase as I stood still. Valerie was standing ahead of me; her smile let me know that she could see everyone was in position waiting to receive me. I was hidden behind wispy trees and large shrubbery. The only one visible to me was Valerie, but I could hear Michael's muffled voice coming from behind the greenery.

My legs were begging me to move. I took a step towards the opening that would lead me to Michael, then another, and another. The path opened and I saw my closest friends waiting for me. They were standing to the side of an aisle shaped with rose petals that was created for my arrival. The smiles on their faces elevated my joy, but I looked beyond them in an effort to see Michael. I couldn't see him as I began my walk, but as I continued down the curved path towards the lakeside gazebo, he appeared, and I picked up my pace.

"Oh wow," I heard him say.

My pace bordered on the edge of a power walk and I arrived in front of Michael before the violinist had a chance to finish the first thirty seconds of our wedding song. Thirty seconds, possibly less. That's how long it took me to walk down the floral-laced aisle that likely took several minutes to create.

As with the hair and makeup artist, I did not know ahead of time who would be officiating our wedding. A woman was standing to the right of Michael, waiting to bring us together as husband and wife. I noticed her for only a moment as I approached. My eyes were focused on the Irishman standing in front of me; he was wearing a dark blue suit, accented with a light blue shirt and a softly colored gold tie. He was devastatingly handsome; I watched his eyes dance across my face with a smile that appeared to translate every thought in his mind. I was lost in my own thoughts when a woman's voice brought me back to earth.

"Family and friends, it means the world to both Jennifer and Michael that you're here..." her accent was unfamiliar to me and when I turned to face her, I noticed her beautiful features and effortless smile. "...if you all agree to love and support Jennifer and Michael in marriage now and forevermore, please say 'we will.'"

Instantly I heard the voices of Katie, Felicia, Mahal, Johnny and Will: "we will!!"

The officiant, Elisabeth, brought Michael and I close to her. As she began to speak, I turned my attention towards her, but I could feel that Michael's attention was entirely on me. I glanced up to find him radiating with adoration as he stared in my direction. Elisabeth's voice continued on in the background, "you've come to one of the most romantic places in all the world, New York City! You're a couple who likes to do things their own way."

Giggles erupted from all of us.

"Now, they do say that coincidences are God's way of staying anonymous, and there was no doubt that God had something in store for the two of you. Nothing, not even the distance, could stop this love from blossoming."

As Elisabeth began to read from the book of Psalms, Michael grabbed my hands, refusing to take his eyes off me.

"Jennifer, do you always promise to enjoy the night sky and continue to travel with Michael and love each other for the rest of your life?"

"I do."

"Jennifer, do you take Michael to be your lawful husband? Do you promise to love, honor, and care for him with tenderness and affection for the rest of your life?"

Holding back tears while looking at Michael, I answered softly, "I do."

Elisabeth asked Michael the same questions to which he proclaimed, "I do!"

"Ladies and gentlemen, come close as Michael and Jennifer

will read their vows to each other." Elisabeth handed me a printed version of the vows I emailed the night before. I felt myself take a deep breath as I prepared to read my promise to Michael. Still holding my left hand, Michael gently squeezed it to encourage me as I began to speak.

"Michael, you are proof that God listens to our hearts more than he listens to our words. I prayed for you only once, but quietly hoped for you every day. ... God has used the heartache of our past to orchestrate the beginning of our future."

My vows were full of promises to keep God at the center of our marriage and appreciate what has been given to me through taking Michael as my husband. I promised more than my heart to him. I promised to rise up for our children and be a place of safety for each of them. I promised to respect his ideas, chase our dreams, and be his companion in every moment. More importantly than all, I promised to see him through the lens of God's love for him.

"I make these vows to you today, as we begin our lives together. These are promises made in love, kept by faith, and will be honored by me all the days of my life."

I was surprised that not a single tear fell from my eyes as I read the translation of my heart out loud. I could see that despite my eyes not releasing any tears, Michael's eyes were ready to surrender what he had been holding in. He leaned in to kiss me, and with a giggle, I backed away while playfully saying, "you can't kiss me yet!" Laughter filled the gazebo as everyone watched Michael try to kiss his bride.

Elisabeth handed Michael his printed vows. His emotion

was caught in his throat as he tried to read his vows to me. I reached for his hand and held it in both of mine.

He cleared his throat in an effort to push his tears away from the surface.

"From this day, before God," his accented voice cracked, "I take you, my beautiful Jennifer, to be my wife."

I sighed as I caressed the back of his hand.

"I promise to love you, to lead you and to protect you. To honor you and our children, to respect your past, support your dreams and encourage you as you strive to fulfill the desires of your heart."

I didn't take my eyes off him. I was lost in every syllable of his carefully written vows. I studied his eyes as he stared into mine with devotion. He gave me promises of love and loyalty, along with the vow to stand beside me as we walked through life together.

"I'm honored to have you in my life. Praise God for all He has done."

Upon hearing the end of his vows, I understood his urge to kiss me as I had to hold myself back from reaching up and placing my lips on his.

Elisabeth's perfect timing distracted me from the desire to kiss the man in front of me when she asked for the rings which Johnny had been holding. As Michael placed the delicate wedding band on my finger, he said, "Jennifer, please take this ring and wear it every day to remind you of this moment and how much I love you."

The words Michael said to me were echoed by my voice as

I placed the ring on his finger. Elisabeth reappeared beside us, "on behalf of all your loved ones, we wish for you a love that's powerful and rich enough to inspire others."

We held each other's hands tightly and Elisabeth's voice filled the space between us when she said, "as long as the two of you keep holding hands and remain a team, everything you wish for can be realized."

Elisabeth closed our wedding ceremony reminding us of the covenant we were entering into together. She stepped aside but her voice carried as she loudly announced, "by the power vested in me, I may now pronounce you husband and wife! Michael, **now** you can kiss your bride!"

Cheers erupted into the air, the violinist picked up where I forced him to leave off, and rose petals were tossed around us as Michael wrapped me in his arms, held the back of my head and lowered me into a romantic kiss.

The world slipped away from me. I heard nothing. The only presence I felt was Michael's against my body. I felt his tenderness as he held me close. I felt his strength as he allowed me to melt into his arms. The passion in his kiss made me feel wanted, needed, and loved. With his lips still pressed against mine, I felt tears fall from my eyes. He pulled his lips away and as we stood, he noticed my tears. He tenderly kissed my cheek and softly asked, "are you okay?"

I nodded as I wiped away the tears and then wrapped my arms around his waist. Immediately, he brought me in close, burying me into his embrace. I closed my eyes and soaked him in.

§

"Good morning, Mrs. Bolton."

I woke to find my husband propped up on his elbow watching as my eyes fluttered open to meet his. I offered a sleepy smile and whispered, "good morning, Mr. Bolton."

He brushed the hair out of my face with a tender touch, allowing his fingers to rest against my cheek. I wanted to take in every detail of this first morning together as husband and wife. I closed my eyes in an effort to preserve this moment. I felt his lips kiss my forehead. My eyes opened in response to his sweet gesture and we stared at each other with smiles of satisfaction.

Despite knowing our friends were most likely awake in their rooms and ready to explore the city, we decided to savor our time alone and order room service, letting everybody know we would meet up with them later.

When the food arrived, Michael arranged the table in a way that allowed us to enjoy our meal while overlooking Central Park from the 39th floor. The night before, I placed my wedding bouquet in a glass filled with water. I moved it from the table to the large window sill, but not without first tracing the penny tucked inside the ribbon. I felt Michael approach behind me. He wrapped his arms around my waist and lowered his chin onto my shoulder.

"I forgot to show this to you yesterday," I said as I pulled the bouquet out of the water. I tilted it to expose the top of the penny peeking out from behind the ribbon I used nineteen years earlier.

"Oh wow, babe," he said quietly. I told him the story of the penny and the conversation I had with God just before finding it. He squeezed my waist to let me know he understood what that penny meant to me. As he released me to pour each of us a cup of coffee, I returned my bouquet to the glass of water, positioning it so that the penny faced me as I sat next to my husband.

"Do you think Ryan would be happy?"

I turned to look at Michael, appreciating the way he continually honored Ryan's love for me. I returned my gaze to the penny staring back at me.

"Yeah, I do."

Michael reached for my hand. "He will always be your husband, you know."

I felt tears instantly spring to my eyes and squeezed his hand in response. The lump in my throat prevented words from escaping my mouth. I nodded and looked at Michael praying my eyes would tell him everything I was feeling.

Had I been able to speak, I would've said, *"you were the one. The one I wrote about and the one I wrote to; the one I prayed for and the one I was scared to meet. You allow me to love you for who you are, while giving me permission to love Ryan for who he was, and that is something I didn't actually believe was possible. Thank you for loving me. All of me."*

As though he could read my thoughts, he said, "what happened to Ryan was awful and I hate that you had to go through so much pain." He squeezed my hand again. "I'm thankful that I'm the one who gets to continue loving you."

My mind flashed back to that day in 1995 when a shy,

blonde-haired, blue-eyed boy entered into my life. I had no idea how greatly his presence would frame the course of my future, and I could've never imagined how deeply his absence would alter it. Ryan's life shaped my own, and his death changed me. Every part of who I am is a result of the love and life I shared with Ryan. Even in his death, he is part of everything I do. He is the reason I love better, appreciate deeper, and live bigger. He is the heartbeat that echoes behind mine. He is the memory cemented in my soul. He is the reason I believed I might never be loved again. I was convinced nobody would be able to love me as Ryan did: wholly, sacrificially, and unconditionally.

And then came Michael.

Epilogue

2025

While sitting at the kitchen table I can see the bright green rolling hills surrounding my home in Banbridge, Northern Ireland. Property lines are marked by trees and in the distance cows are roaming the lush pasture. It's February and the trees in my neighborhood are a mixture of bare branches and permanent green leaves. The air is crisp and chilly at 40 degrees, a temperature southern California doesn't feel often. It's drizzling enough to wet the ground, but it's a rain so gentle it looks like glitter falling from the sky.

My eyes are lost in the beauty of gray skies and my thoughts are circling around the upcoming firefighter's retreat at Hume Lake. It's difficult to believe this will be our sixth retreat with Firefighters for Christ. I recall a conversation with Lori shortly after Michael and I married; she told us that out of all the attendees the year we met, we were the only two single people registered for the event. I am continually in awe of God's divine orchestration. I think about the day He nudged me to take off my wedding ring, one week before Michael and I would meet.

I asked Michael about it one day, "if I had been wearing my ring, would you have talked to me?" Michael's answer was quick: "absolutely not." As I'm lost in reflection of God's perfect timing, my husband appears at the back door. He's wearing a coat to protect him from the chilly elements while he tends to the back garden.

The door creaks as he opens it. Calling out to me in his Belfast accent, he says, "babe, can you put the kettle on?"

As quickly as he entered, he was gone again. I smiled as he closed the door and went back into the weather that still feels foreign to my California blood. I slowly crossed the room into our kitchen, thinking about the vocabulary that has been added to my internal dictionary since we met. I discovered that "putting on the kettle" meant he wanted a cup of tea, which I also learned is known as "a cuppa."

I stared out the kitchen window, watching as three large sheep wander on a hillside not far away. I watch my husband tend to the lawn that's been neglected during the weeks while we were away. We will be returning to Los Angeles next week, back to our California home and Michael's work schedule. This is our life now; we travel between our two homes and four children, two countries and one dog. My once-empty passport now has multiple stamps acknowledging my growing familiarity with the island of Ireland.

Although I am becoming acquainted with cars on the opposite side of the road and referring to cookies as biscuits, gaining emotional familiarity was not as straightforward. As with any new relationship, including with our children, there were bumps and wrinkles that required verbal ironing. I would love to say that learning to balance the duality of loss and love, past and present, has been easy but there is nothing simple about blending two well-lived lives into one never-before-lived life. While working to learn new cultures, new patterns, and new routines with the help of God's wisdom to blend our family of six, our first three years of marriage were spent living apart.

Occasionally it felt as though everything was stacked against us: physical distance, emotional separation, and a global pandemic to top it off. There seemed to be no end to our physical divide. We didn't have any direction and nothing was being made obvious to us.

There were times when I didn't know if my heart could keep going. I wondered if I misread God's signs. *'Was Amy right? Did this only appear to be from God but it really wasn't?'* It was difficult to fight against those thoughts. I would often revisit my journals and recount the ways in which God confirmed every detail of our relationship, even down to the timing of our elopement in New York. Had Michael and I not married when we did, we would not have been able to see each other during the pandemic. The United States closed its borders to everyone except those married to American citizens. As well, the United Kingdom may not have closed its borders, but foreign travelers were discouraged from entering. During one of my visits to Northern Ireland, I was turned away at the Dublin airport after being told that traveling to see my husband was not considered "essential." Thankfully, a very kind police officer saw my tears of desperation and helped me get to my husband.

§

God had been so evident, but as the days wore on it became easy to forget. Revisiting my journals reminded me of everything God had already done and restored my faith that He wasn't done yet. Each time doubt entered my mind, I heard, "don't quit. I brought you here. Keep going." I could hear those words above the apprehension. But it wasn't just about the distance.

My heart was tortured with this new love. Each time I left Michael at the airport, I cried for hours. I refused to sleep if his flight was at night. I obsessively tracked the airplane and would busy myself with household projects if his flight was during the day. The time difference created panic each morning; I became heavily reliant on waking up to a text message from him, and if I woke too early and there was no text, I immediately assumed something happened to him.

I remember a day when we barely spoke because he was incredibly busy working on the home we purchased in Banbridge. Seeing that it was nearing four o'clock in the afternoon in California and I hadn't heard from him (which meant it was nearly midnight in Northern Ireland), I called Michael to make sure he was okay. No answer. I called again and again. Over twenty times I tried calling, while texting in between calls. I asked Felicia's husband, Will, to call him. No answer. My mind went into a tailspin. I imagined he had fallen from the ladder and was either paralyzed or dead. I had no way to check on him. I burst into tears and felt my heart pounding in fear. I kept calling. Nothing. Finally, after nearly thirty minutes of unanswered attempts, he answered. He had fallen asleep on the couch and didn't have his phone near him. After hanging up, I collapsed on the floor and sobbed. I hated the way in which my trauma forced me to react. I felt vulnerable to heartache and believed that every worst-case scenario I imagined was not only realistic, but inevitable.

I doubted my ability to love freely without fear or worry. My heart felt troubled as I blindly entrusted my husband's safety and wellbeing with God. Being married in the fire service trained me to be separated from my husband for days (sometimes weeks) at a time, but then my worst nightmare became a reality. How could I be sure it wouldn't happen again? I found myself clinging to God and begging for His reassurance and comfort. The enemy wanted fear to replace my faith and every day I asked God to fight that battle for me so I could rest in His plans. In addition to pleading for peace within my soul, Michael and I were begging for wisdom and patience as we waited on God's direction for our family.

§

While we waited for answers, we focused on building intimacy and trust between the six of us, which initially felt difficult while physically separated more than we were physically together. On February 22nd, 2020, we honored our blended family with a wedding celebration in California. Friends and family gathered with us to commemorate the start of our new life together; however, less than one month later, the world shut down due to a pandemic and our plans to spend more time together as a family were put on hold indefinitely.

Our family dynamic was unique and our future was uncertain,

but one thing it wasn't: empty. Building a family the way in which we did gave us something deeper than we anticipated. Because our communication was primarily via telephone, FaceTime and text, our connection was cerebral and profound. We couldn't use entertainment to fill the gaps. We didn't have to wonder if we liked each other because of the good time we had or the satisfying food we ate. We had to talk. We had to listen. We had to fill the gaps with questions and find conversation to learn about each other, and most importantly, we had to make the effort. We couldn't use a day of entertainment to hold us over until the next day of fun. We had to be intentional with each other, which in return built deep-seeded trust knowing that we were actively choosing one another. The distance allowed for gradual trust-building and gave each of our children the opportunity to grow into the idea of being a family. It wasn't rushed. It wasn't forced. It was slow and intentional, which allowed strong roots to grow between us.

§

Social media pounded me with questions about our marriage and opinions about our family dynamic, and I fell victim to the antagonism at times. I knew our situation was uncommon. I knew it didn't make sense. I knew it seemed like it would never work. But I also knew it wasn't a mistake. I admit to having my doubts on occasion (a result of my own fear) but the unfiltered opinions of so many encouraged doubt more than they did faith.

It was Michael who taught me about taking leaps of faith and he often reminded me about the miracle of our meeting, silencing the noise outside of our relationship. "We'll keep pushing doors until God opens one, and eventually He will," he'd say. We trusted God would lead us where He needed us to be, and our prayer was that He would guide us to the place best suited for our blended family - even if it meant staying in a long-distance marriage for several more years.

Subsequently, I stepped back into the level of trust I had after Ryan died. Instead of focusing on the days Michael and I were apart, I began asking God to use those days to develop deeper relationships within our family. Rather than wishing our circumstances were different, I asked God to use our story as a testimony of His faithfulness. I begged for His wisdom and guidance to get us through, what seemed to be, unanswered prayers. I refocused my mindset on God and allowed Him to use each day as He needed, instead of controlling how I felt each day should be spent. My mind relaxed as we pressed on in surrender. As much as we desperately wanted to close the physical gap between us, we weren't going to force it. We were willing to wait on God.

Three years after we first met, God opened a door. Michael applied for Kern County Fire Department in California and did well with their process. He was placed third on their list, meaning that as long as he passed the background check and medical exam, he was nearly guaranteed a job with their department. Just as Michael was ready to commit to Kern County, he received a phone call on June 21, 2022, exactly three years from the day he arrived in California and first held me in his arms. It was a conditional offer of employment from Ventura County Fire Department; the same department that has held and honored Ryan's memory for years. Although this felt like an obvious answer, we spent a lot of time praying over it. My heart was biased to Ventura County Fire, but I also knew this was a conditional offer, and he would have to leave the process for Kern County Fire if he went forward with Ventura's offer. Letting go of an opportunity like that was a risk and required a great deal of faith. Michael didn't hear back from Ventura County for another four months; it was torture on his conscious. *Did he make the right decision to leave Kern County's process? He'll have to go through an academy all over again. What if he gets hurt and it ends his career as a firefighter? Is it even wise for him to leave his established career in Belfast and start over?*

The call came in on October 21st. One month later, Michael stepped away from his thirteen-year career with Northern Ireland Fire and Rescue Service to start over with Ventura County Fire. The first time I ironed Michael's uniform, I traced my fingers over the Ventura County emblem recalling the days when I would iron Ryan's uniform for the same department. It was all similar, but felt completely different. I still have trouble finding the words to depict my heart when I think about the way God orchestrated the blending of my past and my future.

On the first day of a driving exercise during the fire academy, Michael was assigned to engine 142. The department had recently implemented new fire engines and many that previously existed were dispersed throughout the county as reserve apparatus. Ryan's fire station received a new engine, which means the engine he used to drive was placed into reserves; now known as engine 142. That day, as Michael prepared to sit in the seat

Ryan once occupied and place his hands on the steering wheel Ryan once operated, he felt a surge of emotion come over him. He took a deep breath and as he did, he caught something out of the corner of his eye. He looked down and couldn't believe what he saw. A penny. To this day, God continues to let us know He is near through the pennies we find at our feet.

God's detail in our lives didn't stop there. On March 5th, 2025, exactly six years after I wrote an open letter to my unknown future husband, I watched as my Northern Irish husband took an oath of citizenship with the United States of America. Throughout the bible, God showcases his attention to detail and connection between the old and new testaments; the only thing we have to do is pay attention to it. He does this for our sake; his continuity gives us security, allowing us to freely trust His word, His character, and His love. When I look at the details of our own story, I can see God's continuity. He has been present throughout, and when I pay attention to the details, I can see His hand in everything - reassuring me that I can trust Him without fear, love Him without limits, and live for Him without worry.

§

After leaving the International Churches of Christ, we were part of a small house-church for five years, leaving behind legalistic religion and untying the knots of indoctrination. We focused on building spiritual depth and connection with God through slow and profound examination of His word. I enrolled in courses at Liberty University to study biblical history, feeling myself draw naturally closer to God as I examined His words with the help and discernment of the Holy Spirit. There was no agenda to my study other than to know more of God. There was no bias or narrative, no manipulated outline of scripture, no desire to prove anyone wrong. I just wanted to know more. We once spent an entire year studying the book of John - I couldn't believe its depth! Books of the bible were examined chapter by chapter, verse by verse with historical context applied, making the clarity of God's message jump off the pages. I had no idea the importance of historical application when reading scripture and I am eternally grateful for those years I spent deep in quiet study with God.

I lost many friendships when I chose to step away from ICOC, and my once-busy social calendar was suddenly silent and empty. I've done hours of grief work and healing since leaving. I have no animosity towards the organization and I have since reconciled many of those friendships. I don't know if they've made any changes to their doctrine about salvation or dating. I hope they have, but even if they haven't, I hope others have been inspired to look beyond the outlined belief system of the ICOC and discover the truth about God's church.

Michael and I have since become members of a local church whose doctrine we trust and whose teaching includes historical context. We have found fulfillment in being spiritually fed and are enjoying the community that surrounds us.

§

I hear the back door open and the sound of my husband's heavy boots hitting the tile floor. "It's baltic, proper freezin'," he says as he quickly closes the door to keep the cold from entering our home. I hand him the steaming cup of tea and his eyes smile as he takes a careful sip. "Do you have the time, babe? I want to get to the shop before it closes."

I tap the screen on my phone. Beneath the date and time is a picture from our most recent family photoshoot during our summer together in California. Evie, Sarah, Amanda, myself, Michael and Brandon. Our arms are wrapped around each other and our smiles are the result of laughter in that moment. It's my favorite photo. I can see the comfort and security shared between the six of us; only because of genetics do we appear to be a blended family. From the start, our kids didn't refer to each other as step-siblings; they considered themselves family right away and eliminated boundaries placed by biology.

During a conversation with Evie that summer, she shared how much she enjoyed spending summers in California.

"It's like a breath of fresh air," she said, "all of us being together."

It was during a night when she realized she hadn't experienced living as a family. Simple things like seeing her dad come home from work and witnessing marriage in action were new occurrences for her. Although Sarah and Evie lived as a family unit with their mum and dad in their very early years, their young ages at the time of separation couldn't hold onto the memories of their experiences as a family.

Amanda and Brandon have years of memories with their own family unit but were forced to live as an incomplete household when their dad died. They have memories of oneness and unity, but as time has pressed forward, those memories are being held together by videos and photographs as the physical memories are fading away.

All four children had been hurt by the dissolution of the family they were originally given, which left all four children craving the operation and solidarity of a family unit. Years and distance taught us that family is not determined by bloodlines or proximity. It's in the way we communicate and connect, the approach in which we listen and love, and our relentless practice of grace and patience. Family is what we created within the six of us, which is how we are able to maintain lives in two countries without losing the connection we share. Our home is not defined by where we live, it's defined by how we love.

§

I think about Ryan every single day. I am left to wonder what he would be like as a father of young adults and as a man approaching his 50s. When I close my eyes, I can hear his voice and my fingertips can trace the hair on his forearms. I see him in my son's smile; his dimples and strong chin branding our son's face with unmistakable Osler genetics. Through our daughter, I relive his love for the ocean and lose myself in her blonde hair and blue eyes that matched his. He is everywhere I look. Even in the time and places he never experienced, I see him there. His presence will never leave me because he is forever a part of me.

§

While reading through the pages of this book, Amanda said to me, "isn't it crazy to think that when Daddy was alive, he knew someone who knew Michael?" I wondered if Ryan heard about Michael through stories told by Jeremy Bower. Chances are he could've. I asked Jeremy about it and he said he talked to "all the guys" about his time in Northern Ireland, which means it's quite possible Ryan heard about the Irish firefighter who would one day protect his name, honor his life, and love his family.

Our story makes me think about Cornelius in the bible; the man I read about when I was originally seeking a deeper relationship with God. Cornelius and Peter had no reason to ever cross paths, and they likely would've never known each other had it not been for God connecting them. Without their knowledge, God was preparing the both of them long before they met.

Michael and I had no reason to ever cross paths. We likely would've never met had it not been for God connecting us years before we'd actually meet. He spent so much time preparing our hearts for the day we'd meet at Hume, neither of us expecting what He had planned for us.

The details of God are indescribable, and years later, it is still difficult for me to find the words. When I think about the way God has planned and orchestrated the details of my life, I can see that He is constantly working behind the scenes, navigating paths towards an unknown future. Despite all the words I've written, there are words still stuck inside my heart. I can't find them; truthfully, I don't even know if they exist. Nothing I write illustrates what I feel when I think about God, so I will leave with this: if you ever wondered if God is real, if He is good, or if He is trustworthy...

He is.

Oh, how He is.

Hello again, Reader,

It might appear as though Michael coming into my life is proof of God's redemption, and while he is part of it, the redemption began long before we met.

It appeared in my nourished body after eating nearly nothing for weeks after the death of my husband. It appeared in my beating heart and breathing lungs when I believed I wouldn't be able to live. It appeared in the days I made my bed. The days I drove to work and the days I helped with homework. It appeared in the smiles upon my face and the laughter from my soul, when I felt I might not have joy again. It was in the signs God revealed to me as a reminder that He was near, which pushed me to keep trusting Him.

God's redemption appeared in the days I was given, not in *what* I was given. His redemption was in me.

We've been conditioned to think that big, obvious, miraculous events are the only proof of God's presence and work - the obvious renewal of life. But redemption is in the smaller moments, the ones the world takes for granted and the heartbroken beg to feel. Michael was God's obvious redemption for the rest of the world to see; the ones who need a clear sign that He is present and miracles still happen. But God's most precious work is done *within* us, not *for* us.

It's easy to hear my story and believe it was new love that rescued me from the depths of grief, but it wasn't. I had already emerged from the ashes into something new. I was a new creation before Michael came into my life. He didn't rescue me, he found me.

I don't know where you are in your journey and I don't know what your path looks like, but I do know this: God will rescue you and you will emerge as something new. Who you are today is not who you will be tomorrow, and who you are tomorrow is not who you will be in a week, a month or a year.

God uses each day to refine you and each moment to transform you. Where you feel pain, God sees growth. What you see as hopeless, God sees as promising.

The story of God's redemption in your life is happening now.

It's in the opening of your eyes, the beating of your heart, and the sound of your voice. You don't need to wait for the obvious renewal of life to see the promise of God's deliverance. Consume yourself with His love, immerse yourself in His devotion and you will find that His redemption is already happening.

It's taking place within YOU.

Xoxo,

Jenn

As for me,
I WILL ALWAYS HAVE HOPE
Psalm 71:14

Acknowledgments

Michael – it takes a certain kind of man to love a widow; he has to encompass equal amounts of security and humility. Thank you for being that man. Not everyone can live and love as you do; thank you for leading our family and loving our children. I was afraid to love again, but you showed me that I had nothing to fear; thank you for asking me to be yours. I am grateful for you beyond words and I love you more than you'll ever know.

Amanda - being my first born, you were forced to grow up with me. Thank you for your patience as we learned together. You were my co-pilot as we navigated rough waters, my right hand as we faced uncertainty, and now one of my most treasured friends. My heart explodes with gratitude for you. I adore you, Rosie Pie.

Brandon – you are like your Daddy in so many ways: strong, tender, and compassionate. So many of my darkest days were made light by you and those qualities you share with your dad. I am so proud of who you are and who you're becoming. I love you endlessly, buddy.

Sarah and Evie – I couldn't imagine how my heart would expand when you came into my life. Thank you for loving me and allowing me to be part of your lives. I love you each as though you've always been mine and am so grateful I get to "keep you forever."

Mom and Dad – I hate to think about where I would be without you. I have tried to write this out so many times and nothing captures what I feel for you. 'Grateful' doesn't cut it. You have laid down your life for me countless times and yet, I know you would do it again and again. You are what every child deserves to have. I love you both so much. Thank you – for everything.

Tom - You graciously welcomed me into your family before knowing what our future held. Your confidence in Michael and our marriage is what I hope to be like as parent: unconditionally supportive. Thank you for making me feel so loved; I am honored to share your last name.

Grandma & Grandad - My testimony of faith begins with the seeds you planted long ago. Your obedience to God brought me to this moment; without faith, I don't know that I would've made it through. You gave me the hope of eternity, and for that, I could never thank you enough. I love you so much. I wish you were here for this, Grandad. I miss you.

Katie – my first reader, my loudest cheerleader, my bestest friend. You have been a pillar in my life in more ways than I can count. Thank you for loving me as a cousin, discipling me as a sister, and believing in me as a friend. I would be lost without you (literally). I love you beyond words, Deeky.

Roger & Mahal – Rog, thank you for loving Ryan so deeply; he truly thought of you as his brother. Holly, watching your husband and your best friend grieve forced you to wait on your own grief; thank you for showing up through your silent heartache. Thank you both for welcoming Michael and trusting me with the story being written by God. I love you both – especially you, Loser.

Cherie, Julie and Jeanine – 30 years ago I met the cutest kid and fell in love with not only him, but his entire family. Thank you for allowing me to love him; as long as there is breath in my lungs, I will protect his memory, speak his name and live for him.

My widow community - You carry strength beyond measure, wisdom beyond years, faith beyond comprehension, and empathy beyond understanding. You house the most beautiful souls, and anyone in your presence is privileged to be there. Hate that I know you, but love that I do.

Everyone who has supported us – as desperately as I wish I could individually thank the thousands of people who have supported our family over the years, I wouldn't know where to begin. On my darkest days, the love and prayers of so many kept me afloat. You watched my children grow and cheered them on, helping me to feel less alone in parenthood. You witnessed my healing and watched as my heart began to open again. You've shared your stories with me and have trusted me with your vulnerability. Although I can't individually thank everyone, I have felt the love of each person who has been kind enough to share with me. Thank you for being on this journey with us. You are part of my story, too.

Ryan - For years you told me to write a book. You believed I had something to give to the world long before I had a story to tell. I've often cried while writing because I'm doing what you believed I could, but it took losing you to finally do it. I'm sorry I waited so long to write. I promise this won't be the first and last book. I promise I'll do what you believed I could. I hope I've made you proud. I will love you for eternity. 143-25

God - You are the perfect author and a flawless story-teller. Thank you for trusting me to narrate this story You've written. These words are Yours and this book belongs to You; I am merely the messenger. I am humbled by Your love for me and the faithfulness of which You promised. Like the apostle John said, You have done many more miraculous things that I have witnessed, "which are not written in this book" (John 20:30 ERV). It would be impossible to record everything, but I pray this book is a glimpse into the miracles I have seen. Lord, please allow these words to further Your kingdom by showing to the world that You are a God of hope, a Father of love, and a Savior for all. I will follow You anywhere and worship You everywhere. I am Yours.

Here I am, send me.

Isaiah 6:8

I love You. I trust You. I need You.

In Loving Memory

Ryan Stewart Osler

August 29, 1978 - September 21, 2016

Photo of Ryan taken by Jennifer Osler-Bolton
August 31, 2013
as he was leaving home for the Rim Fire

For information about the
Grief Recovery Method:

www.griefrecoverymethod.com
800-334-7606

Made in the USA
Middletown, DE
21 April 2025

74535678R00198